THE DISCERNING TRAVELER'S GUIDE TO

Special Places

THE BEST OF NORTH AMERICA'S
INDEPENDENT INNS, RESORTS, RANCHES AND
HOTELS FOR ROMANCE, ADVENTURE AND
GOURMET CUISINE.

By Fred And Mardi Nystrom

7TH WESTERN EDITION

ACKNOWLEDGMENTS

We are dedicating this edition to our son Tyler, who passed away. We miss his good spirits, laughter and gusto. For years when we discovered some place we knew our children Chad, Tyler and Makenna would love, we made plans to bring them back with us to share in the experience. Sadly, we were not always able to make those visits together. Now, when we find some special area of the country, we bring home a small memory stone and place it in the garden in hope that Tyler's spirit will enjoy and share in the discovery.

This little poem speaks to not overlooking the opportunity of the moment.

Yesterday is history,
tomorrow is a mystery
and today is a gift.
That is why we call it the present.
-author unknown

Special Credits

Edited by Alex Jones and Scott Holter
Design and Maps by Kristy Ewing
Separations and Film by Seattle ImageSetting
Photographic Contributions:
Jack Affleck...146-147
Paul Beswick...184
David Livingston...36-37
Charles Mann...155
John Marshall...86
Milroy McAleer...16
Patti McConville...189
Karl Neumann...148
Doug Peebles...120
Doug Plummer...67-68
T.L. Schermerhorn...178-179
Rob Drake - Back Cover

Copyright @ 1997
ISBN 0-936777-04-4

Library of Congress Catalog
Number 97-066798

Rates shown in this edition are correct as of the time of printing. Please note that all rates are subject to change without prior notice.

Nystrom Publishing LLC
Tel: 425.392.0451
Fax: 425.392.7597

Printed in Tulsa, OK by PennWell Printing Company

For the past 12 years, my wife Mardi and I have been working full-time to discover the very best independently owned and operated lodgings, restaurants and adventure providers in North America. This edition will highlight our selections in the western states and Provinces. We have also included a shorter editorial listing of 30 equally Special Places in the East. These and many others will be featured in our next edition covering the remainder of North America.

———◆◆◆◆———

WHAT MAKES A PLACE SPECIAL?

We are often asked what makes one place special while another, down the road with many of the same features, is not. After several thousand incognito inspections, we have come to realize that the critical ingredient is quite simple. It is not the amount of money spent per room. It is not the quality of the antiques or furnishings. It is not even the expense of the setting that makes a place special. The common trait shared by all the "Special Places" in this book is that they all evidence a highly developed sense of hosting. Good hosts will treat you as a welcome guest in their home. Their goal is to help you enjoy your time and to come away feeling that you were well cared for. This personal approach to hospitality is the hallmark of all the places in this book. No amount of money invested in a property will take the place of good, honest hosting.

HOW DO YOU FIND THESE SPECIAL PLACES?

We do it the old fashioned way. We get in a car and drive to each place, spending our time and money to check out both the place and the hosts. Each year we visit hundreds of places, and only the exceptional ones are contained in this edition.

HOW TO USE THE TOLL-FREE TELEPHONE PROGRAM

Each of the places in this book are reachable by using one toll-free number—800.954.8585. When your call reaches the automatic switchboard and you are welcomed to Special Places, enter the four-digit code of the property you want to reach. Your call will be automatically routed to the property. It is that simple.

ON-LINE INFORMATION

You can visit out active travel web site at www.specialplaces.com to discover hundreds of Special Places. We work to carefully keep the information accurate and up to date. After each trip, the editorials are first created for the web site and then the information is printed in the guide books. Before you plan any trips consult our site for the latest information.

GIFT CERTIFICATES

You can now give travel as a gift to any of your friends or relatives. You may purchase a Special Places Gift Certificate from us in any denomination. We will send it gift wrapped to your recipient, or back to you to give. The certificate is good at any of the Special Places in North America. It can be used for lodging, food or adventure. It is an easy gift to give and allows the recipient to use it in a way that fits their wishes. A book and a certificate are a great combination.

TO ORDER

Call us at 800.954.8585. When your call is answered, enter the extension 9000 and your call will be routed to our office.

TABLE OF CONTENTS

CALIFORNIA

Map 6
Heritage Park Inn 8
The Willows Historic
  Palm Springs Inn 10
Blue Lantern Inn 12
Inn At Playa Del Rey 14
Inn on Summer Hill 16
Villa Rosa 18
Simpson House Inn 20
Alisal Guest Ranch & Resort . . .22
Ballard Inn 24
The Martine Inn 26
Inn At Depot Hill 28
Babbling Brook Inn 30
Casa Madrona 32
Amber House 34
La Residence Country Inn 36
The Wine Country Inn 38
Belle De Jour Inn 40
The Honor Mansion 42
Applewood Inn 44
The Inn At Occidental 46
The Stanford Inn By The Sea . . .48
The Gingerbread Mansion Inn . .50
Carter House & Hotel Carter . . .52

PACIFIC NORTHWEST

Map 54
Romeo Inn 56
Campbell House Inn 58
Rock Springs Guest Ranch 60
Black Butte Ranch 62
The Heathman Hotel 64
The Shelburne Inn 66
Shoalwater Restaurant 68
Inn At The Market 70
Sorrento Hotel 72
Herbfarm 74
Birchfield Manor 76
Run of the River 78
Domaine Madeleine 80
Home By the Sea 82
Inn At Swifts Bay 84
Turtleback Farm Inn 86
Alaska Adventurer 88

WESTERN CANADA

Ocean Pointe Resort
  Hotel and Spa 90
Abigail's Hotel 92
The Beaconsfield Inn 94
Sooke Harbour House 96
The Aerie 98
Oceanwood Country Inn 100
Yellow Point Lodge 102
Middle Beach Lodge 104
Ships Point Beach House 106
Durlacher Hof 108
Tyax Mountain Lake Resort . . .110
Park Royal Hotel 112
Teahouse Restaurant 114
The Wedgewood Hotel 116
Seasons In The Park Restaurant .118
Emerald Lake Lodge 120
Deer Lodge 122
Buffalo Mountain Lodge 124

ROCKIES

Map 126
River Street Inn 128
Kandahar Lodge 130
Flathead Lake Lodge 132
Triple Creek Ranch 134
Lone Mountain Ranch 136
Mountain Sky Guest Ranch . . .138
Teton Pines Resort 140
Vista Verde Ranch 142
Romantic RiverSong Inn 144
Trapper's Cabin 146
SaddleRidge At Beaver Creek . .148
San Sophia 150
The Lightner Creek Inn 152
Blue Lake Ranch 154

SOUTHWEST

Hermosa Inn 156
The Wigwam Resort 158
Rancho de los Caballeros 160
Canyon Villa 162
Casa Sedona 164
Territorial Inn 166

EASTERN

Map 168
Monmouth Plantation 170
Chalet Suzanne Country Inn . . .172
Marquesa Hotel 174
Greystone Inn 176
Fearrington House Country Inn 178
The Boulders Inn 180
Inn At Pelican Bay 182
Paradise Inn 182
Hotel Place St. Michel 182
First Colony Inn 183
The Swag Country Inn 183
L'Auberge Provençale 184
Thomas Shepherd Inn 184
Inn At Antietam 184
The Rittenhouse 185
Glendorn A Lodge in the Country .185
Ever May On The Delaware . . .185
Troutbeck 186
The Cliffside Inn 186
Captain Ezra Nye House 186
Old Harbor Inn 187
Old Inn On The Green 187
Egremont Inn 187
Chambery Inn 188
Historic Merrell Inn 188
Stage Neck Inn 188
Captain Lord Mansion 189
Old Fort Inn 189
Black Point Inn 189
Inn By The Sea 190
Harraseeket Inn 190
Inn At Canoe Point 190
Lindenwood Inn 191
Adair Country Inn 191
Kedron Valley Inn 191

To Order Additional Copies . . .192

ALPHABETICAL LISTING OF PROPERTIES
PROPERTIES WITH PAGE NUMBER AND TOLL FREE INSTANT ACCESS NUMBER

Property	Page #	Access #
Abigail's Hotel	92	1018
Adair Country Inn	191	2033
Alaska Adventurer	88	7000
Alisal Guest Ranch & Resort	22	6000
Amber House	34	1008
Applewood Inn	44	2017
Babbling Brook Inn	30	1005
Ballard Inn	24	2000
Beaconsfield Inn	94	1068
Belle de Jour	40	1010
Birchfield Manor	76	2001
Black Butte Ranch	62	3000
Black Point Inn	189	3009
Blue Lake Ranch	154	1034
Blue Lantern Inn	12	1000
Buffalo Mountain Lodge	124	2008
Campbell House Inn	58	1035
Canyon Villa	162	1025
Captain Ezra Nye House	186	1059
Captain Lord Mansion	189	1048
Carter House/Hotel	52	5001
Casa Madrona	32	5000
Casa Sedona	164	1026
Chalet Suzanne	172	2014
Chambery Inn	188	2038
Cliffside Inn	186	2027
Deer Lodge	122	2036
Domaine Madeleine	80	1055
Durlacher Hof	108	1019
Egremont Inn	187	2030
Emerald Lake Lodge	120	2007
Ever May on the Delaware	185	2026
Fearrington House Country Inn	178	2015
First Colony Inn	183	1037
Flathead Lake Lodge	132	6002
Gingerbread Mansion Inn	50	1013
Glendorn	185	2025
Greystone Inn	176	2018
Harraseeket Inn	190	4009
Heathman Hotel	64	4000
Herbfarm	74	8003
Heritage Park Inn	8	1033
Hermosa Inn	156	2037
Historic Merrell Inn	188	1057
Home By The Sea	82	1016
Honor Mansion	42	1047
Hotel Place St. Michel	182	4006
Inn At Antietam	184	1054
Inn At Canoe Point	190	1065
Inn At Depot Hill	28	1004
Inn At Occidental	46	1028
Inn At Pelican Bay	182	4010
Inn At Playa Del Rey	14	1039
Inn At Swifts Bay	84	1041
Inn At The Market	70	5002
Inn By The Sea	190	1064
Inn On Summer Hill	16	1046
Kandahar Lodge	130	6001
Kedron Valley Inn	191	2029
L'Auberge Provençale	184	2020
La Residence Country Inn	36	1038
Lightner Creek Inn	152	1030
Lindenwood Inn	191	2032
Lone Mountain Ranch	136	6003
Marquesa Hotel	174	4002
Martine Inn	26	1003
Middle Beach Lodge	104	1031
Monmouth Plantation	170	2011
Mt. Sky Guest Ranch	138	6004
Ocean Pointe Resort	90	4005
Oceanwood Country Inn	100	2005
Old Fort Inn	189	2035
Old Harbor Inn	187	1056
Old Inn On The Green	187	2028
Paradise Inn	182	1044
Park Royal Hotel	112	4001
Rancho de los Caballeros	160	6012
River Street Inn	128	1020
Rock Springs Guest Ranch	60	6007
Romantic RiverSong Inn	144	1022
Romeo Inn	56	1014
Run of the River	78	1050
SaddleRidge At Beaver Creek	148	6008
San Sophia	150	1023
Seasons In The Park Restaurant	118	8004
Shelburne Inn	66	1015
Ships Point Beach House	106	1061
Shoalwater Restaurant	68	8001
Simpson House Inn	20	1001
Sooke Harbour House	96	2003
Sorrento Hotel	72	4007
Stage Neck Inn	188	2031
Stanford Inn By The Sea	48	1012
Teahouse Restaurant	114	8005
Territorial Inn	166	1024
Teton Pines Resort	140	3002
The Aerie	98	2004
The Boulders Inn	180	2013
The Rittenhouse	185	4003
The Swag	183	2039
The Wedgewood Hotel	116	4011
The Willows Historic Palm Springs Inn	10	1060
Thomas Shepherd Inn	184	1052
Trapper's Cabin	146	6009
Triple Creek Ranch	134	3007
Troutbeck	186	6011
Turtleback Farm	86	1017
Tyax Mountain Lake Resort	110	3003
Villa Rosa	18	1002
Vista Verde Ranch	142	6006
Wigwam Resort	158	3004
Wine Country Inn	38	1009
Yellow Point Lodge	102	2006

You can make toll free reservation calls to all of these properties by dialing 800.954.8585. This number takes you to the Special Places routing center. After your call is answered, enter the 4-digit Instant Access number of the property you want to reach. Your call will automatically be routed to the reservation office for that property. If you receive a busy signal or no answer, repeat the process again later. When making your reservation, please tell them you are calling because of their editorial in the Special Places book.

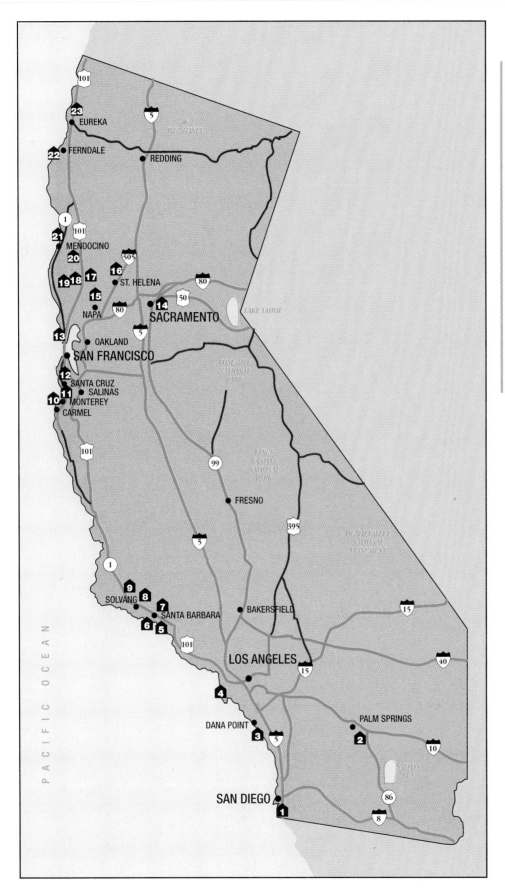

CALIFORNIA

1. HERITAGE PARK INN - San Diego
2. THE WILLOWS - Palm Springs
3. BLUE LANTERN INN - Dana Point
4. INN AT PLAYA DEL REY - Los Angeles
5. INN ON SUMMERHILL - Santa Barbara
6. VILLA ROSA - Santa Barbara
7. SIMPSON HOUSE - Santa Barbara
8. ALISAL RANCH - Solvang
9. BALLARD INN - Solvang
10. MARTINE INN - Pacific Grove
11. INN AT DEPOT HILL - Capitola
12. BABBLING BROOK INN - Santa Cruz
13. CASA MADRONA - Sausalito
14. AMBER HOUSE - Sacramento
15. LA RESIDENCE - Napa
16. WINE COUNTRY INN - St. Helena
17. BELLE DE JOUR - Healdsburg
18. HONOR MANSION - Healdsburg
19. APPLEWOOD INN - Guerneville
20. INN AT OCCIDENTAL - Occidental
21. STANFORD INN - Mendocino
22. GINGERBREAD MANSION - Ferndale
23. CARTER HOUSE / HOTEL - Eureka

HERITAGE PARK INN
~ CALIFORNIA ~

LOCATION: IN VICTORIAN VILLAGE, ONE BLOCK ABOVE OLD TOWN.

ADDRESS: 2470 HERITAGE PARK ROW, SAN DIEGO, CA 92110

HOSTS: CHARLES AND NANCY HELSPER

TELEPHONE: 619.299.6832

TOLL FREE: 800.954.8585, EXT. 1033

FAX: 619.299.9465

ROOMS: 10 ROOMS. ONE TWO-BEDROOM SUITE

RATES: $90 TO $225, INCLUDES FULL BREAKFAST.

REMARKS: NO PETS. CHILDREN WELCOME. SMOKING ON VERANDA. COMPLIMENTARY BEACH CHAIRS AND TOWELS. CLASSIC VINTAGE FILMS SHOWN NIGHTLY IN THE PARLOR.

During a time when most cities were giving little thought to their past and focusing on growth, San Diego paused long enough to save a piece of its architectural history. The county established a new neighborhood for seven historically significant Victorian buildings. Meticulously moved and reassembled, these homes now sit on a bluff overlooking Old Town, the first Spanish settlement on the California coast. The Harfield Christian House and Edward Bushyhead House, now sit next to each other, as they did originally, and together form the Heritage Park Inn.

TWIN MANSIONS

Set among cobblestone walkways and colorful gardens, the 1889 Queen Anne-style main house is characterized by a variety of chimneys, a turreted tower, fish-scale shingles, and an encircling veranda. From the front parlor to the well-decorated rooms, the entire inn exudes warmth and Victorian charm. The formal front parlor with its twin, rose-colored settees, Eastlake fireplace and ever-present jigsaw puzzle beckons guests to sit and relax. Each evening a film from the inn's collection of classics is shown in the parlor and popcorn is served. *It's a Wonderful Life* and *Casablanca* are two of our favorites.

Guests are invited each afternoon for for tea on the veranda. It was during the tea time, while enjoying dainty sandwiches, tarts and cookies that Charles and Nancy Helsper told us how they became a part of this wonderful historic inn.

When they first visited the Heritage Park in 1992 for an advertised distress sale, they had no plans to become innkeepers. Nancy explained: " Our plans changed in a flash once we saw the inn. We came to buy a four-poster bed and instead we bought the whole inn." Charles, a retired naval commander, had long wanted to try his hand at innkeeping and Nancy's 10 years in the hospitality business made the decision an easy one for them.

As innkeepers, Charles and Nancy bring their natural and engaging personal style to everything from decorating the inn to making guests feel welcome, comfortable and relaxed.

Guest rooms all have private baths and follow themes in both name and decor. They are extremely well done and offer claw-foot tubs, four-poster, canopy and sleigh beds, ornamental fireplaces, period antiques and collectibles. Next door, the 1887 Italianate houses a sumptuous turn-of-the-century two-bedroom suite with a large jacuzzi. This suite is our destination of choice when ever we get back to San Diego.

Each morning, the carved wooden doors open and guests are invited to the 13-foot ceiling dining room for a full breakfast by candlelight.The Helsper's creativity and personality begins to show during breakfast, as each guest has a personalized card at their place setting. Freshly squeezed orange juice is followed by a fruit course that varies daily, from poached pears to broiled grapefruit with maple glaze. Then a warm from-the-oven entree is presented on antique china garnished with edible flowers. Our recent breakfast course was baked Victorian French Toast with Apple Cider syrup and Eggs Florentine. Mardi found her own cozy-covered teapot with several tea selections waiting for her arrival.

A SPA FOR THE HEART

Charles and Nancy believe the inn is a spa for the heart and soul, so they set out to do everything possible to make your stay memorable. Their special touches range from fresh flowers in your room, plush terry robes, turned-down beds with chocolates on your pillow, to Charles' homemade cookies.

San Diego is a city for all seasons. Our favorite time to come is in February, when the hills are green, the days sunny and bright and all the attractions are open and uncrowded. Within walking distance is historic Old Town and there are a variety of excellent restaurants selections within a three block circle.

GETTING THERE

From San Diego International Airport: Take I-5 north to Old Town Avenue exit. Turn right on Old Town Avenue and then left on San Diego Avenue and right on Harney into Heritage Park.From the north: Take I-5 south to Old Town exit and follow the directions above.

THE WILLOWS HISTORIC PALM SPRINGS INN

~ CALIFORNIA ~

LOCATION: AT THE BASE OF THE SAN JACINTO MOUNTAINS IN OLD PALM SPRINGS VILLAGE

ADDRESS: 412 W. TAHQUITZ CANYON WAY, PALM SPRINGS, CA 92262

HOSTS: TRACY CONRAD AND PAUL MARUT

TELEPHONE: 619.320.0771

TOLL FREE: 800.954.8585, EXT. 1060

FAX: 619.32.0780

ROOMS: 8

RATES: WINTER $250-$550; SUMMER $175-$375

REMARKS: FRENCH AND SPANISH SPOKEN. CHILDREN OVER 16 WELCOME. FULL GOURMET BREAKFAST INCLUDED. NO PETS. SWIMMING POOL. CONFERENCE FACILITIES. TRANSPORTATION AVAILABLE.

The Willows, built in the style of a lavish Mediterranean villa, rests at the base of California's San Jacinto Mountains. Built in 1927, it was the home of Samuel Untermyer, former U.S. Secretary of the Treasury. Members of the 1930's intelligentsia graced these elegant halls, surrounding themselves with magnificent Italianate architecture, lush gardens, a sparkling waterfall and stunning mountain landscapes. Albert Einstein and his wife, Elsa, often vacationed at the home of their dear friend, as did Hollywood greats Marion Davies, Clark Gable and Carole Lombard, who came to this private oasis for rest and relaxation. Today, after meticulous restoration, Tracy Conrad and Paul Marut proudly present guests with the charming grandeur of a bygone era. Their goal was and is to provide guests with an "unrivaled sense of luxury and the intimacy of a private home."

This is a labor of love for Paul and Tracy, as they both maintain active professional careers in medicine. We found their excitement and personal involvement infectious. Finally, there is a special place in the valley.

Today, guests enter through ornate iron gates, discovering a mansion bathed in warm beige stucco, embellished with iron balconies, private patios and a verandah. Southern European ambiance sweeps indoors as the decor highlights a fusion of antique and neoclassical styles. The extensive living room features a grand piano, upholstered chairs and a sofa, and an enticing fireplace. Framed with an immaculately polished hardwood floor and a mahogany-beamed cathedral ceiling spotlighting two delicate chandeliers, the room speaks of elegance and refinement. You can step out onto the veranda to enjoy the magnificent frescoed ceilings and views of the pool, spa and Tahquitz Canyon.

SUMPTUOUS LUXURY

Each of the eight guest rooms is named for its distinguishing features or for a former celebrity guest. Though each room is unique, warm wood and soft desert colors embrace period antiques, queen or king size beds, comfortable sofas, slate or hardwood floors, individual climate control, cable television, two line telephones and a luxurious private bathroom. Gaze up at the stars tiptoeing over the mountains on one of many private balconies or nestle in front of your fireplace for an intimate moment.

UNPARALLELED STYLE

The dining room, with its frescoed ceiling, stone floor and magnificent tiled fireplace is distinctly Italian in feeling. Opposite the fireplace, through sliding glass doors, is a small formal garden that features a spectacular 50-foot waterfall that spills into a crystal pool below. Each morning, guests can relax here over a gourmet breakfast and perhaps a bottle of fine champagne. Complimentary afternoon wine tastings and hors d'oerves are available as the sun sets over the ever-changing desert landscape.

DESERT REFLECTION

Head outside for a stroll along the stone footpaths through the spectacular hillside garden. The mystical qualities of the property led Einstein to "Inspiration Point," a secluded corner in which he spent early morning hours meditating. Terraces throughout the gardens provide fabulous vistas and quiet contemplation. After your walk, relax by the pool, or allow the Jacuzzi spa to invigorate you. Visit the Desert Museum next door, or The Living Desert in nearby Palm Desert.

Take the tram ride up into the mountains and the scenery changes dramatically. Hiking the many trails provides a complete alpine experience. There are several points to overlook the entire valley.

Plan at least one evening dining at the famous Le Vallauris restaurant right across the street. As you stroll back in the warm desert air, you will have no difficulty imagining Mr. Gable and Ms. Lombard walking this same path back to their room.

GETTING THERE

From Los Angeles: Take 10 East to Highway 111. Right on Tahquitz Canyon Way. The inn is on your right, across from Le Vallauris restaurant.

BLUE LANTERN INN

~ CALIFORNIA ~

LOCATION: OVERLOOKING THE DANA POINT YACHT HARBOR.

ADDRESS: 34343 STREET OF THE BLUE LANTERN, DANA POINT, CA 92629

HOST: LIN MCMAHON, INNKEEPER

TELEPHONE: 714.661.1304

TOLL FREE: 800.954.8585, EXT. 1000

FAX: 714.496.1483

ROOMS: 29

RATES: ROOMS $135 TO $275, DEPENDING ON VIEW; TOWER SUITE $350; INCLUDES GOURMET BREAKFAST, AFTERNOON TEA, WINE AND HORS D'OEUVRES

REMARKS: CHILDREN WELCOME. HANDICAPPED ACCESSIBLE. NO SMOKING.

Perched above the Dana Point Yacht Harbor with one of the best ocean views in town is an enchanting Cape Cod bed-and-breakfast called the Blue Lantern Inn. Full of romance and charm, the inn is a storybook hideaway that every newlywed couple dreams of. The panoramic views of the Pacific, spectacular sunsets, dramatic accommodations and lovely park next door are all ingredients for a heavenly stay.

You'll find the coastal town of Dana Point surprisingly charming and full of history. A life-size replica of the ship Pilgrim and a statue of Richard Henry Dana Jr., the city's namesake, help to retrace the discovery of the cliff-lined cove in 1835. And though there's no need to leave delightful Dana Point, Southern California and all of its amenities are easily explored from the inn.

CAPE COD CHARM

Open since late 1990, the inn reflects the Cape Cod theme of Dana Point with its gabled slate roof, cobblestone paths and flower borders. Its 29 lavish guests rooms are individually decorated with elegant, traditional furnishings and the soft colors of the coast-seafoam green, lavender, periwinkle and sand. Print wallpapers, patterned carpet and thick quilts create a joyful, romantic atmosphere. Each room offers a fireplace, large private bathroom, some with two sinks, Jacuzzi tub, fluffy terry robes, a color television and refrigerator, complete with complimentary beverages. Almost all of the rooms have views of the Pacific and private terraces where you can enjoy the sunset or eat a leisurely breakfast. If you have the opportunity, you must try the Tower Suite, as it is the ultimate in opulence and luxury. It comes with a 20-foot vaulted ceiling, a king-sized bed and a breathtaking 180-degree view of the coast and harbor, 2,500 vessels strong.

BEGIN WITH BREAKFAST

Each morning, guests awaken to a breakfast buffet of home-baked breads, sweet rolls, cereals, fruit, hot entrees, juices and freshly brewed coffee. Lin and her attentive staff serve afternoon tea, wine and hors d'oeuvres in the spacious library. A fireplace, small bar, game tables and good reading light make the library a popular spot. We have often used the library for a convienent place to meet our friends who are arriving to join us for dinner.

Other little touches that we think make the Blue Lantern Inn special include an evening towel change and turndown service with chocolates, and an endless supply of fresh fruit and cookies.

WITH THE BUSINESS TRAVELER IN MIND

In addition to the library, which will accommodate a gathering of 40 people, business travelers will appreciate the Blue Lantern's fully equipped exercise room and two conference rooms, one which seats up to six people, the other up to 10. A fax machine, audiovisual equipment and catering services are also available. Ask about the Blue Lantern Inn's corporate guest program, which among other things, offers special rates, one-day laundry service and early morning coffee.

A wide variety of activities await Blue Lantern guests. Several superb restaurants are within walking distance, and golf courses and tennis courts are a short drive away. Dana Point also offers whale watching, sailing, windsurfing, deep-sea fishing and para-sailing for you thrill seekers.

Dana Point and the arts-oriented community of Laguna Beach are home to interesting shops and art galleries. If your stay finds you at the Blue Lantern during July and August, "a must" is the Laguna Art Festival and The Pageant of the Masters, an extraordinarily impressive showcase of life-size renditions of famous fine art pieces using real people.

GETTING THERE

From the south, travel north on the Pacific Coast Highway (Highway 1) through Dana Point. Turn left onto the Street of the Blue Lantern. The inn is on your right at the dead end. From the north, travel five miles south of Laguna Beach on the Pacific Coast Highway. As you approach Dana Point, take a right onto the Street of the Blue Lantern.

INN AT PLAYA DEL REY

~ CALIFORNIA ~

LOCATION: FIVE MINUTES NORTH OF LOS ANGELES
    INTERNATIONAL AIRPORT

ADDRESS: 435 CULVER BOULEVARD, PLAYA DEL REY,
    CA

HOSTS: SUSAN ZOLLA

TELEPHONE: 310.574.1920

TOLL FREE: 800.954.8585, EXT.1039

FAX: 310.574.9920

ROOMS: TWO SUITES; 19 SINGLE ROOMS

RATES: $85 - $225

REMARKS: RESERVATIONS RECOMMENDED. ALL ROOMS
    WHEELCHAIR ACCESSIBLE. NO SMOKING INSIDE, NO
    PETS, FREE PARKING, SPANISH, FRENCH AND
    JAPANESE SPOKEN. BREAKFAST INCLUDED.

This lovely Cape Cod-style inn is just three blocks from the beach at Playa del Rey, and only minutes from the bustle of urban Los Angeles. The Inn at Playa del Rey overlooks the Ballona Wetlands, a 350-acre bird sanctuary and beyond to the main channel into Marina del Rey. This stunning location provides easy access, relaxing views and fresh sea breezes.

Innkeeper Susan Zolla, owner of the highly regarded Channel Road Inn, saw a niche for an inn that would serve as a close-by retreat from city life as well as offer a convenient, relaxing home-away-from-home for both business travelers and pleasure seekers.

Like many successful innkeepers, Susan calls forth a number of talents gleaned from her past professional lives. She uses her experience as history major, teacher, mom, serious cook and general contractor to create and deliver on her promise to "Listen carefully to my guests and to do everything possible to provide for their needs."

After a five-year endeavor, Susan was able to open the 21-room Inn at Playa del Rey in 1995. The Inn has become a sanctuary that brings the beauty of the natural surroundings inside. Guest rooms are designed to be fresh and comfortable for the corporate traveler, yet rich and sumptuous for a special romantic getaway.

The true sanctuary here at Inn at Playa del Rey (Beach of the King), is provided by Susan, Carol, and the attentive staff. Guests are encouraged to take off their shoes, put up their feet and watch the sailboats tack out to the blue Pacific Ocean.

Mardi and I will never travel in or out of Los Angeles again without at least one night at this wonderful inn. This is one of the very few places where I could come as a business traveler or vacationer and feel equally comfortable.

Fresh, Simple, Seaswept

All the rooms are different, designed to accommodate a variety of needs and tastes. Some have decks or porches. Some have high canopied beds, eight have Jacuzzi tubs, many have fireplaces and two have a fireplace in the elegant bathroom. With forethought for the business traveler, each room features telephone, voice mail, data outlets and cable TV. "They're like the beach," says Susan of the airy rooms decorated in natural tones. "They're luxurious, yet comfortable."

Birds and Breakfast

The sunny dining room has pinewood floors and beautiful art hanging on the walls. The inviting room overlooks the wetland bird sanctuary, and the sound of birds adds warmth and charm to an already comfortable environment. Guests awake to the aroma of freshly brewed coffee, and dishes like Cherry and Pecan cake, or Chili Cheese Puff with Fresh Salsa, Apple or Peach French Toast stuffed with Cream Cheese or an Artichoke Souffle. You can enjoy the full buffet breakfast in front of the fireplace and watch the egrets, herons and mallards outside. The fragrant lemons from the inn's garden make wonderful fresh lemonade in season. Enjoy it as you relax in the garden hot tub.

Every afternoon, guests can gather in the living room for wine and cheese, and tea is available. Bicycles are available for those wanting some exercise or just for a leisurely ride on the spectacular 30-mile Oceanside bike path. Dinner is within walking distance, or just a short drive to many great restaurants in Marina del Rey.

The most popular day trip from Inn at Playa del Rey is a bike ride to famous Venice Beach. Disneyland and Universal Studios are each 45 minutes away and downtown Los Angeles is only 25 minutes drive. Beverly Hills shopping is close by, and of course, the beach runs for miles, just a few blocks away.

Getting There:

From LAX airport, take Sepulveda Blvd. North to Lincoln Blvd. (Hwy 1). Bear left onto Lincoln, go 2.5 miles to Jefferson Blvd., left on Jefferson 1 mile to Culver Blvd. Left on Culver one-half mile to the Inn.

From other points, take 405 north or south and exit on #90 freeway. Go west toward Marina del Rey. Freeway ends at Culver Blvd., turn left, go west 2 miles on Culver to Inn.

INN ON SUMMER HILL

~ CALIFORNIA ~

LOCATION: 4 MILES SOUTH OF SANTA BARBARA IN THE VILLAGE OF SUMMERLAND

ADDRESS: 2520 LILLIE AVE., SUMMERLAND, CA 93067

HOSTS: VERLINDA RICHARDSON, INNKEEPER; DENISE LABLANC, ASSISTANT INNKEEPER

TELEPHONE: 805.969.9998

TOLL FREE: 800.954.8585, EXT. 1046

FAX: 805.565.9946

ROOMS: 16

RATES: $165 - $295

REMARKS: NO SMOKING, RESERVATIONS RECOMMENDED, COMPLIMENTARY BREAKFAST, HOR D'OEURVES, AND DESSERT. NO PETS. WHEELCHAIR ACCESSIBLE, AAA FOUR DIAMOND AWARD; RATED ONE OF THE TOP TWELVE INNS OF THE NATION.

Paul and Mabel Shults had a vision. To design, build and operate an inn that would showcase Mabel's considerable talents as a designer while providing all the amenities and warmth of European hospitality. As collectors of fine antiques and art, and after years of extensive travel all over the world, they built their dream in the seaside village of Summerland on a sun-drenched hillside overlooking the blue Pacific Ocean. The Inn opened in 1989, and has earned numerous awards and accolades from hospitality industry experts. The philosophy at Inn on Summer Hill consists of "making each guest's experience your top priority and maintaining a congenial atmosphere in all areas." Recognized as one of the finest Bed and Breakfast Inns in North America, we are proud to consider it one of our outstanding Special Places.

In the rolling foothills near Santa Barbara, Inn on Summer Hill is a quiet retreat which combines the best of yesteryear with the tasteful comforts of today. The California Craftsman-style Inn features arbors and balconies which reach to the commanding views of the ocean. The setting is tranquil with brick pathways lacing through lush gardens bursting with fragrance and color. The captivating interior has an English country ambiance combining custom-woven fabrics, hand-embroidered settees, original art, antiques and collectibles usually found only in fine old-country estates. The pine-paneled walls and floors of the lobby and meeting room are set off by the glowing fireplace and French doors which open to views of the ocean and gardens.

COMFORTERS AND CANOPIES

Each individually designed mini-suite has a view of the ocean and the Channel Islands from a private balcony or deck. Each also features original art, antiques, carpets and custom-made down-filled duvets. Canopy beds, with imported draperies to match, are a signature touch at the inn, creating a luxurious and romantic Old World atmosphere.

SUMPTUOUS BREAKFASTS ABOVE THE OCEAN

The pine-paneled dining room looks out over the ocean and features Mabel's extensive tea pot collection. A large pine farm table has whimsical barnyard-animal metal chairs around it or there are two private tables-for-two. Breakfast is seasonally inspired and uses fresh herbs from the gardens whenever possible. The menu, which changes daily, might offer Warm Apple and

Onion Tart served with mild Habanero Sausage and Thyme-laced Manchego Crisps, Black bean Waffles served with an Ancho Chili-cranberry Sauce and topped with Brine-cured Pork Loin. Additional breakfast items include Inn on Summer Hill's famous Bread Pudding, fresh fruit, homemade pastries, muffins and croissants, cereal, juices and distinctive custom-flavored coffees.

Afternoon appetizers are fabulous: Sundried Tomato and Butternut Squash Bruschetta, Avocado and White Bean Salad, Crabmeat and D'Arbol Chili Pastelles or Apple and Goat Cheese Empanadas. Try them with Inn on Summer Hill's featured California wines.

Dinner is available in many fine Santa Barbara restaurants, and the staff at Inn on Summer Hill can direct you to one that suits your mood and appetite. Room service delivery is also available. The perfect end to another perfect day at Inn on Summer Hill means choosing from the nightly pastry selection with such sweet selections as Swiss Apple Tart, Fallen Citrus Souffle and Autumn Ancho Crisp, or content yourself with a selection of cookies and other small treats.

The most popular day activities involve playing on the beautiful beach at Summerland or whale watching. For the truly adventuresome, hike Rattlesnake Canyon or kayak "Hammond's Reef."

GETTING THERE

From U.S. Highway 101 northbound take Summerland exit. Follow signs to Summerland. The Inn is located one-quarter mile down the road. From Highway 101 southbound take Summerland exit. Turn right on Lillie Avenue, and continue for one-quarter mile. From Santa Barbara Airport take Highway 101 south for 12 miles.

VILLA ROSA
~ CALIFORNIA ~

LOCATION: ONE BLOCK OFF THE BEACH, NEAR STEARNS WHARF

ADDRESS: 15 CHAPALA, SANTA BARBARA, CA 93101

HOSTS: ANNIE PUETZ, INNKEEPER

TELEPHONE: 805.966.0851

TOLL FREE: 800.954.8585, EXT. 1002

FAX: 805.962.7159

ROOMS: 18

RATES: $100 TO $210 DOUBLE ON WEEKENDS AND IN SUMMER. TWO-NIGHT MINIMUM ON WEEKENDS AND HOLIDAYS. $150 TO $185 ON WEEKDAYS IN WINTER.

REMARKS: INCLUDES CONTINENTAL BREAKFAST, COMPLIMENTARY WINE AND CHEESE, EVENING PORT AND SHERRY. CHILDREN OVER 14 WELCOME. NO PETS.NO SMOKING IN ROOMS.

Blue ocean views from private verandas, palm trees, avocado groves and a sensual evening breeze make the Villa Rosa an enchanted place that is woven into the colorful tapestry of Santa Barbara.

Immediately upon entering Santa Barbara, you are aware that this is no ordinary beach town. The thing that sets the different cast is the architecture. The thick adobe walls with deeply recessed doors and windows, the graceful balconies and the red-tiled roofs are all reminiscent of villages along Spain's Mediterranean coast. Perhaps this should be expected since Santa Barbara was under Spanish and Mexican control from 1782 until 1846. However there is little left from that period. After the 1925 earthquake, the Architectural Board of Review decided to promote the Spanish Colonial look, which can now be appreciated throughout the town.

PRESERVING THE PAST

In keeping with the preservation spirit, many of the centrally located historic hotels have been restored to their former elegance. The Villa Rosa, built in 1932 is a good example of the Spanish Colonial Revival. During its history, the building was used as an apartment house, a motel and as off-campus housing for students. The decline in fortunes for the building continued until its renovation in 1981.

Transforming the dilapidated building into an immaculate 18-room inn was no easy feat. The total interior was gutted and a completely new tile roof installed. Creative architectural additions included an enclosed courtyard, a solar heated pool and jacuzzi. A space for small meetings has also been created. Rooms are furnished in a Spanish Colonial style with the traditional flair of the Southwest.

The hospitality that Annie shows to each of her guests has made Villa Rosa one of our favorite places to spend a few quiet days relaxing. Morning walks, afternoon beach times and early evenings around the secluded pool are essential parts of our visit.

VILLA PERFECTA

We have heard contented guests refer to the inn as "Villa Perfecta." This aptly describes this romantic retreat. Guests receive a range of amenities that would be found in a European resort and the pampering of a domestic bed and breakfast inn.

The pale pink, two-story building presents a facade of visual diversity, with turreted corners, cupolas, arched porticos and wrought iron balconies. Views of the beach, Stearns Wharf and mountains lining the south coast are rewarding sights from the inn. In typical Spanish tradition, there is also a serene garden courtyard complete with spa and pool.

SPANISH INFLUENCES

The rooms are decorated with Spanish and Mexican art and exotic potted plants. The terra cotta-tiled baths add to the Mediterranean feel. Three rooms include small kitchen facilities ideal for longer stays. Four deluxe rooms feature fireplaces and sitting areas. All rooms have telephones. TVs may be available on request.

FLAIR WITHOUT FANFARE

A complimentary breakfast of croissants, muffins, fruit and freshly brewed coffee is served in the lobby. In-room or poolside service can be easily arranged. Wine, cheese and social congenialities are offered in the lobby from 5-7 p.m. daily

Santa Barbara is home to California's oldest continually running cinema house, the Lobero Theater. Take a trolley ride to the mission, the zoo or a historic museum. Whether you prefer active or restful pastimes, Santa Barbara offers choices that appeal to both.

GETTING THERE

From the north take US 101 south to Castillo Street. Turn right at the stoplight on Castillo Street to Cabrillo Blvd. Turn left and follow Cabrillo Blvd. to Chapala Street. Turn left on Chapala and the Villa Rosa is on the left side of the street. From the south, take US 101 north to Cabrillo Blvd. Exit. Turn left at the stop sign and follow Cabrillo Blvd. to Chapala Street. Turn right on Chapala and the inn is on the left.

SIMPSON HOUSE INN
~ CALIFORNIA ~

LOCATION: IN A QUIET RESIDENTIAL NEIGHBORHOOD

ADDRESS: 121 E. ARRELLAGA STREET, SANTA BARBARA, CA 93101

HOSTS: GLYN AND LINDA DAVIES

TELEPHONE: 805.963.7067

TOLL FREE: 800.954.8585, EXT. 1001

FAX: 805.564.4811

ROOMS: 14 ROOMS, SUITES AND COTTAGES

RATES: $150 TO $350 DOUBLE

REMARKS: NO SMOKING OR PETS INSIDE THE INN. COMPLIMENTARY WINE AND MEDITERRANEAN HORS D'OEUVRE BUFFET, TEA AND SHERRY. BICYCLES, ENGLISH CROQUET, BEACH TOWELS AND CHAIRS. SPA SERVICES. FITNESS FACILITY AND POOL NEARBY. AWARDED AAA FOUR-DIAMOND.

Traveling to the Simpson House Inn in Santa Barbara is considerably easier today than it was when the house was built in 1874. Though modernization of travel has made the inn easily accessible, once you've entered its hedge-lined interior, you'll forget all about the 20th century. Glyn and Linda Davies purchased the Simpson House, one of the oldest wooden buildings in Santa Barbara, and opened it as the Simpson House Inn in 1985. "From the start," Glyn says, "we all had a vision of preserving this old house as a piece of living history." The Davies have woven a sense of permanence into the inn with art, antiques, fine Oriental carpets and handprinted Victorian wall papers.

A HOUSEFUL OF HERITAGE

In the halls and stairways of the Historic Landmark inn, the Davies' family portraits are displayed. In the downstairs sitting room, historical books and photo albums are open for fireside investigation. The formal dining room, with large windows overlooking the garden, is an ideal setting for meetings and retreats of up to 30 people.

The six rooms inside the Simpson House are named in honor of the family of Robert Simpson, its original owner. Each has a private bath and is furnished with antiques, including such authentic accents as handprinted Victorian wallpapers, antique beds and claw-foot tubs. In the 1878, fully reconstructed barn behind the inn is where you will find us doing one of our visits. The barn has four spacious suites, two up and two down, each with private baths, fireplaces, original pine floors covered with Oriental rugs. Antique pine armoires conceal televisions wet bars and VCRs.

Three English garden cottages are luxuriously appointed with canopied featherbeds, fireplaces, Jacuzzis and private courtyards with fountains.

Each evening, turn down service with housekeeping and the delivery of fresh truffles, leaves your room refreshed. We appreciate this quiet service.

Many guests take advantage of another of the unique services available at the inn. Glyn and Linda have elected to provide a range of European spa treatments which are available in the comfort of your room. Professional spa therapists provide treatments such as facials, massages, aroma therapy and reflexology.

For the very active, the inn provides guest passes to a nearby private athletic/health club. Amenities include a complete fitness facility and pool.

ENGLISH BREAKFAST

Breakfast is served on the veranda, or on private patios and decks overlooking the sunlit garden. Begin with yogurt, a variety of fresh fruits and cereal, or homemade granola from the cereal bar. Strawberry blintzes or French toast made with fresh apples, baked and covered with caramel syrup, may be among the entrees that follow. "Then spoon homemade lemon curd over scones hot from the oven and add a bit of whipped cream," Linda directs. "It's heaven."

BEYOND THE GATE

The Simpson House Inn is located within walking distance of many local attractions. On foot, you can explore the Museum of Art, the Alice Keck Gardens, and Alameda Park, or walk through the historic downtown area. We often walk over to State Street and make an evening of sampling appetizers at several of the restaurants.

Complimentary Santa Barbara Trolley passes are given to each guest on arrival. They may use the trolley for a 90 minute narrated tour, or hop on and off at points of interest. The trolley will pick you up right in front of the inn.

GETTING THERE:

From the south on Highway 101, take the Garden/Laguna Street Exit. Turn right onto Garden Street. Go one block to Guittierez, turn left and go one block to Santa Barbara Street; turn right. Continue on for 13 blocks to Arrellaga and turn left. The Simpson House Inn is mid-street on your right. From the north, take the Mission Street Exit and turn left onto Mission Street. Drive six blocks to Anacapa Street, and turn right. Continue for four blocks to Arrellaga Street and turn left. the inn provides secure off-street parking.

ALISAL GUEST RANCH & RESORT

~ CALIFORNIA ~

LOCATION: 40 MILES NORTH OF SANTA BARBARA AND 3.5 MILES SOUTH OF SOLVANG.

ADDRESS: 1054 ALISAL ROAD, SOLVANG, CA 93463

HOST: DAVID S. LAUTENSACK, GENERAL MANAGER

TELEPHONE: 805.688.6411

TOLL FREE: 800.954.8585, EXT. 6000

FAX: 805.688.2510

ROOMS: 73

RATES: $325-$400 DOUBLE OCCUPANCY. TWO-NIGHT MINIMUM. ROUND-UP VACATIONS INCLUDE ALL ACTIVITIES AND ARE AVAILABLE FROM MID-SEPTEMBER THROUGH MID-JUNE, EXCLUDING HOLIDAYS.

REMARKS: RATES INCLUDE BREAKFAST AND DINNER. RESERVATIONS REQUIRED. NO SMOKING, NO PETS. ALL ROOMS HAVE WOOD-BURNING FIREPLACES, COFFEE MAKERS AND REFRIGERATORS. WHEELCHAIR ACCESSIBLE. GOLF, TENNIS, HORSEBACK RIDING, BOATING, FISHING AND SWIMMING ON PREMISES.

Surrounded by gently rolling hills that are golden in the summer and emerald green with splashes of wildflowers in the spring, the Alisal Guest Ranch nestles in the secluded Santa Ynez Valley. An original Spanish land grant, Alisal has remained a working ranch since 1804. The ranch's 10,000 acres are populated with eagles, hawks, deer, coyotes and mountain lions. Huge century-old live oaks dot the hillsides, but it is the sycamores that gave the place its name. In Spanish, Alisal means "grove of sycamores." The present owners, the Jackson family, acquired the ranch in 1943. It soon became popular as a family gathering place and a getaway for entertainment celebrities. The Jacksons maintain the property as a working cattle ranch where some 2,000 calves are raised each winter.

Only 40 miles north of Santa Barbara, the Alisal Guest Ranch is a private retreat that captures the feeling of warm, western hospitality. The guest portion occupies approximately 350 acres of the land and can accommodate 200 guests.

ROOMS WITH A VIEW

The Alisal offers a selection of 34 suites, 29 studio cottages, seven executive studios and three executive suites. All accommodations offer views of hills, gardens or pastures, complete with frolicking horses. Guest cottages are clustered around manicured lawns and are decorated in California Ranch design. Bungalows that line the long entrance drive to the ranch have front porches, two and three bedrooms, and a large living room. Studios and two-room suites can be arranged for either king or twin beds. All have working fireplaces, which the Alisal staff keeps well stocked with firewood.

FUN AND ACTIVITIES

A ride into the oak-studded hills will tempt even the slickest of city slickers. Two-hour guided horseback rides are scheduled each morning and afternoon. Lessons are also available. Our favorite is the breakfast ride out to the old "Adobe." Upon arrival, the crew prepares a hearty meal of eggs, flapjacks and other warm goodies. Coffee brews next to the open fire. The ranch also offers half-day lunch rides and moonlight dinner rides. Once back to the ranch, you can wash off the trail dust with a dip in the free-form swimming pool or relax in the spa.

The ranch has two golf courses available to guests. A resident PGA pro, a fully equipped pro shop, lounge and restaurant make the package complete. If tennis is more your game, you'll be glad to hear of the seven championship tennis courts and pro shop. For the late afternoon and evening try the relaxed atmosphere of the Oak Room lounge which features live entertainment nightly.

The Alisal has its own 100-acre lake, for sailing, fishing and canoeing. The lake is stocked with bluegill, bass and catfish. There is no license requirement and the ranch will supply you with tackle. Other activities include volleyball, ping pong, billiards, croquet, bicycling and nature walks in the lovely hills.

RANCH CUISINE AND RODEOS

Alisal offers a full breakfast buffet, or you may order from the menu. Dining at the Alisal is not typical of rustic ranch life. Chef Pascal Gode began cooking when he was 13 in his native France, and by his twenties had become chef at the famous Adolphus Hotel in Dallas. His career continued as executive chef at the Four Seasons, and his own highly acclaimed restaurant, La Vie en Rose. The Santa Ynez Valley drew Pascal to the Alisal as a great place to raise a family. In the Ranch Room, you will find California cuisine at its best. The menu is different for every day. In the warmth of summer evenings, the ranch often does barbecues with live entertainment.

Just three miles away is the Danish village of Solvang. Within a 30 minute drive there are 14 wineries to visit, as well as two historic California missions.

GETTING THERE

Take Hwy. 101 to Buellton and exit at Hwy. 246 (Solvang/Lompoc). Go east through Buellton to Solvang. Once in Solvang, turn right on Alisal Road, go over the bridge and continue past both golf courses to the main ranch entrance.

BALLARD INN

~ CALIFORNIA ~

LOCATION: IN THE HEART OF THE SANTA BARBARA WINE COUNTRY.

ADDRESS: 2436 BASELINE AVENUE, BALLARD, CA 93463

HOSTS: STEVE HYSLOP AND LARRY STONE

TELEPHONE: 805.688.7770

TOLL FREE: 800.954.8585, EXT. 2000

FAX: 805.688.9560

ROOMS: 15

RATES: $150 TO $220 DOUBLE. FULL BREAKFAST AND LOCAL WINE TASTING WITH SPECIALTY HORS D'OEUVRES INCLUDED.

REMARKS: NO PETS. SEVEN-DAY CANCELLATION NOTICE REQUIRED. TWO-NIGHT MINIMUM. ATTACHED RESTAURANT (CAFE CHARDONNAY) SERVES DINNER WEDNESDAY THROUGH SUNDAY. NO SMOKING. FOUR DIAMOND AWARD.

Just 40 minutes from Santa Barbara, nestled in a country neighborhood of orchards and vineyards, the Ballard Inn offers an intimate country retreat from the stress and strain of city living. Located in the center of the tiny township of Ballard, in the Santa Ynez Valley, this modern 15-room country inn is close to everything the country has to offer: quiet strolls, blossoms in the orchards, sampling the newest harvest at one of the world-renowned wineries nearby, countryside bicycle rides and picnics amidst fabulous wildflower displays in the springtime.

COMFORTABLE ELEGANCE

Guests arriving at the two-story inn pass through flowering gardens framing a covered veranda with welcoming white wicker furniture. Once inside, you'll see a stunning three-sided fireplace of Green Italian Marble, while on the left is a hand-polished oak staircase cascading from the second floor.

The living room is flanked by a large warming fireplace and is our favorite spot for relaxed reading. Antique cabinets display award-winning local wines, along with winery tour information. In the comfortable Vintners Room, guests enjoy outstanding food and wine. The Stagecoach room has a round table for games and cards and a soft leather sofa in the perfect spot for watching the big screen television.

ROOMS FOR EVERY MOOD

Ballard Inn offers fifteen distinct guest rooms, each possessing its own special charm and character, and reflecting Santa Ynez Valley's local history and its residents. All of the rooms have California king-size beds (longer than regular kings), queen, or twin-sized beds. Seven rooms have fireplaces, and several offer cozy down comforters. All rooms have private baths, air conditioning and heating. The Mountain Room, our most recent choice, is decorated in warm earth tones and offers stunning views of the local mountains from the private balcony. The inn keeps all of the rooms open for tour when not occupied, so you can choose the room for your next visit.

A GOURMET'S HAVEN

Owners Steve Hyslop and Larry Stone pay special attention to the food and wine served at Ballard Inn. Their experience in the restaurant business in Santa Barbara and Sun Valley for many years shows in everything they do. Every day at 4:30 p.m., guests are treated to a tasting of great local wines served with carefully selected hors d'oeuvres.

Mornings at the inn offer full breakfasts, cooked to order and served in the dining room. The inn's attached restaurant, Cafe Chardonnay, is superb. Its creative wine-country cuisine makes leaving the inn nearly impossible.

SPORTS NEARBY

Exceptional golf courses are within a 30 minute drive, including a new course at Alisal Ranch, which is open to the inn's guests. You'll find tennis courts nearby as well.

GREAT CHARDONNAY

The word is getting out: World-class wines are being produced in the Santa Barbara Wine country, and the Ballard Inn is located right in the middle of all the most interesting wineries to visit and sample.

Bicycle riding has become as big a part of the Santa Ynez Valley as the wineries. The inn has mountain bikes available, or you can bring your own. There is a covered and secure bike rack at the inn for storage. Ride out to Figueroa Mountain, which, in the spring, turns brilliant orange and purple with California poppies and lupine; or choose from several itineraries available from the inn's staff.

Autumn is the time for the Celebration of harvest. this annual event applauds the diverse wines and foods of Santa Barbara county. At nearby Lake Cachuma, you can take an "eagle cruise" to nesting and sighting areas for golden eagles.

GETTING THERE:

From Highway 101, take the Solvang Exit. Follow Route 246 east through Solvang to Alamo/Pintado Road, turn left. Drive three miles to Baseline Avenue, turn right. The Ballard Inn is 50 yards down the street to your right.

THE MARTINE INN
~ CALIFORNIA ~

LOCATION: FACING THE WATER ON MONTEREY BAY

ADDRESS: 255 OCEANVIEW BLVD., PACIFIC GROVE, CA 93950

HOST: DON MARTINE

TELEPHONE: 408.373.3388

TOLL FREE: 800.954.8585, EXT. 1003

FAX: 408.373.3896

ROOMS: 19

RATES: $135 TO $245 DOUBLE, INCLUDES BREAKFAST

REMARKS: NO PETS. SMOKING IN FIREPLACE ROOMS ONLY. OFF STREET PARKING.

The Martine Inn is a gracious bed and breakfast overlooking the rocky coastline of California's famous Monterey Bay. Built in 1899 as a 59 room family compound, the original home was true Victorian. It was the family retreat of the Parke family of Parke Davis Pharmaceuticals who remodeled the exterior to Mediterranean in 1927. The Martine family purchased the home in 1972, and Marion and Don fully renovated it in keeping with the Victorian traditions. "Everything we do helps to create an authentic turn-of-the-century environment, from our antique silver service to the recipes we use to prepare our food," says Don. "Our goal is to treat our guests in the same gracious manner as if they had been guests of the Parke family during the early 1900s." And for judging from our many stays, their mission has been successful.

COMPLETE SUITES

In renovating the inn, the Martines took particular care with details. Inlaid oak and mahogany floors were hand restored, and the wall coverings and paint carefully selected in keeping with the era. Each of the 19 rooms is individually decorated with elegant museum-quality antiques. The Martines searched extensively for complete bedroom suites for each room and have unearthed some interesting finds. The Edith Head Room contains her bedroom suite and a commissioned portrait; the McClatchy Suite is furnished from the estate of C.K. McClatchy; The Park Room features a 1860 Chippendale Revival four-poster bed, complete with canopy and side curtains.

Thirteen of the rooms have wood-burning fireplaces. Many have ocean views, and all have private baths. Two oceanside parlor areas give those without view rooms a place to enjoy the water vista.

ELEGANT SERVICE

The oceanside dining room contains an impressive collection of silver and china, all carefully selected by Don and Marion. A 1765 Old Sheffield server, Victorian condiment and pickle service, and signed Tiffany loving cups are but a few of the treasures they've found. A lovely Victorian-style china service is used for breakfast, and freshly brewed coffee is served in individual Victorian silver pots.

Our favorite time at the inn is in the evening, when guests gather for hors d'oeuvres and a glass of wine in the parlor. There is something magical about enjoying good food and wine while watching the sea otters enjoying their social rituals in the kelp beds just across the street. The glass-enclosed pool room and Jacuzzi hot tub are located off the courtyard. The inn's library is stocked with literature on nearby attractions as well as menus from most restaurants. Winter is the best time to watch for migrating whales and to curl up by the fire as the storms come in over the ocean.

THE MOST IMPORTANT MEAL

Breakfast is not to be missed. The inn's long-time chef prepares fresh and wonderful creations such as Eggs Castroville, salmon Wellington, or Monterey eggs and salsa. Fresh fruit juice, and homemade breads accompany the meal. Gourmet picnic lunches are available upon request, encouraging a full day of exploration.

Monterey, Pacific Grove and the nearby town of Carmel-by-the-Sea are filled with excellent choices for lunch or evening dining. The Martines will be happy to make your reservations or offer suggestions.

ON THE PENINSULA

The Martine Inn is within easy walking distance of many attractions. The Monterey Aquarium is just four blocks away, and features nearly 100 habitat galleries and exhibits. Monterey's historic Fisherman's Wharf houses a large fishing fleet, shops and seafood restaurants. A walking tour of historic Monterey, called the Path of History, winds past the wharf on its lovely garden-lined route.

GETTING THERE:

From Highway 1, take the Pacific Grove/Pebble Beach turnoff. Stay on Highway 68 to Pacific Grove (it becomes Forest Avenue). Stay in the right lane to Ocean View Blvd. Turn right and go 1/2 mile. Park on the lawn under the trellises.

INN AT DEPOT HILL

~ CALIFORNIA ~

LOCATION: FOUR MILES SOUTH OF SANTA CRUZ OFF HIGHWAY 1

ADDRESS: 250 MONTEREY AVENUE, CAPITOLA-BY-THE-SEA, CA 95010

HOST: SUZIE LANKES AND DAN FLOYD

TELEPHONE: 408.462.3376

TOLL FREE: 800.954.8585, EXT. 1004

FAX: 408.462.3697

ROOMS: 12

RATES: $165 TO $250 DOUBLE

REMARKS: TWO-NIGHT MINIMUM OVER A SATURDAY NIGHT. NO PETS. HANDICAPPED ACCESSIBLE. SMOKING ON OUTSIDE PATIO AREA ONLY. FULL BREAKFAST, AFTERNOON TEA OR WINE AND HORS D'OEUVRES, AFTER-DINNER DESSERT AND COMPLIMENTARY OFF-STREET PARKING. MOST ROOMS HAVE PRIVATE HOT TUBS IN GARDEN PATIOS. MOBIL FOUR-STAR AWARD.

For an exotic get-away, try Paris or the Italian Riviera. But if your time is limited, visit the Inn at Depot Hill, two blocks from Monterey Bay in the town of Capitola. Designed in the grand style of the old-world, it's the next best thing to a romantic European escape. We always try to time our trips along the Northern California coast, so that we can include a night at this wonderful inn.

In the main room you can feel the history of this 1901 building, which was originally a depot for the

Southern Pacific Railroad connecting the Santa Clara Valley to the sunny shores of Capitola-by-the-Sea. This Corinthian-columned building welcomed thousands who alighted from the "Sun Tan Special," to enjoy a seaside retreat from the intense heat of the valley.

PERIOD FURNISHINGS

The parlor is lined with bookshelves to its 14-foot ceilings. An unusual round sofa may have held visitors awaiting their return home. A 1909 baby grand piano has been augmented with silicon chips to play a variety of music, and a fireplace warms this as well as the adjacent dining room, which once housed the depot's ticket windows. Two wing chairs and a table sit in front of a trompe l'oeil scene that creates the illusion of looking through a dining car window at an ocean vista.

EXOTIC DESTINATIONS

Owner Suzie Lankes attributes her interest in railroads to her grandfather who once worked as chief architect for Southern Pacific. Suzie explains, "I traced the railroads on the maps of Europe to the exotic destinations that lay at the tracks' end. We designed the rooms to reflect these beautiful, elegant places."

All 12 rooms are individually decorated. The Cote d'Azur has a lovely needlepoint rug on terra-cotta tile floors and a canopied iron bed. Portofino, in shades of green and camel with a hand-painted grape wreath above the marble fireplace, is fully handicapped accessible. The Paris Suite, in vivid black and white, is upholstered in French toile with large windows covered in French lace. A fireplace opens to both bedroom and sitting area.

The pink and green floral draperies and striped sofa of the Sissinghurst English Garden Room reflect the beautiful gardens found there. From the canopied bed you can view the fireplace at eye-level. A pillow-filled windowseat is the highlight in the Stratford-on-Avon. The Delft Room is our favorite, with the soothing blue and white, from the Delft tile surrounding the fireplace to the chaise. Its feather bed is covered in a white Belgian linen comforter and has floor to ceiling white linen bed drapes.

The Railroad Baron gives a taste of how railroad barons lived. Overstuffed red velvet chairs invite you to read in the sitting area, which is separated from the bedroom by white columns with heavy draperies of gold silk. The focus of the bathroom is a two-person soaking tub.

The books and paintings in each room reflect their themes, and each room is equipped with amenities to make your stay comfortable: concealed color televisions and VCRs, in-room stereos, Egyptian cotton robes, hair dryers and coffee makers are just a few. All rooms have fireplaces and private marble bathrooms. There is even a small TV in each bathroom. Ground-level suites have private patios and Jacuzzis.

MORNING DINING

Breakfast is served in the main dining room or delivered to your room: fresh fruits from the local farmer's market, granola, fruit juices, croissants, cinnamon rolls and muffins. There is always a hot dish, from eggs Benedict to delicious quiches. Take afternoon tea or wine and hot hors d'oeuvres onto the patio and relax among flowers that surround a reflecting pool and a herringbone brick patio and pergola. The courtyard is often used for parties and a conference room is available for business guests.

GETTING THERE

From Santa Cruz, go south on Hwy. 1 four miles to Capitola. Take the Park Ave. Exit and turn toward the ocean and follow Park to Monterey Avenue. Turn left on Monterey and immediately left into the inn.

THE BABBLING BROOK

~ CALIFORNIA ~

LOCATION: 90 MINUTES SOUTH OF SAN FRANCISCO ON MONTEREY BAY.

ADDRESS: 1025 LAUREL STREET, SANTA CRUZ, CA 95060

HOST: SUZIE LANKES & DAN FLOYD

TELEPHONE: 408.427.2437

TOLL FREE: 800.954.8585, EXT. 1005

FAX: 408.427.2457

ROOMS: 14

RATES: $105 TO $180 DOUBLE OCCUPANCY. INCLUDES FULL BREAKFAST, AFTERNOON WINE AND CHEESE.

REMARKS: TWO NIGHTS REQUIRED FOR SATURDAY RESERVATIONS. SMOKING ON PATIOS OR DECKS ONLY. HANDICAP ACCESSIBLE. NO PETS.

As you pull into the parking lot of this lovely Santa Cruz inn, prepare yourself for the smell of cookies wafting out the French doors to greet you.

AN HISTORIC MASTERPIECE

Beside the Babbling Brook's cascading waterfall lies an ancient protected Ohlone Indian burial ground. The property has hosted an 18th-century grist mill run by Mission fathers and a tannery, complete with water wheel, during the Gold Rush days. In 1924, Charles Chandler and his wife turned the site into a Roaring

'20s retreat. Mrs. Chandler expanded the existing log cabin, added stone retaining walls, an enormous wine press, an outdoor stone bread oven and rotisserie, and elaborate gardens. Lloyd Wright bought the home in 1942 and used it as a restaurant, christening it "The Babbling Brook." The Babbling Brook Inn opened as the first bed and breakfast inn in Santa Cruz in 1981.

GARDEN OF EARTHLY DELIGHTS

A small handcrafted sign on the inn's front deck reads "Time began in a garden." That's easy to believe here. Surprisingly, you are situated in the heart of town, near the beach and the boardwalk, but secluded in the oasis of the inn.

The inn's comfortable living room is filled with soft chairs and sofas. Here, you can sit by the fire playing backgammon or cards, listen to the soothing piano music in the background, or read through the restaurant book, in which guests have written their reviews of more than 100 local restaurants. Suzie and her gracious staff make a visit to the inn indeed feel like a trip home.

ROMANTIC RETREAT

The Babbling Brook has 14 guest rooms: six in the main house, and eight in chalet-style cottages in the gardens. All rooms have private baths; all but two offer fireplaces, and these feature Japanese deep soaking whirlpool tubs. Two newly enlarged baths have jet tubs for two. Rooms in the cottages have a view of the hillside, overlooking gardens and brook. All rooms reflect the style of a particular French Impressionist artist. This is a place to discover, or rekindle, romance.

The Honeymoon Suite has a large antique bathtub and canopied bed, with a private balcony where the waterfall and brook enter the grounds. Most rooms have balconies with French doors that open onto decks. The rooms are filled with special, "homey"

touches, such as fine Laura Ashley linens and hand-woven Kennebunk throws.

GOURMET BREAKFAST

A breakfast at Babbling Brook is no ordinary experience. You are presented with a buffet of homemade croissants, a variety of breads, muffins, orange almond granola, an egg dish, and coffee and juices. When you return from an afternoon of beach-town browsing, wine and cheese are available as you decide what to do for dinner. The special "Irresistible" cookes always seem to appead just when needed.

ON THE BOARDWALK

An engaging Bohemian throwback to the surf cities of yesteryear, Santa Cruz maintains a refreshingly carefree air. Surfers paddle by on their boards. Early morning docks are lined with fishermen drinking strong coffee and predicting the day's forecast, and the music of the boardwalk's carousel swells to meet the day. Scenic jogging paths take you along the coastal cliffs. You will find the shops, galleries and restaurants filled with the creations of innovative artists.

Fall brings migrating whales close to the coast and the sea lions to nearby Ano Nuevo State Park. The Monarch butterflies call the beautiful Natural Bridges Beach Park home. The University of California at Santa Cruz's Shakespeare Festival, and the Cabrillo are touted as among the best in their categories.

GETTING THERE

From the north, take Hwy 17 to Hwy 1, toward Half Moon Bay. Follow Hwy 1, and at the signal turn south on Laurel Street. The inn will be on your right. From the south, take Highway 1 through town to Laurel Street. Turn left and proceed almost two blocks toward the ocean. The inn will be on your right.

CASA MADRONA

~ CALIFORNIA ~

LOCATION: IN DOWNTOWN SAUSALITO, 15 MINUTES FROM SAN FRANCISCO ACROSS THE GOLDEN GATE BRIDGE

ADDRESS: 801 BRIDGEWAY, SAUSALITO, CA 94965

HOST: JOHN MAYS

TELEPHONE: 415.332.0502

TOLL FREE: 800.954.8585, EXT. 5000

FAX: 415.332.2537

ROOMS: 34

RATES: $138 TO $260. BREAKFAST AND EVENING WINE-AND-CHEESE SOCIAL HOUR INCLUDED.

REMARKS: TWO NIGHT MINIMUM STAY ON WEEKENDS. VALET PARKING AVAILABLE. RESERVATIONS RECOMMENDED. MOBIL THREE-STAR DESIGNATION. BEST SMALL HOTEL IN NORTHERN CALIFORNIA

The Casa Madrona is one of those sophisticated, "highbrow" places your parents would have exposed you to as a youngster. While many of its counterparts have fallen into decline, however, the Casa Madrona has only become more refined. At once charming and stately, this 1885 inn is an elegant blend of 19th century Victorian hotel and New England-style inn. It's a vertical structure, elegantly blending into its environment as it cascades down the side of a steep hill. This unique design provides spectacular, uninterrupted views of the San Francisco Bay, from Tiburon on your left and around to the Bay Bridge on your right.

ELEVATED ELEGANCE

The entrance to the hotel gives little indication of the true character of the hotel. Aside from the reception desk, there's only a set of unassuming elevator doors off to the side. Take the elevator to the main landing. There's an entirely different world on the floors above.

HILLSIDE COTTAGES

The Casa Madrona has 34 individually decorated accommodations. Twelve rooms are in the historic Victorian House, and 17 are in the hotel's more recent addition, the New Casa. In addition to these rooms, five cottages dot the premises, most with woodburning stoves and private entrances. Most rooms have fireplaces, private decks with spectacular views, televisions and wet bars. All have cotton robes that you can wear out to the spacious outdoor Jacuzzi.

Many of the hotel's guest rooms are perfect for celebrating special occasions. A clawfoot tub surrounded by a hand-painted garden scene is the centerpiece of the "Renoir Room." The room has an Impressionist decor, a sundeck and fireplace. In the two-room "La Belle Provence," you'll find a French-country style atmosphere with stunning views from the private balcony. The stately "Katmandu" has a fireplace and tub for two, overstuffed cushions and intimate alcoves.

DINING ROOM WITH A VIEW

On the uppermost floor of the hotel is the Mikayla Restaurant, candlelit and cozy with floor-to-ceiling windows that offer a dramatic view of San Francisco Bay. Entirely renovated in 1995 by artist/designer Laurel Burch, the restaurant features natural colors, whimsical furniture and a 12-foot hand-painted mural

of "The Legend of Mikayla," a sea goddess with flowing hair entwined with sea creatures and flowers. A dining terrace with a retractable roof and sliding glass walls is no less than sublime. The restaurant serves healthy American West coast cuisine nightly and a fabulous Sunday brunch. A Continental breakfast, featuring housemade pastries, fresh fruits and cereals, with juices, tea and coffee, is included in your room rate.

Executive chef Terry Lynch uses fresh local organic produce from the farmer's market. His cuisine is a delectable blend of ingredients such as a Napoleon of potato and Bellwether Farms Ricotta cheese with roasted pepper oil, or seared rare Ahi Tuna in a spice crust with beet-tamari sauce and sesame crackers.

Meals like these, combined with the staff's impeccable service, have earned the restaurant rave reviews. Dinner here is a must-do during your stay at lovely Casa Madrona.

AT THE END OF THE BRIDGE

Sausalito is a great jumping-off spot for exploring the lower Sonoma coast. Drive up through Muir Woods and down the west slope to Stinson Beach and the Point Reyes National Seashore. Perfect areas for beachcombing, picnics and backcountry exploration. The Casa Madrona gives you easy access to San Francisco to the south and all of the Wine Country to the north. For an interesting day trip head over to Tiburon, or take a ferry to neighboring Angel Island.

GETTING THERE

Leaving San Francisco, once over the Golden Gate Bridge, take the first Sausalito exit to the right and stay on the main road into downtown Sausalito. The hotel will be on your left. From the north, take the Marin City/Sausalito exit. Turn left under the freeway and follow the road into the heart of town. The hotel will be on your right.

AMBER HOUSE

~ CALIFORNIA ~

LOCATION: EIGHT BLOCKS EAST OF THE CAPITOL
ADDRESS: 1315 22ND STREET, SACRAMENTO, CA 95816
HOSTS: JANE RAMEY AND MICHAEL RICHARDSON
TELEPHONE: 916.444.8085
TOLL FREE: 800.954.8585, EXT 1008
FAX: 916.552.6529
ROOMS: 14
RATES: $129 TO $249
REMARKS: RATES INCLUDE FULL GOURMET BREAKFAST.
NO SMOKING. NO PETS.

The Amber House is a wonderful combination of three meticulously restored, decorated and adjacent historic homes. The 1905 Craftsman style, original Amber House has five guest rooms all named after famous poets. Its beveled glass front door and wide porch welcome you to an elegant retreat near the center of the city. The adjacent house, an Eclectic with a Mediterranean flair has four deluxe guest rooms, all with marble baths and whirlpool bathtubs for two. The third, an 1895 Colonial Revival also offers deluxe rooms and a beautiful garden courtyard.

Back in 1986 Michael Richardson, his wife Jane Ramey and daughter Hilary were living in Southern California. Realizing that their babysitter was getting more time with their young daughter than they were, they reached a quality verses quantity of life decision. Luckily for the rest of us, they decided that a lifestyle change was required and they ended up buying the original home which would eventually become the Amber House of today.

Their personal efforts and refined tastes are easily spotted. The main parlor of the Amber House reflects a marked attention to detail–an old rubbed brass chandelier, oil paintings and antique Victrola evoke an era of refinement. The bookcase-lined library is a perfect spot for morning coffee or quiet conversation. The dining room features stained-glass windows that replicate the leaded glass in its built-in hutches. Outdoors, the garden has a soothing fountain surrounded by iron benches.

TIME TO READ A BOOK OF POETRY

The five guest rooms in the Poet's Refuge are all named for poets. Longfellow's Room has a queen bed and a romantic marble bathroom with a jacuzzi tub beneath a skylight. Lord Byron has an iron queen bed and Jacuzzi bath tub for two. Emily Dickinson features a see-through fireplace and heart-shaped Jacuzzi tub. Each is provided with a telephone, clock radio, cassette player and cable television with VCR.

The Artist's Retreat, the 1913 Mediterranean-style house next door offers a parlor/meeting room, dining room and four luxurious guest rooms. Rooms are designed in colors and fabrics to reflect the vibrant artists for whom they are named. Renoir is an elegant mini-suite with a king canopy bed, sofa and antiques. The full-canopied queen bed in Degas is washed in pinks and mauves. In Van Gogh's green and white

marble tiled solarium bath, a waterfall flows into the heart-shaped Jacuzzi for two. These rooms are furnished with antique armoires that hold a color television and VCR. Each features separate phone lines with voice mail. One of the special touches we like is that the inn charges no fees for local or credit card calls.

The Musician's Manor is the latest addition to the Amber House. Mozart's is the favorite room. It features a fireplace, heart-shaped jacuzzi tub surrounded by luxurious marble and a private deck.

GUESTS' NEEDS COME FIRST

Jane and Michael make sure that the inn offers only the highest quality service and amenities. The gourmet breakfast can be served right in your room, in the dining room or on the sunny garden courtyard, at the time you request. Pre-breakfast coffee or tea is delivered to your door, along with a newspaper. A a little plate of home-baked cookies is delivered to your room each evening, and wine and champagne are always ready. "We take it as a very personal trust that each of our guests leaves here feeling that they got much more than they expected and would love to come back," says Michael.

HISTORICAL HUB

Just eight blocks from the capitol and convention center, the inn is situated in a quiet residential neighborhood of historic homes, small shops and great restaurants. The state capitol and its surrounding grounds offer a rich walking tour. The heritage of this historically rich area is centered in Old Sacramento, throughout 28 acres of Gold Rush-era buildings.

GETTING THERE

In Sacramento, stay on Business 80. Take the 15th Street Exit. The inn is eight blocks east of the capitol between Capitol and N streets.

LA RESIDENCE COUNTRY INN
~ CALIFORNIA ~

LOCATION: ONE HOUR FROM SAN FRANCISCO. JUST NORTH OF NAPA WHERE THE VINEYARDS BEGIN.

ADDRESS: 4066 ST.HELENA HIGHWAY, NAPA VALLEY, CA.

HOSTS: DAVID JACKSON AND CRAIG CLAUSSEN

TELEPHONE: 707.253.0337

TOLL FREE: 800.954.8585, EXT.1038

FAX: 707.253.0382

ROOMS:20

RATES: $150 TO $235. RATES INCLUDE FULL BREAKFAST.

REMARKS: RESERVATIONS SUGGUSTED.

Most wine aficionados recognize the name Carneros from the many fine vintages produced in this area north of San Francisco. With the perfect climate of warm, sunny days and cool starry nights, this is one of the world's premier wine-growing regions. Near-perfect weather, combined with fabulous restaurants, world-class wineries, cozy bed and breakfasts, chic hotels and luxury inns, make it one of our top choices for a romantic weekend.

Situated just north of the town of Napa, La

Residence is delightfully nestled among two acres of heritage oaks and towering pines. This beautiful inn is a wonderful place from which to explore the wine country in comfort and style. A marriage of decorative restraint and architectural intelligence, La Residence offers a sophisticated, yet comfortable ambiance.

The entry drive weaves past the inn's small vineyard and courtyard, where an Italian stone fountain splashes pleasantly. The main entrance is through double French doors to a small Spanish-tiled lobby. Following this international arrival, the smell of American chocolate chip cookies baking might draw you to the inn's large, immaculate kitchen. Here, chef and co-owner David Jackson prepares sunset hors d'ouevres, tempting pastries and the generous breakfasts for which La Residence is famous.

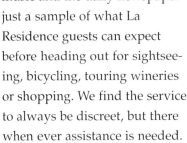

La Residence is comprised of two buildings, The Mansion, an elegantly restored Victorian home built by a river captain in 1870 and the Cabernet Hall, a contemporary building in the "French-barn" style. A charming white gazebo, with pool, umbrellas and chaises, visually spans the distance between the two structures. Beautifully landscaped grounds lead to the spacious new spa, cloistered by gardens and trees.

SIMPLE ELEGANCE

There are 20 generous rooms at La Residence, decorated with deep colors and beautiful fabrics. Suites all have luxurious features including private verandas, French doors, antique furnishings, fireplaces, CD players, hair dryers, thick towels and classic European-style bed linens, freshly ironed for your pure indulgence. Rooms overlook the gardens or pool, and are decorated with handsome designer fabrics, fireplaces, CD players and luxurious linens. Each of the rooms in the French Barn have private patios. Our room on the ground floor had a cozy brick patio which came in

handy for relaxing at the end of the day. Wine, cheese and hors d'oeuvres are served on the veranda each afternoon at sunset or by the fireplace when the weather turns chilly.

BREAKFAST FOR TWO

The inn's breakfast is served at tables for two in the delightful and casually elegant dining room. Homemade caramel-nut rolls, scrambled eggs, fresh fruit, hot coffee, soft classical music and the daily newspaper-just a sample of what La Residence guests can expect before heading out for sightseeing, bicycling, touring wineries or shopping. We find the service to always be discreet, but there when ever assistance is needed.

EASY ADVENTURES

In the Carneros wine-growing region, there is a marriage of the best of the old and new worlds. Vineyards stretch as far as the eye can see and prestigious wineries flourish, many the fruits of American and European collaboration. Here, the unique soil and temperate climate are perfect for production of outstanding Pinot Noirs, Chardonnays and fine sparkling wines. Cordorniu, Domaine Carneros, Acacia, Sonoma Creek, Saintsbury and Carneros Creek, are just a few of the Carneros wineries close by La Residence. Carneros Alambic is a collaboration between two prestigious European names, Remy Martin and Schramsberg. Carneros Alambic is the region's only fine brandy distillery and is just a few minutes away by car, or an easy afternoon bike ride.

GETTING THERE

Driving north on Highway 29 through the town of Napa, turn right off the highway between Salvador and Oak Knoll Avenue. The inn is along the frontage Road towards Napa.

THE WINE COUNTRY INN
~ CALIFORNIA ~

LOCATION: IN THE MIDDLE OF THE NAPA VALLEY WINE-
   GROWING REGION.
ADDRESS: 1152 LODI LANE, SAINT HELENA, CA 94574
HOST: JIM SMITH, INNKEEPER
TELEPHONE: 707.963.7077
TOLL FREE: 800.954.8585, EXT. 1009
FAX: 707.963.9018
ROOMS: 24
RATES: $135 TO $180 DOUBLE; $20 PER ADDITIONAL
   GUEST. RATES INCLUDE CONTINENTAL BREAKFAST.
REMARKS: NO PETS. NOT SUITABLE FOR CHILDREN.

The Wine Country Inn sits among the cultivated vineyards of Napa Valley, in California's famous wine producing region. Just as fine vintage wines are wrought through total dedication and love, so is this family-operated country property.

One of the oldest continually operated inns in the region, The Wine Country Inn began as Ned and Marge Smith's dream. Intent on opening an inn, they traveled extensively to gather ideas. They wanted to recreate the look and character of older inns, yet add the comforts available today. The entire Smith family engaged in the creation of their inn. The men did the masonry, building, and furniture refinishing; the women stitched quilts, comforters and pillow slips. Their efforts resulted in a three-story stone and wood structure that blends beautifully with neighboring wineries. The strong family involvement continues with the active involvement of Jim Smith as the General Manager of the inn.

COUNTRY VIEWS

Because of the inn's placement on a knoll, almost every room offers a country view. Wild mustard, lupines and poppies flourish, and a row of Chinese pistachios line the driveway. Each of the inn's 24 rooms has a character trait setting it apart from the others. Private balconies, large patios edging the lawn, snug window alcoves, a hand-painted canopy bed, or a Victorian headboard reworked to handle a queen-sized mattress all await your discovery. Fifteen of the rooms have a free-standing fireplace. All rooms have a private bathroom and air conditioning, while some have piped-in classical music with individual volume control.

What all of the rooms have in common is comfort. There are no televisions or radios, yet there are plenty of books and quiet reading nooks. There are pastoral views and intimate rooms ideal for romance. The inn has an outdoor swimming pool with plenty of lounge chairs, and a large bubbling spa nearby. Pool towels and robes are provided.

NEARLY CONTINENTAL BREAKFAST

The inn's Common Room is the gathering place for a hearty Continental breakfast served daily from 7:30 a.m. to 9:30 a.m. Homemade granola, a variety of breads, from zucchini to banana, fresh juice, fruits and coffee comprise the morning meal. Guests can eat around the large refectory table or outside on the deck.

The Common Room is also well stocked with books and games to keep you entertained during other times of the day.

The Wine Country Inn is close to more than a dozen fine restaurants that serve lunch and dinner. Menus are stacked on a Common Room table for guests to review, and the staff will be glad to make the phone call to secure a reservation.

THE WINE COUNTRY

Over 260 wineries dot the valley between the cities of Napa and Calistoga. Most wineries in the valley are open to the public and offer tours and tasting; a few wineries may be visited by appointment only. Among the valley's old and great wineries are Beringer, Louis Martini and Charles Krug. Sterling Vineyards, accessible by tram, sits on a knoll over the upper valley. The Wine Country Inn staff will provide information on wineries and wine tastings, and make appointments for you.

St. Helena, the wine country's capital, is noted for its 40 wineries and historic buildings. Shops, restaurants and scenic parks line the main street through town. The Silverado Museum features Robert Louis Stevenson memorabilia, over 7,000 items recount his life and global adventures.

Calistoga, Yountville and St. Helena are artist communities, where galleries are filled with local paintings, crafts and photographs. One of the best ways to view the wine country is via an early morning hot air balloon ride.

GETTING THERE

From Napa go north on Highway 29 through St. Helena. Two miles past downtown, turn right on Lodi Lane. Go east one-quarter mile to the inn, which will be on your left.

BELLE DE JOUR INN
~ CALIFORNIA ~

LOCATION: 70 MILES NORTH OF SAN FRANCISCO
ADDRESS: 16276 HEALDSBURG AVENUE, HEALDSBURG, CA 95448
HOSTS: TOM AND BRENDA HEARN
TELEPHONE: 707. 431.9777
TOLL FREE: 800.954.8585, EXT.1010
FAX: 707.431.7412
ROOMS: 5
RATES: $135 TO $245 SUITES
REMARKS: RATES INCLUDE FULL COUNTRY BREAKFAST. TWO-NIGHT MINIMUM ON WEEKENDS. NO SMOKING. NO PETS.

When Tom and Brenda Hearn found themselves talking by car phone while stranded in traffic jams on separate Los Angeles freeways, they knew it was time for a change. Within five months, the Hearns had purchased Belle de Jour.

Driving into this pastoral country setting, one understands the motives for such a move. Roads and wineries in the heart of this wine-producing valley are less crowded and more scenic than what many city dwellers expect. Belle de Jour's setting on six rolling acres is uncluttered and relaxing. Hammocks hang from the olive trees. A well-used wine vat has found new life as a "cold tub" on the inn's redwood deck.

INDIVIDUAL COTTAGES

Tom and Brenda designed the inn to reflect the amenities they most enjoy—individual cottages that provide privacy and relaxation. "Guests have an opportunity here to feel at ease, to be alone, to choose when and if they wish to socialize," said Brenda.

A Battenberg lace canopy and comforter bedeck the Shaker pencil post king-size bed in the Caretaker's Suite. Antique English and American pine mix with wool area rugs and an invitingly soft loveseat. Rough-hewn walls that once enclosed a grain and tack room have been transformed into a natural, refreshing space. The bathroom is a delight, with a teal blue-tiled whirlpool tub for two.

From the whirlpool tub in the Terrace Room, you have a view of rolling pastures and a private patio. Soft florals cover the brass king bed. The airy feeling of Atelier is enhanced by Ralph Lauren florals and rag rugs. A suspended canopy from the vaulted ceiling envelopes the queen bed. Rattan sofa and chairs in the sitting area front the blue-enameled Vermont castings fireplace. The tub and shower have Jacuzzi jets.

The Adirondack chairs on the lawn outside The Morning Hill Room overlook trees and rolling pastures. Furnished with antiques and warmed by an enamel fireplace, this suite has a lace-curtained bay window and large armoire in the foyer. Florals in soft greens and pinks cover French doors and queen English cottage bed. The shower and steam bath holds two people. Suites are furnished with fresh flowers, ceiling fans, air conditioning, refrigerators, hair dryers and sun-dried sheets.

The newly created Carriage House is the latest addition to the Belle de Jour Inn. Completed in late 1996 this is now our favorite place to stay. The entire second floor is a deluxe country suite with nearly 700 square feet of relaxing space. The suite is set with 10 foot vaulted ceilings, plank wood floors, Old World antique pine furniture and upholstered seating. There is a gas fireplace to take the chill off cozy winter evenings and a reading nook utilizing first growth redwood salvaged from the original barn. We were pleasantly surprised to discover that from the king size four-poster bed, you have a stunning view of the valley to the east. The Carriage House lacks for nothing. The whirlpool tub (which fits two quite nicely, thank you!) sits in its own tile alcove, surrounded with lush plants. Through the 15th century stained-glass window, you have another wonderful view of the green valley. The bathing experience is completed with the addition of a two-person tiled shower.

FARM-STYLE BREAKFAST

A full country breakfast is served every morning. Guests sit around the French farmhouse harvest table to enjoy fresh fruit, hot muffins and whole grain breads, freshly brewed coffee, tea and juice, and hot entrees like hashbrown Quiche or Parmesan Eggs.

For a special day, have Tom give you his customized back road and winery tours in his 1923 Star open touring car.

GETTING THERE

Follow Hwy. 101 north to Healdsburg. Take the Dry Creek Road Exit. Turn right at the bottom of ramp and go a quarter mile to the second light. Turn left on Healdsburg Avenue. The entrance to the inn is across from Simi Winery Tasting Room. The tree-lined driveway goes up the hill to the Inn.

THE HONOR MANSION
~ CALIFORNIA ~

LOCATION: SEVENTY MILES NORTH OF SAN FRANCISCO IN THE SONOMA WINE COUNTRY, BETWEEN ALEXANDER AND DRY CREEK VALLEYS.

ADDRESS: 14891 GROVE ST. HEALDSBURG, CA 95446

HOST: CATHI FOWLER

TELEPHONE: 707.433.4277

TOLL FREE: 800.954.8585, EXT. 1047

FAX: 707.431.7173

ROOMS: 6

RATES: $120 - $220.

REMARKS: BREAKFAST AND AFTERNOON REFRESHMENTS INCLUDED. POOL ON PREMISES. ONE COTTAGE IS WHEELCHAIR ACCESSIBLE. NO PETS. NO SMOKING EXCEPT IN DESIGNATED OUTSIDE AREAS.

The Honor Mansion is an elegant Bed and Breakfast in charming Healdsburg, in the heart of the Sonoma Wine Country. Owner Cathi Fowler had a successful decorating business in nearby Santa Rosa, California, when Steve, her husband conceived the idea of Cathi running an elegant and comfortable inn. He knew it would be a perfect use of Cathi's talents. Soon after she decided this was where her talents and heart were taking her, things began to happen very quickly. In just a few short months, Cathi found the perfect house, put a deal together, swapped houses with the sellers, and found all the furnishings at one antique auction. Says Cathi, "I just knew it was meant to be."

The house that had been waiting for Cathi to come along was known as the Honor house. Full-time residence of Dr. Honor, and part-time hospital, the house had been in the original family for 108 years. Cathi engaged the services of a contractor who had apprenticed as a Victorian restoration artist, and the renovation began. Today, the Honor Mansion is a beautiful example of Italianate Victorian architecture, and Cathi will gladly share the rich history of the house with you during your stay.

Cathi's philosophy about hosting is very simple: "We manage to anticipate needs, but never be intrusive." She personally greets every guest, and is always available. Every guest's stay begins with a welcome tour of the house, so that they will be completely at home during their stay. Cathi showed us how to help ourselves to wine glasses, and even how to operate the automatic cappuccino machine. We knew we had discovered a special place. The Honor Mansion is quiet and peaceful, but with the sophisticated amenities of much larger city properties, including winter and summer bathrobes and comforters on feather beds, and full turn down service each evening. One guest had written in the guest book "It's like staying at your best friend's home and at the Ritz all in one."

TIMELESS TREASURES

All six of the luxurious rooms of The Honor Mansion are furnished with fine antiques and eclectic Victorian pieces. Each has a private bath with clawfoot tub or shower, and each has a distinct theme or identity. The Dogwood Room is decorated in rich burgundy and cream tones, has a sitting area with a view of the koi pond and the dogwood trees. The Magnolia Room has a four-poster carved bed, a comfortable sitting area

and overlooks the fragrant 100-year-old magnolia tree. Two rooms have fireplaces and all have queen beds. The newly completed cottage offers a king-size bed, TV and VCR, refrigerator, wet bar and fireplace. Privacy and luxury in a peaceful garden setting.

BREAKFAST IN ELEGANT TRADITION

The Honor Mansion breakfast is served in a high-ceilinged dining room, with a view of the lovely Koi pond garden, which opens just beyond the open French doors. During our recent stay, the weather was perfect for enjoying breakfast on the deck, next to the waterfall. Breakfast is always a full gourmet affair, freshly prepared each morning and may offer Vegetable Frittatas, Caramel Apple French Toast, fresh-squeezed juices, fresh fruit and home baked muffins, scones and breakfast items.

During the warm summer months, you can start or end your day with a dip in the swimming pool. Afternoon lemonade, cappuccino and baked goodies are available for refreshment after the day's winery tours, bicycling adventures, beachcombing or antique shopping...or after a day relaxing with a good book beside the pond.

Your host will be happy to help arrange dinner reservations, winery tours, a round of golf, or even a hot air balloon ride over the lovely Sonoma Valley. Sonoma County has plenty of activities to fill your days. End the day by the parlor fireplace with a glass of smooth local sherry or some award-winning Sonoma wine.

GETTING THERE:

From San Francisco, take Highway 101 north to Healdsburg. Take the Dry Creek Road exit; turn right onto Dry Creek Rd., take first right onto Grove St. The white picket fence of Honor Mansion is easy to spot.

APPLEWOOD INN
~ CALIFORNIA ~

LOCATION: 90 MINUTES NORTH OF SAN FRANCISCO.

ADDRESS: 13555 HIGHWAY 116, (POCKET CANYON) GUERNEVILLE, CA 95446

HOSTS: JIM CARON AND DARRYL NOTTER

TELEPHONE: 707.869.9093

TOLL FREE: 800.954.8585, EXT. 2017

FAX: 707.869.9170

ROOMS: 16

RATES: $125-$250. TWO-NIGHT MINIMUM ON WEEKENDS. DINNERS TUESDAY THROUGH SATURDAY. RESERVATIONS REQUIRED. RATES INCLUDE FULL COOKED-TO-ORDER BREAKFAST.

REMARKS: NOT APPROPIATE FOR CHILDREN.

Applewood Inn is one of those places that, once found, you want to keep a secret. Redwoods, apple trees and vineyards surround this historic landmark. Just minutes from the rugged Sonoma Coast, this romantic hideaway has built a reputation for impeccable style and hospitality.

The Inn is located on six acres close to the Russian River, the Sonoma coast, golf, biking and many award-winning local wineries. Guests are pampered with comfortable elegance in a friendly, relaxed and romantic atmosphere. While elegant inns are not uncommon, finding one that also serves fresh, delicious, local fare is not so easy. Applewood Inn offers that rare combination of a relaxed, intimate inn and a world-class restaurant that is open to the public for dinner.

A ROMANTIC RETREAT

When Applewood owners Jim Caron and Darryl Notter bought the property known locally as "The Estate" they never thought their country inn would become a nationally acclaimed destination. The house was built in 1922 for a wealthy San Francisco banker. After a downturn in fortune, it was sold, and then sold again, this time to an underfinanced entrepreneur who converted the home into an inn. Jim and Darryl saw the property in 1985 while on vacation and bought it the same day. They've created their own version of paradise, and we find that it's pretty close to the real thing!

COUNTRY-HOUSE ELEGANCE

Decor is handsome with a mix of contemporary pieces and antiques. Drawing on his background in art and interior design, Darryl wanted the inn to be comfortable and elegant, but not cutesy or pretentious. What he envisioned were the large old country houses of Europe that are furnished with pieces from many generations. As he scoured the countryside for the antiques and almost-antiques that grace Applewood's comfortable interior, the vision became a reality that is both stylish and familiar.

Three beautifully appointed common rooms include an inviting sitting room, and a solarium dining room and a place to cozy up to a crackling fire in the river rock fireplace. There is an excellent selection of jazz and classical music CDs, and there are fresh flowers everywhere. A delightful patio surrounds the pool and Jacuzzi, with several outdoor seating areas away from the main house.

DISTINGUISHED INDIVIDUALITY

Sixteen rooms and suites are scattered over three floors in two Mediterranean-style villas. Each of the guest rooms is individually decorated, complemented by European down comforters on comfy queen-sized beds, over-sized Egyptian cotton towels and hand-pressed linens. Rooms have restful views of the towering redwoods or the inn's terraced gardens and courtyards. Each suite has all the above, plus fireplaces facing the bed, and either a shower- or Jacuzzi-for-two, VCRs and private verandas or spacious-courtyards for soaking up the warm sunshine.

INDULGENT IMAGINATIVE DINING

After a day exploring the Sonoma coast or nearby wineries, you can enjoy four-course dinners at candlelit tables for two. Dress is casual. The dining room has an inviting fireplace and solarium windows which view the surrounding redwoods. Specialties of the evening might include Chicken Breast with Fennel sauce, Risotto with Prosciutto, Grilled Parmesan Asparagus and Crostini Pommodoro. Salads are made with fresh greens from a nearby farm in such presentations as Field Greens with Wild Mushrooms and Tuscan Salad with New York Strip Steak. Desserts will tempt you with offerings of such diversity as Plum Pie, Strawberry and Brandy Cream Cake or Chocolate Souffle Roll Cake with Cappuccino Cream.

As Darryl puts it, "We feel best when...we look around the room and see people looking satisfied, rested and relaxed."

GETTING THERE:

From San Francisco, take Highway 101 north to Cotati. Take Highway 116 west about 22 miles to Guerneville. One mile before Guerneville you'll see the sign for Applewood Inn. Turn in and start to unwind.

THE INN AT OCCIDENTAL
~ CALIFORNIA ~

LOCATION: ABOVE OCCIDENTAL'S MAIN STREET.

ADDRESS: 3657 CHURCH STREET, OCCIDENTAL, CA 95465

HOSTS: INNKEEPER JACK BULLARD, ASSISTANT INNKEEPER HILARY AVALON & ANDY JEFFERSON

TELEPHONE: 707.874.1047

TOLL FREE: 800.954.8585, EXT. 1028

FAX: 707.874.1078

ROOMS: 8

RATES: $135 TO $195 MIDWEEK. $165 TO $250 FRIDAY AND SATURDAY. INCLUDES FULL GOURMET BREAKFAST; WINE IN THE LATE AFTERNOON.

REMARKS: NO PETS. NO SMOKING. CHILDREN OVER 10 WELCOME. TWO DAY MINIMUM STAY ON WEEKENDS AND HOLIDAYS. SPECIAL DINNERS FOR UP TO 50 PEOPLE CAN BE ARRANGED.

Driving north from San Francisco, over the Golden Gate Bridge, most travelers take either the scenic and winding Highway 1 or the faster Highway 101. But between these two roads is a vast and continuous band of rolling hills. Because there are relatively few roads through these foothills, many don't know of the beautiful, secluded valleys. Occidental is a small village within one of these valleys. Innkeeper Jack Bullard happened upon Occidental when looking to relax after retiring from managing the business affairs of legal firms. He wanted to be surrounded by friendly people, to be able to showcase his many collections, and to live in a wonderful setting. Opening an inn in this quaint community was his answer and is travelers' good fortune. Be sure to ask Jack for a personal tour of the inn. We were delighted to have him point out his treasures, tastefully displayed in each room.

VICTORIAN DETAILS

As soon as the inn was Jack's, the remodeling began. One of his first projects was to restore the original Victorian touches to this 1877 home. The result is the stunning Inn At Occidental. Fir floors shine, and the bright white wainscoted hallways lead to eight beautifully decorated guest rooms. The meticulous attention to detail in every stage of the remodeling allows the classic architecture of the original home to blend seamlessly with contemporary comforts and amenities.

Each of the guest rooms is furnished with antiques and original art from Jack's private collection. The Ivory Suite features Jack's grandparents' beds which join to make a king-size bed, a brick corner fireplace, and a large French window. The Sugar Suite has a private patio and a new fireplace which can be enjoyed from the king-sized bed. The Quilt Suite is a wonderful sunny room with fireplace, 10-foot ceilings and a Jacuzzi spa for two. The Cut Glass Room has doors which lead onto a private patio, complete with bent willow chaise lounges and a new six-person hot tub. Each accommodation is individually decorated with comfortable furnishings and elegant fabrics.

GARDEN DINING

Breakfasts at the inn are always memorable, filled with warmth, friendly conversation and delicious foods. During our last visit, we were served a selection of fresh fruit, juices and homemade granola. This was promptly followed by a lavish serving of Orange-Thyme Pancakes. During our second morning, the weather was perfect for enjoying the entire process again, this time outdoors on the patio. The only part of the delicious breakfast which was the same as the morning before was the quality of the selections and the service.

DOWN TO THE WINE CELLAR

The Inn's wine cellar is no dark and damp closet, rather a large and well-loved room below the Inn. It is an ideal location for a gathering of friends, for hosting a wedding reception or a private meeting.

Jack often hosts the Sonoma County winemakers at multi-course gourmet dinners. With a little pre-planning, you can arrange your visit to coincide with the Sonoma County Tastemaker's Dinner, which is attended by the owners and producers of some of the county's finest food products.

A STONE'S THROW

Occidental is ideally located within an hour of San Francisco, close to the Sonoma wine country, and near Bodega Bay's coastal area. The Russian River "Wine Road" begins a few miles from the Inn and meanders through the Russian River Valley. With six grape-growing appellations, you must sample some of the Chardonnay and Pinot Noir grown in this cooler region. When driving toward the coast, be sure to stop at Theresa's church and the schoolhouse, just south of Bodega. This is where Alfred Hitchcock filmed his horror classic, "The Birds."

GETTING THERE

From Hwy. 101, take the Rohnert Park/ Sebastopol exit and go 7.4 miles to Sebastopol. Turn left at light and follow signs to Bodega Bay for 6.4 miles. Turn right at sign for Freestone and occidental and continue for 3.7 miles to stop sign in Occidental. A right turn at the light brings you up the hill to the Inn.

THE STANFORD INN BY THE SEA
~ CALIFORNIA ~

LOCATION: FACING THE OCEAN, JUST SOUTH OF MENDOCINO. AT COAST HIGHWAY #1 AND COMPTCHE-UKIAH RD.

ADDRESS: P.O. BOX 487, MENDOCINO, CA 95460

HOSTS: JOAN AND JEFF STANFORD

TELEPHONE: 707.937.5615

TOLL FREE: 800.954.8585, EXT. 1012

FAX: 707.937.0305

ROOMS: 33

RATES: $195 TO $245 SINGLE; $250-$350 SUITES. RATES INCLUDE BREAKFAST.

REMARKS: TWO DAY MINIMUM STAY ON WEEKENDS. PETS ACCEPTED.

The century-old town of Mendocino perches on a broad headland of Northern California's rugged coast. Once a thriving logging community, Mendocino's Victorian buildings are now home to art galleries, handicraft shops and fine boutiques. We find Mendocino to be one of those rare travel discoveries that needs to be slowly savored. There is no better way to appreciate the Mendocino area than by staying a few days at The Stanford Inn by the Sea.

Adjacent to the inn, the Big River winds through a forested canyon and flows into Mendocino Bay. The estuary's undeveloped shores are home to a host of wildlife such as deer, black bears, beavers and blue herons. Nothing intrudes upon this inn's secluded grounds except nature.

INVITING HAVEN

Innkeepers Joan and Jeff Stanford have created a truly special place. They have dedicated themselves to building what Jeff calls "a truly unique and healthy place— a place for re-creation." Joan adds," The inn provides an opportunity for people to get excited about life again." Walking through the gardens, visiting the inn's llamas and horses, canoeing, sitting on a rock by the ocean, or just taking some time to unwind, guests love being at the Stanford Inn.

Each of the 33 rooms opens onto a deck, offering spectacular panoramic views of the ocean and the grounds. All rooms have private bathrooms and wood-burning fireplaces and are beautifully decorated with sleigh or four-poster queen- or king-size beds, authentic antiques and fine reproductions. When you arrive, a bottle of local vintage wine is placed on a silver platter in your rooms and this completes the picture.

A small Nantucket-style cottage near the river contains two lovely suites, each equipped with its own full kitchen, living room and bedroom. The suites overlook the canoes gathered on the shore of the river.

LAVISH GROUNDS

After a full breakfast, we love to sit pool-side by the greenhouse where, in this tropical environment, you will find orchids, fishtail palms and lush bougainvillaeas surrounding the large pool, sauna and spa. A visit here is more than a physical workout; it is a sensual seduction. We begin and end our days here soaking in the fragrant plants, the classical music and the views.

BIG RIVER NURSERIES

The Stanford's have created the Big River Nurseries as a certified organic garden to produce lettuce, herbs, spices, onions, garlics and other vegetables for local restaurants. They use French intensive, biodynamic and organic growing methods to produce their fresh and healthy crops. Some of the nursery's raised beds also provide roses and other varieties of flowers. You will find the dried herbs and floral wreaths throughout the inn.

A BIKE'S RIDE AWAY

With Big River near by, the inn has canoes and kayaks available at Catch-a-Canoe and Bicycles Too! The Class I river is great for excursions. The Stanfords also have top-of-the-line mountain bikes for guest use. Take a ride down the bicycle route along Highway 1, or explore off-road through forests of redwoods and firs.

COASTAL WANDERINGS

The northern California coast offers intriguing sights in any season. Our favorite time to visit is in January when the windswept shore is often battered by storms which bring in driftwood, shells and the occasional glass fishing net float. Ask the inn for directions to some of the more secluded beaches.

Strolling along Mendocino's boardwalk, you will find about 75 galleries and shops. The staff at the inn can direct you to the best of the shops and to the restaurants for casual to fine dining.

GETTING THERE

From the north on Highway 1, cross the Mendocino bridge and then turn east on the Comptche-Ukiah Road. The inn will be on your left. Coming from the south on Highway 1, turn right on Comptche-Ukiah Road, which is the last road before the bridge.

THE GINGERBREAD MANSION INN
~ CALIFORNIA ~

LOCATION: NORTHERN CALIFORNIA, 20 MILES SOUTH OF EUREKA, 280 MILES NORTH OF SAN FRANCISCO.

ADDRESS: 400 BERDING STREET, FERNDALE, CA 95536

HOST: KEN TORBERT

TELEPHONE: 707.786.4000

TOLL FREE: 800.954.8585, EXT. 1013

FAX: 707.786.4381

ROOMS: 10

RATES: $140 TO $350. RATES INCLUDE FULL BREAKFAST. OFF-SEASON RATES AVAILABLE.

REMARKS: TWO-NIGHT MINIMUM STAY ON WEEKENDS, HOLIDAYS AND SPECIAL EVENT PERIODS. NO SMOKING. NO PETS. RESERVATIONS RECOMMENDED.

The entire town of Ferndale has been declared a state historic landmark. It is here, in one of the country's best-preserved Victorian villages, that you'll find the Gingerbread Mansion. A beacon of warmth and hospitality, this brightly painted bed and breakfast is set just off Ferndale's Main Street. The 19th century turreted building evokes a world of enchantment and serenity.

The Victorian structures of Ferndale were nicknamed "Butterfat Palaces" by the Portuguese and Scandinavian dairymen who settled the area in the late

1800s. The ornate houses are still maintained by descendants of the "Cream City's" founding fathers. With no parking meters or stoplights, Ferndale is a perfect place to spend a weekend.

A blend of Queen Anne and Eastlake architecture with intricately detailed "gingerbreading," the Gingerbread Mansion was built in 1899 for a local physician, who turned it into the Ferndale General Hospital in the 1920s. Partially restored in the 1960s, Ken Torbert bought the mansion in 1981, where, over the course of two years he created an elegant, romantic retreat.

MANY EXTRAS

Four parlors offer opportunity to relax. Two, with fireplaces, are stocked with an excellent collection of books and games. In the afternoon, we have enjoyed gathering with other guests for tea and a variety of cakes and confections around the fire. The Gold Parlor invites guests to participate in completing two 1,000-piece jigsaw puzzles of the mansion. No radios, televisions or telephones can be found in the mansion's serene guest rooms, but a parlor guest phone is available.

HIS AND HER BUBBLE BATHS

Ken's meticulous care is evident in all guest rooms and suites, which are large and individually decorated with antiques, stained-glass windows, period art pieces and comfortable, firm beds. Bathrobes are tucked in the dresser drawers, and hand-dipped chocolates are left by the bedside when the staff turns down your bed. Many rooms have fireplaces, some have verandas, and some have sitting areas. All rooms have private baths with showers, and five have wonderful old-fashioned, claw-footed bathtubs. The Empire Suite offers a claw-footed tub in front of the fireplace, and a marble-lined walk-in shower with two shower heads and five massage jets.

BOUNTIFUL BREAKFAST

In the morning, a tray of coffee or tea waits on the hall sideboard for you to enjoy in your room. But it won't be long before enticing aromas lead you into the elegant dining room for breakfast. The two tables are beautifully set with Ken's rare collection of green cameo Depression glass.

A generous breakfast includes fresh fruits, juices, baked egg dishes and homemade granola. Locally made cheeses (salmon cheddar and caraway jack) are also served, with a variety of homemade breads, muffins and cakes. As you polish off the last few crumbs, Ken prepares you for a day of exploring with anecdotes about Ferndale's history and its colorful cast of characters.

THINGS TO DO

The inn is located only a block from the many Victorian shops and galleries, and although not visible from the inn, the Pacific Ocean is a mere five miles away. The highly acclaimed repertory theater hosts seven productions a year.

State and National Redwood parks are north and south of town. A long, untamed walking beach is just five miles from Main Street. There is a very special driving loop from Ferndale out to the Lost Coast (the most unexplored region of the California coastline). The loop continues over the mountains and comes back to Highway 101 through the giant redwoods.

GETTING THERE:

The Gingerbread Mansion is located 260 miles north of San Francisco. Take the Fernbridge/Ferndale Exit off Highway 101. Follow the Ferndale-Victorian Village sign to Main Street (about five miles). Turn left at the Bank of America. Go one block to Berding Street. The mansion is on the corner.

CARTER HOUSE & HOTEL CARTER

~ CALIFORNIA ~

LOCATION: IN THE "OLD TOWN" SECTION OF EUREKA

ADDRESS: CARTER HOUSE, 1033 3RD STREET, EUREKA, CA 95501; HOTEL, 301 L STREET, EUREKA

HOSTS: MARK AND CHRISTI CARTER

TELEPHONE: 707.445.1390

TOLL FREE: 800.954.8585, EXT. 5001

FAX: 707.444.8067

ROOMS: 31

RATES: $140 TO $280 DOUBLE; INCLUDES FULL BREAKFAST.

REMARKS: COMPLIMENTARY WINE AND HORS D'OEUVRES SERVED FROM 5 TO 6 P.M. IN HOTEL CARTER LOBBY. NO PETS. TEA AND COOKIES BEFORE BED. WINE SHOP IN LOBBY.

Mark Carter, a native Eurekan with a penchant for Samuel and Joseph C. Newsom designs, scratched an itch when he came across plans by those same architects which detailed an 1884 mansion that stood in the middle of San Francisco until the great earthquake and fire of 1906. Inspired by these old Newsom drawings, the Carter House, a romantic bed and breakfast inn opened in 1982 to rave reviews.

NEW CHALLENGES

Always ready for new challenges, Mark built Hotel Carter. across the street, to provide gracious accommodations for those who want the benefits of a classic hotel. The peach and ivory lobby of the Hotel Carter is enhanced by an eclectic display of contemporary art and bleached pine antiques, and the spacious 23-room establishment also houses an innovative restaurant which blends a contemporary California style with old-fashioned values: greet guests with open arms, offer a warm fire, a glass of wine and a houseful of laughter.

DETAILS AND DELIGHTS

Lavish detailing in the five guest suites of the Carter House is complemented by simple interior design. Crisp white walls, polished oak floors spread with Oriental carpets, splashes of modern art all add to the bright, uncluttered feel of the rooms. Cozy down comforters and thick robes are part of the ambiance.

All rooms in Hotel Carter have private baths (some with Jacuzzis), telephones and televisions. The deluxe suites on the hotel's third floor are appointed with marble fireplaces, double-headed showers and honor bars stocked with regional specialties. What we love best about these rooms, however, are the whirlpool spas, some of which have great views.

A fews doors down the street is the Bell House Cottage. The three rooms in this 1889 Victorian may be reserved as a unit or individually. Each room has a private bath, done in white marble, with a whirlpool tub; two have fireplaces. All have complete kitchens and living rooms with TV, VCR, stereo, and video and CD libraries. Mark and Christi are now remodeling another of the neighborhood Victorians into a one-bedroom retreat with a state-of-the-art kitchen. He plan this new cottage will become a cooking school and test kitchen.

EXPERIENCE IN DINING

Breakfast delicacies include fresh fruit, homemade granola, pastries and just-baked muffins. Sumptuous entrees highlight the generous and varied breakfast.

Christi Carter and her team of chefs produce innovative meals. "Everything is harvested from our garden and prepared the same day," says Mark. The hotel offers a multi-course dinner service five nights a week. With "fresh" as the key ingredient, the hotel's cuisine features a changing menu of regional delicacies, including North Coast seafood and garden herbs and vegetables. Make reservations early for their monthly Winemaker and Guest chef Dinners dinners.

Your appetizer might be Humboldt Bay oysters with Asiago or baked local Chevre with garden greens. Flavorful entrees may include grilled duck breast with Zinfandel-blueberry sauce, scallops sauteed in garlic, lemon and fresh herbs, or a special vegetarian creation. To finish off the meal, choose from a variety of pastries and desserts that Christi's crew prepares daily.

Carter's extensive wine list has twice been awarded the *Wine Spectator's* Best Award Of Excellence. They have also added full bar service

AROUND EUREKA

The clean ocean air invites a tour through Eureka's Old Town. Explore the boutiques and antique shops or take a Victorian home tour in a horse-drawn carriage. You'll find sights associated with a historic working seaport in addition to contemporary establishments.

GETTING THERE

From the north, follow Hwy 101 into town, it becomes 4th Street. Turn right on L Street and go one block. From the south, follow Hwy 101 through town and it becomes 5th Street. Stay on 5th for about 13 block to L Street. Turn left and go two blocks. the Hotel Carter is on the corner of 3rd and L Streets.

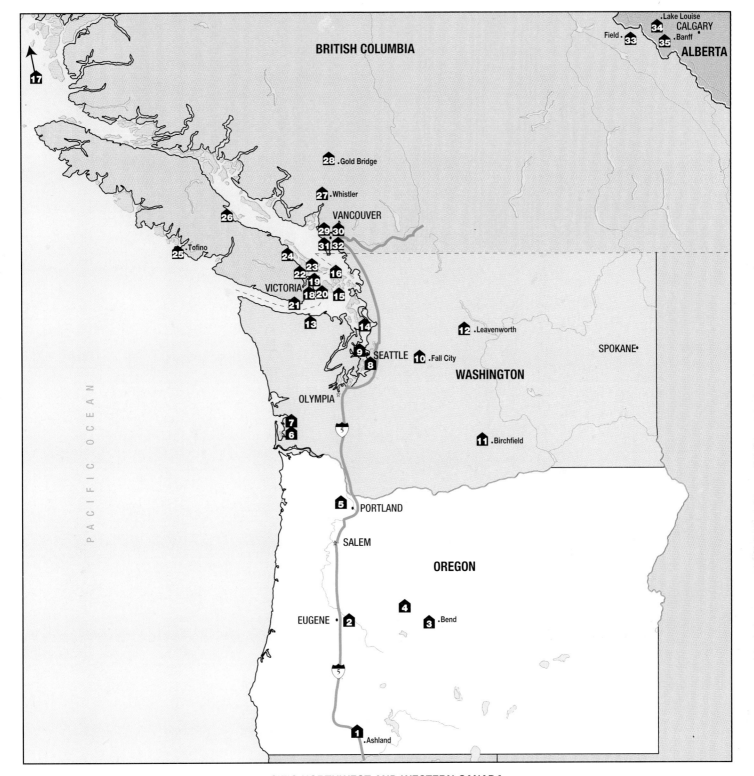

PACIFIC NORTHWEST AND WESTERN CANADA

1. ROMEO INN - Ashland, OR
2. CAMPBELL HOUSE - Eugene, OR
3. ROCK SPRINGS RANCH - Bend, OR
4. BLACK BUTTE RANCH - Sisters, OR
5. HEATHMAN HOTEL - Portland, OR
6. SHELBURNE INN - Seaview, WA
7. SHOALWATER REST. - Seaview, WA
8. INN AT THE MARKET - Seattle, WA
9. SORRENTO HOTEL - Seattle, WA
10. HERBFARM - Fall City, WA
11. BIRCHFIELD MANOR - Yakima, WA
12. RUN OF THE RIVER - Leavenworth, WA

13. DOMAINE MADELEINE - Port Angeles, WA
14. HOME BY THE SEA - Clinton, WA
15. INN AT SWIFTS BAY - Lopez Island, WA
16. TURTLEBACK FARM - Orcas Island, WA
17. ALASKA ADVENTURER - Juneau, AK
18. OCEAN POINTE RESORT - Victoria, BC
19. ABIGAIL'S HOTEL - Victoria, BC
20. BEACONSFIELD INN - Victoria, BC
21. SOOKE HARBOUR HOUSE - Sooke, BC
22. THE AERIE - Malahat, BC
23. OCEANWOOD - Mayne Island, BC
24. YELLOW POINT LODGE - Ladysmith, BC

25. MIDDLE BEACH LODGE - Tofino, BC
26. SHIPS POINT BEACH HOUSE - Fanny Bay, BC
27. DURLACHER HOF - Whistler, BC
28. TYAX MOUNTAIN LAKE RESORT - Gold Bridge, BC
29. PARK ROYAL HOTEL - Vancouver, BC
30. TEAHOUSE REST. - Vancouver, BC
31. WEDGEWOOD - Vancouver, BC
32. SEASONS REST. - Vancouver, BC
33. EMERALD LAKE LODGE - Field, BC
34. DEER LODGE - Lake Louise, AL
35. BUFFALO MOUNTAIN LODGE - Banff, AL

ROMEO INN

~ OREGON ~

LOCATION: IN SOUTHERN OREGON NEAR THE CALIFORNIA BORDER

ADDRESS: 295 IDAHO STREET, ASHLAND, OR 97520

HOSTS: DON AND DEANA POLITIS

TELEPHONE: 541.488.0884

TOLL FREE: 800.954.8585, EXT. 1014

FAX: 541.488.0817

ROOMS: 6

RATES: $95 TO $180 DOUBLE, INCLUDES FULL BREAKFAST.

REMARKS: TWO-NIGHT MINIMUM STAY JUNE THROUGH SEPTEMBER AND ON WEEKENDS FROM MARCH THROUGH OCTOBER. CHILDREN 12 AND OVER WELCOME. NO SMOKING AND NO PETS.

Just as 17th century England was marked by Shakespeare's prolific genius, so has 20th century Ashland been transformed by its internationally renowned Oregon Shakespeare Festival. Whether you're in town to catch a performance of Richard III, or simply searching out a romantic refuge, you'll find what you need at the Romeo Inn. And more. The elegant Cape Cod style inn was built in the early 1930s and is set in a quiet residential neighborhood just eight blocks from the festival's center stage.

Don and Deana purchased the inn in 1996 and created a place that guests have said, "feels just like home." "No, better than home." "This is a place where guests can relax by the fire in the living room, read a book in the library or enjoy the outdoor pool, spa and lovely gardens. And they do, over and over again." explains Deana. At least half of the guests at the inn are repeat visitors, and many lasting friendships have been forged on the back patio and around the inn's swimming pool. The inn's relaxing atmosphere and central location is also ideal for small conferences of up to 15 people.

ROOMS FOR WHAT YOU WILL

Accommodations at the inn consist of four spacious guest rooms and two deluxe suites. Each of the rooms have telephones, king-sized beds and private baths, with traditional and antique furnishings. Beds are covered with custom-made hand-stitched Amish quilts.

The Coventry Room is upstairs and looks out over the flower gardens to the mountains. Downstairs, the Canterbury Room features a floor-to-ceiling brick fireplace. The downstairs rooms both have private entrances, which also accommodate guests with limited mobility, and daybeds for reading or lounging.

The Cambridge Suite has a comfortable sitting area under a vaulted ceiling, where you can look out onto the pool and garden. French doors open onto a private patio with a view of the Cascade Mountains. Set apart from the inn for complete privacy is the Stratford Suite. With a full kitchen and living room, this suite offers a sweeping view of the Cascades, the Rogue Valley and the gardens of the inn. The marble fireplace provides warmth, as does the two-person whirlpool tub with a skylight view.

LOVE'S LABOR

Breakfast at the Romeo Inn encourages early ris-

ing, as the smell of baked scones, muffins and freshly brewed coffee winds its way under the door to your room. A fresh fruit dish, such as a pineapple with maple cream and granola, starts the meal right. The fruit course is always accompanied by fresh-squeezed juices. New entrees are always being created as they have continued the inn's tradition of trying not to serve the same meal twice to any previous guest. We like to take our morning coffee in the warm sunshine of the back garden.

A ROSE IS A ROSE

After breakfast, we suggest you follow our normal pattern and relax in the Jacuzzi, enjoy a swim in the pool, or explore the inn's gardens. Here, over 200 varieties of flowers bloom throughout the year. A pine-strung hammock and two garden benches encourage relaxation among the flowered grounds, and a fountain entitled "First Love" completes the English garden atmosphere.

Ashland has hosted the Oregon Shakespeare Festival since 1935. From March through October, the festival presents the work of Shakespeare and other playwrights, with as many as nine plays running concurrently. The town's theatrical offerings also include productions by SOSC, The Oregon Cabaret Theatre, and the Actor's Theatre Company. The Britt Festival in nearby Jacksonville features jazz, dance, bluegrass, and classical music under summer stars.

GETTING THERE

From the south on Interstate 5, take Exit 11 to Sherman Street. Turn left and proceed two blocks to Iowa and turn right for one block to Idaho, turn left. The inn is on the corner of Idaho and Holly. From the north, take Exit 19 to N. Main (Highway 99). Turn left on 99 and drive through downtown to Gresham. Turn right, drive four blocks to Iowa and turn left. Proceed one block and turn right onto Idaho.

CAMPBELL HOUSE INN
-OREGON-

LOCATION: TWO BLOCKS FROM DOWNTOWN EUGENE
ADDRESS: 252 PEARL STREET, EUGENE, OR 97401
HOSTS: MYRA & ROGER PLANT
TELEPHONE: 541.343.1119
TOLL FREE: 800.954.8585, EXT. 1035
FAX: 541.343.2258
ROOMS: 12
RATES: $85 TO $275; INCLUDES FULL BREAKFAST.
    PACKAGES AVAILABLE
REMARKS: INCLUDES WINE AND CIDER IN EVENING, SAME-
    DAY LAUNDRY SERVICE. ADJACENT TO HIKING TRAILS
    AND BIKE PATHS. MINIMUM STAYS REQUIRED ON SOME
    WEEKENDS AND HOLIDAYS.

Back in 1892 when the John Cogswell wanted to build a home for his daughter, he chose a site on Skinner Butte because of the territorial views to the South over Eugene. Now over 100 years later this three-story home is once again as lavish and sophisticated as it was originally.

After standing vacant for over 20 years, the "old Campbell place" needed more than just a good scrub and some tender loving care. It was through the interest of a local couple, Roger and Myra Plant, that the

8,000 square foot Campbell House Inn came to be. After five years of waiting and hoping, followed by a prodigious amount of effort, resources and pluck, they have opened the old Queen Anne style mansion as a "City Inn."

As you walk up the winding walkway to the inn, notice the well-manicured green lawns, acres of flowers and briskly busy tree squirrels. Entering on the main level through the French doors, you pass through the elegant marbled floor reception area into the parlor, dining room and library. The renovation restored all the parts of the old home which had character and charm. To this they have added the modern amenities that travelers require. Close to 2,000 square feet were added to the home to house the spacious guest rooms.

BELLS AND WHISTLES

All 12 rooms have large private baths. The suites all offer a variety of decor ranging from the Frazier Room, which is decorated in an English fishing and hunting lodge theme, complete with fly-fishing paraphernalia and knotty-pine paneling, to a two-room honeymoon suite, on the second floor. The Dr. Eva Johnson Suite is beautifully appointed in evergreen, melon and beige colors, giving the suite a country English ambiance. The room features a cherrywood four-poster king-size bed and a jetted tub for two tucked in a gabled window.

The Campbell Family is the premiere suite and is named after the original owners. This is a bright, spacious suite decorated in English hunting lodge decor. It is our favorite, with its incredible view of the city from its dormer window.

The rooms all have TV, VCR (video selections are in the library), and telephones. We appreciate the services available for the business guests, such as the fax machine and copier, and small conference rooms. Myra can even provide computers for pre-planned meetings.

We love the sound of trains. The whistle and distant clatter of the wheels conjures a haunting and romantic images. If you do not share this fascination, ask for a room facing the lush hillside.

Make no mistake, this is a romantic place. You feel this as soon as you come onto the grounds. Your treatment by the staff and the little extra efforts they go to on your behalf, all combine to make a stay here a very romantic experience. It is no wonder brides vie for the honeymoon suite. On our most recent visit, there was a wedding ceremony taking place outside under the spreading oak tree. Crisp white linens, gardenia flowers and the soft flickering of candles all added to the intimate attraction of the inn.

Before breakfast, we found a wooden butler outside our door, waiting with a serving of freshly brewed coffee. Myra offers a full breakfast each morning, including some freshly baked goodies. If you have any special dietary requirements, just let her know in advance of your arrival.

The inn is an easy three block walk down the hill to the historic district, the performing arts Hult Center, the 5th Street Public Market. Throughout the area you will find great restaurants, shops and Steelhead's, a wonderful brew pub.

We use the inn as our jumping off spot for exploring this scenic area of Oregon. The rugged coast is just over one hour's drive, as are the Cascade Mountains or the Oregon Wine country. Within 30 minutes you can be golfing or whitewater rafting.

GETTING THERE

From I-5 to I-105 heading west (exit 194B), take Coburg road/Downtown, Exit 2. Follow City Center Mall signs to East 3rd Street, which is the first street on right after crossing over the river. Then turn right on Pearl. The inn will be up the hill on the left.

ROCK SPRINGS GUEST RANCH

~ OREGON ~

LOCATION: NINE MILES NORTHWEST OF BEND
ADDRESS: 64201 TYLER ROAD, BEND, OR 97701
HOSTS: JOHN AND EVA GILL
TELEPHONE: 541.382.1957
TOLL FREE: 800.954.8585, EXT. 6007
FAX: 541.382.7774
ROOMS: 26
RATES: $1,575 PER ADULT-SINGLE, $1,430 PER ADULT-DOUBLE, $1,065 PER CHILD 6-16, $865 PER CHILD 3-5. SATURDAY TO SATURDAY. OPEN LATE JUNE THROUGH AUGUST. AMERICAN PLAN. HOLIDAY RATES AVAILABLE FOR THANKSGIVING.
REMARKS: BABY-SITTERS HOUSED AND FED FOR SMALL CHARGE WHEN TRAVELING WITH FAMILY. NO PETS.

Nestled among the Ponderosa pine and juniper forests in the foothills of central Oregon's Cascade mountains, Rock Springs Guest Ranch is a comfortable, self-contained resort where guests quickly become part of an extended family. The ranch is situated in a small valley with lush green pastures and dramatic rim rock. The main lodge overlooks a spring-fed pond with 30-foot high volcanic boulders as a backdrop. It is a place with strong traditions and ties; in fact, over half of the guests return year after year.

Donna Gill, the dynamic founder of the ranch, is a bit of a legend in this part of the country. Listed among the Great Women of Oregon, Donna was one of the pioneers in the area's recreation industry. She built Rock Springs Guest Ranch in 1969 with families in mind and ran the ranch until she passed away in 1983. Her nephew John, and his wife Eva, now continue the family tradition for which Rock Springs is famous-dedication to service.

CATERING TO FAMILIES

Rock Springs Guest Ranch caters to families with a week-long package that includes lodging, all meals, horseback riding, youth programs and lots of special activities. The main lodge serves as the common area for hors d'oeuvres, drinks, meals and socializing.

Youngsters gather each morning with the youth counselors and enjoy a well-developed program that includes horseback riding, evening hayrides, lunch rides, organized talent shows, hikes, swimming and an overnight camp-out.

While children are off exploring, learning the mysteries of the outdoors, and listening to tales of the Old West, parents have a chance to spend time together. In the evening the kids meet again for more adventures, while the adults gather for hors d'oeuvres and conversation.

PRIME RIDING

The ranch keeps about 65 horses for its guests. John's sister, Leslie, is a veterinarian, and attends to the care and fitness of the riding stock. Riders go out in groups of six or seven people of similar ability to explore the adjoining Deschutes National Forest. Set against the backdrop of the magnificent snow-covered peaks of the Three Sisters, these are some of the best trails in the country.

Activities and amenities at Rock Springs include horseback riding, a swimming pool, two professional tennis courts, a sand volleyball court, horseshoes, croquet, and fishing in the pond which is stocked with Rainbow trout. At the end of the day, relax in the ranch's custom outdoor spa. Set into a cave-like shelter of boulders, this is perhaps the most romantic setting we have ever found for a hot tub.

RUSTIC AND RELAXING

Eleven cozy, modern cabins sit among the tall ponderosa pines. These duplex and triplex units feature cathedral ceilings and knotty pine walls and accommodate from two to six people per cabin. All have private decks, and most have a fireplace, wet bar and sitting area; the staff stacks the firewood outside the door.

WELL-FED GUESTS

At Rock Springs the emphasis is on food with healthy choices, including flavorful low-fat and vegetarian choices. Breakfasts may include omelettes, homemade sticky buns, French toast, pancakes, waffles, fresh fruit, yogurt, granola, fresh coffee and juices. For lunch you can expect many options on the buffet table, ranging from traditional sandwiches to adventuresome items, plus soup and salad. Dinner includes such entrees as Baked Salmon, Marinated Beef Tenderloin or Chicken Piccata and is always accompanied by at least one meatless entree option. From fresh Northwest seafood to Country French cuisine there's something for everyone, and the view from the dining room is spectacular. The bar offers award-winning Oregon microbrewery beers and wines from Oregon and Washington.

GETTING THERE

To reach Rock Springs Ranch, follow U.S. 20 north from Bend for six miles to Tumalo. Turn west on the Tumalo Reservoir Road for three miles to the ranch.

BLACK BUTTE RANCH

~ OREGON ~

LOCATION: ON U.S. HIGHWAY 20, WEST OF SISTERS IN THE CASCADE MOUNTAINS

ADDRESS: P.O. BOX 8000, BLACK BUTTE RANCH, OR 97759

HOST: MICHAEL JUSTIN, GENERAL MANAGER; CARRIE LARSEN, RENTAL OPERATIONS

TELEPHONE: 541.595.6211

TOLL FREE: 800.954.8585, EXT. 3000

FAX: 541.595.2077

ROOMS: 113 HOMES AND CONDOS

RATES: $95 STANDARD ROOM, $105 DELUXE ROOM, $137 TO $194 ONE- TO THREE-BEDROOM CONDO APARTMENTS, $135 TO $295 TWO- TO FOUR-BEDROOM HOMES.

REMARKS: MINIMUM STAYS DURING THE SUMMER SEASON. NO PETS, FIREWORKS, MOTORCYCLES, SCOOTERS, ROLLER DEVICES OR OFF-ROAD VEHICLES.

On the eastern slopes of Oregon's Cascade range, the Ponderosa pines grow tall and stately, a safe habitat for deer, coyote, porcupine and raccoon. Eagles and osprey build their nests high in the pine's boughs, and squirrels, chipmunks and quail gather their seeds for food. At the 3,300-foot level, where the pines give way to meadows and lakes, you'll find Black Butte Ranch, Oregon's great golf and tennis resort. The ranch is surrounded by seven peaks that range from the 6,415-foot cinder cone called Black Butte to the proud 10,495-foot Mount Jefferson. Sitting on the patios and decks of the ranch's condos and homes to watch the sun's first light on the meadow, you would be hard-pressed to tell where the ranch ends and the rugged Cascades begin.

NOT A CARBON COPY

Black Butte Ranch is a destination resort unlike any other. Each unit in the 1,830-acre development is individually furnished and privately owned, and many are managed by the ranch. Rental manager Carrie Larsen explains, "We offer deluxe hotel-type rooms to one, two, and three-bedroom condominium units. For the vacationing family, we can also provide complete homes." Many of the units have fully stocked kitchens, washers and dryers, rock or brick fireplaces or wood-burning stoves, and all have televisions, telephones and wide inviting decks. Guests receive many of the same privileges accorded the owners; access to two golf courses, four swimming pools, 19 tennis courts, miles of bike and jogging paths, and the lodge. The lodge is a three-story glass, fir and pine building made a little more grand by the scale of the scenery outside its floor-to-ceiling windows. The furnishings combine antique tables and secretaries with modern pine and fabric chairs.

RANCHHOUSE SPECIALTIES

The Restaurant at the Lodge, with its unsurpassed view of the mountains and overlooking Big Meadow, is renowned for its award-winning cuisine. Ranch dinner specialties include generous cuts of Prime Rib, New York steak, roasted duck, fresh Pacific salmon and Oregon oysters. The wine list contains over 90 selections from Oregon, California and Washington.

Breakfast specialties include giant cinnamon rolls, eggs Benedict, and a farmers omelet. Lunch includes an assortment of deli sandwiches, salads, and a hot kettle of soup with fresh fruit.

THE SPORTING LIFE

Golf is the main recreational activity at Black Butte Ranch, which was awarded a silver medal by *Golf Magazine* as one of the top 50 golf resorts in the country. Residents and guests play on two 18-hole courses located amid the trees and within view of the mountains and lakes. Both Big Meadow, a 6,880-yard par 72, course and Glaze Meadow, a 6,600-yard par 72, course are open seven days a week in the spring, summer and fall. The facilities include a driving range, practice green and a pro shop at each course. The ranch offers golf clinics in the spring, along with golf packages. Golf professionals are available to assist you with your game throughout the summer.

If golf has a rival at the ranch, that rival's name is tennis. There are 19 Plexipave courts in seven different locations.

On Oregon's hot summer days swimmers can cool off in any of the four large pools. There is great fishing on the Deschutes and Metolius rivers, or catch and release with barbless hooks on the lake near the lodge. The lodge has a good rental fleet of bicycles to cruise the 18 miles of paved biking trails. In the winter, cross-country ski rentals are available at the Sport Shop.

Sisters, the Western town eight miles east of the ranch, has only three streets, yet more than 70 businesses, shops and restaurants line them. This small ranch community is also known as the llama capital of North America.

GETTING THERE

From the north, drive to Redmond, then turn onto Highway 126 to Sisters. From the south, drive to Bend, take Highway 20 to Sisters. From the west, take Highway 22 from Salem, or Highway 126 from Eugene, which merges with Highway 20. The well-marked ranch turnoff is eight miles west of town.

THE HEATHMAN HOTEL
~ OREGON ~

LOCATION: DOWNTOWN IN THEATER AND SHOPPING DISTRICT
 AT BROADWAY AND SALMON
ADDRESS: 1001 SW BROADWAY, PORTLAND, OR 97205
HOST: PIERRE ZREIK, GENERAL MANAGER
TELEPHONE: 503.241.4100
TOLL FREE: 800.954.8585, EXT.4000
FAX: 503.790.7111
ROOMS: 150
RATES: $160 TO $205 SINGLE; $180 TO $225 DOUBLE; $275 TO $675 ONE-AND TWO-BEDROOM SUITES
REMARKS: WEEKEND AND SPECIALTY PACKAGES ARE AVAILABLE.

At a time when cities across the nation were bursting at their seams, yet ignoring the consequences of traffic and unplanned sprawl, Portland was tearing up freeways and planting parks. At a time when pollution was considered a fact of city life, Portland was turning to hydroelectric power and clean air, and restoring the Willamette River to ensure the purest drinking water in the country. And from the look of Portland's charming neighborhoods, verdant parks and active downtown, their efforts have really paid off. Portland has become one of our favorite places to visit.

REBIRTH OF A LEGEND

As modern spires began appearing on the skyline, the City of Roses inspired the restoration of The Heathman Hotel. The New Heathman Hotel was the toast of the town when it opened in 1927, but by the mid-eighties, it clearly had been up too late and hosted too many parties. In 1984, the hotel reopened after a two-year restoration, its solid 10-story brick exterior in harmonious opposition to the glass and steel highrises.

ORIENTAL FLAVOR

The hotel's subtle oriental flavor is evident throughout, including its Ming pieces and a rare rice paper Japanese Imari screen. The Heathman's mezzanine level includes a secluded library with signed first editions from renowned writers. A bar with bistro-style dining contains art pieces from the Elizabeth Leach Gallery and has a view to the Tea Court below. The mezzanine has a private door that connects to the Arlene Schnitzer Concert Hall.

The hotel's 150 guest rooms and suites have all been designed with the needs of the discerning traveler in mind, and the hotel has available parlor suites with corner view living rooms for a variety of hospitality and business functions. The recently remodeled Grand Suite offers the highest level of comfortable elegance, with its cozy living room, fireplace, and master bedroom and bath.

Warm tones of terra cotta, celery, and ivory accent the polished hardwood and contemporary McGuire rattan furnishings, which are covered in colorful English chintzes. King and queen-sized beds are available and rooms offer every conceivable amenity-private bars, 24-hour room service, plush bathrobes, luxurious hard-milled soaps and bath accessories, and nightly turndown service. Choose a complimentary film from the hotel's collection of over 300 movies, or head to the new third-floor fitness suite for a workout.

DESIGNER DINING

The Heathman restaurant has an enviable reputation for its local Oregon seafood, freshwater fish, game and other hand selected delicacies. Its energetic atmosphere is enhanced with Andy Warhol's "Endangered Species" animal art. For more casual fare, there's the Marble Bar, or the Mezzanine Bar & Library, one of the hotel's "best kept secrets."

Around the corner and up the block is the B. Moloch/The Heathman Bakery & Pub. Its fun-loving decor highlights the work of 19th century French caricaturist, Henri Colomb. A 10-ton woodburning oven adds to the flavor of the cooking that has won the pub a loyal local following. We often order take-out from the Bakery and return to the quiet of our room to enjoy both the food and one of the hotel's videos.

IN THE CENTER OF THINGS

The South Park Blocks area is home not only to The Heathman Hotel, but is the cultural heart of the city as well. The Portland Art Museum, Oregon Historical Society and Portland State University are located here. The neighboring Performing Arts Center is host to the Oregon Symphony and numerous theatre productions. Two blocks away is historic Pioneer Courthouse Square, known as "the living room" of Portland. Nordstrom, Saks, Niketown and other stores are nearby.

GETTING THERE

From the north, Take I-5 to the City Center Exit across the Broadway Bridge. Bear left on Broadway and go 16 blocks to the corner of Broadway and Salmon. The hotel is on the right. From the south, Take I-5 north to I-405 and continue on to the Salmon Street Exit. Go right on Salmon Street to the corner of Salmon and Broadway and make a right turn to the hotel. Valet parking is available.

SHELBURNE INN
-WASHINGTON-

LOCATION: ONE MILE SOUTH OF LONG BEACH ON LONG BEACH PENINSULA.

ADDRESS: 4415 PACIFIC WAY, SEAVIEW, WA 98644

HOSTS: DAVID CAMPICHE AND LAURIE ANDERSON

TELEPHONE: 360.642.2442

TOLL FREE: 800.954.8585, EXT. 1015

FAX: 360.642.8904

ROOMS: 15

RATES: $99 TO $175 DOUBLE. MIDWEEK OFF-SEASON LODGING PACKAGES AVAILABLE OCTOBER THROUGH JUNE.

REMARKS: COMPLIMENTARY COUNTRY BREAKFAST WITH ROOM. NO PETS. NO SMOKING.

The Shelburne Inn, built in 1896, just celebrated its 100th year. It is the oldest continuously operating lodging establishment in the state. Located on the 28 mile Long Beach Peninsula, the inn was originally a Mecca for Oregonians. Summer guests would come down the river on a paddlewheeler to the Port of Ilwaco, then board a narrow gauge railroad to Seaview. The existing inn is now on the National Register of Historic Places and has undergone a series of changes that includes the uniting of two buildings from opposing sides of the street to where the inn now stands.

FINE DINING

On the ground floor, you'll find the nationally acclaimed Shoalwater Restaurant and the Heron & Beaver Pub, which serve lunch and dinner. Recently the Shelburne Inn was selected as one of the "10 Best Country Inns in America." This is the only place we have discovered in the rural Northwest where you can have this quality lodging experience combined with a world-class restaurant experience of the Shoalwater.

David Campiche, a Seaview native, and his wife, Laurie Anderson, purchased the inn in 1977 and began renovation. Both are knowledgeable in antiques, and together they collected the quality pieces that now fill the inn. A new wing added five guest rooms, bringing the total to 15. In 1992, *Conde Nast Traveler* named the Shelburne Inn one of the 25 top inns worldwide.

QUIET VICTORIAN RETREAT

All of the rooms in the three-story inn have private baths; two rooms are suites. Colorful quilts along with crocheted pillow shams and marble-topped dressers add distinction to each room. Regional and European artwork blends gracefully on the walls. Most rooms open onto verandahs bright with potted flowers.

Each morning, guests gather around a large table in the lobby, where they are served a breakfast that we believe to be one of the "best in the world." David, Laurie and their staff devote much of their energies to creating a unique breakfast prepared from a seasonal array of unusual, indigenous foods. The choice of four entrees could range anywhere from oyster frittatas and homemade sausage to herb scrambled eggs kasari and pan-fried oysters. The whole family are mushroom collectors, and often strike out with the famous forager, Veronica Williams, in search of goosetongue and sea greens, and fresh wild watercress. The Shelburne's country-style feast has been featured in *Gourmet* and *Food and Wine*, and is complimentary with your room.

YEAR-ROUND DESTINATION

Winter is our favorite time on the peninsula, when big storms hammer their way along the coast. Bundle up and beachcomb for Japanese fishing floats, driftwood, and shells. The 28 miles of state-owned beach are perfect for favorite oceanside pastimes like kite flying and photography, and expansive wildlife refuges are located at both ends of the peninsula. But, best of all is the simple pleasure of slowly walking along the beach, enjoying this natural setting.

The Shelburne Inn is situated at the juncture of the Columbia River and the Pacific Ocean. Charter fishing for salmon and sturgeon is available out of Ilwaco. Nearby lakes are full of bass and trout. Willapa Bay is the cleanest estuary in the United States, and supplies the country with 20 percent of its oysters, annually. Ask David to show you where to find the biggest razor clams on the beach.

Bring along a canoe or kayak to explore the refuge on Long Island in Willapa Bay. You can hike for hours among its 247-acre stand of red cedars, which provides sanctuary for elk, deer, bear and the great blue heron.

Back on the mainland, horseback riding, tennis and golf are all within easy reach of the inn. Curio shops, museums, and art galleries are great for browsing or picking up special gifts.

GETTING THERE

From Seattle, take Interstate 5 south to Olympia, then Highway 8 and 12 to Montesano. Follow Highway 101 south to Seaview. From the Oregon coast, follow U.S. 101 across the Astoria bridge and turn left to Ilwaco. Head north for two miles until you reach Seaview. The inn is on the left.

SHOALWATER RESTAURANT
~ WASHINGTON ~

LOCATION: IN SHELBURNE INN ON LONG BEACH PENINSULA

ADDRESS: 4415 PACIFIC WAY, P.O. BOX A, SEAVIEW, WA 98644

HOSTS: TONY AND ANN KISCHNER

TELEPHONE: 360.642.4142

TOLL FREE: 800.954.8585, EXT. 8001

FAX: 360.642.8826

CUISINE: NORTHWEST

PRICES: $12 TO $24

HOURS: LUNCH SERVED IN PUB 11:30 A.M. TO 3:00 P.M.; DINNER 5:30 P.M. TO 9:30 P.M. OPEN DAILY, EXCEPT CHRISTMAS DAY AND DECEMBER 1 THROUGH THE 15.

REMARKS: RESERVATIONS RECOMMENDED. AWARDED FOUR STARS BY THE MOBIL GUIDE.

The Shoalwater Restaurant shares what owner Tony Kischner describes as a "symbiotic relationship" with The Shelburne Inn. Linked by a couple of doorways, a strong friendship and a common spirit, the two businesses work in harmony to provide a complete dining and lodging experience. Their combined efforts are among the best you will discover in the west.

Tony, formerly the manager of Seattle's legendary Rosellini's Other Place Restaurant, and his wife, Ann, opened The Shoalwater in 1981. One hundred year-old stained-glass windows salvaged from a 17th century church in England have become the building's trademark facade. Tony blends the best of his international upbringing with his restaurant training to create a superb dining experience. Northwest foods are featured in a seasonally varied menu that changes every three months.

NATIVE PROVISIONS

The Long Beach Peninsula is surrounded by three bodies of water filled with fresh fish and seafood. Willapa Bay is famous for its oysters and steamer clams; the Pacific Ocean yields bottomfish, crab and razor clams, while sturgeon and salmon stream up the Columbia River. Chef Terry Riley combines these ingredients to create uncommon appetizers and entrees. "Terry's a masterful chef who can produce flavor and match foods in unusual ways that come off marvelously," says Ann. Whether you choose spring-run Chinook salmon with cranberry and blueberry mustard sauce, or poached oysters with saffron and ginger in a beurre blanc sauce, you can still steal a bite of your companion's stuffed pork tenderloin in a shallot and garlic cream sauce. Starred menu items are low-calorie or low-cholesterol. Ann's homemade bread accompanies the meal, and her dessert tray merits the rave reviews and awards she has received.

TONY'S FOLLY

"My one folly," is how Tony refers to his collection of over 400 wines that has received the *Wine Spectator's* Award of Excellence. To showcase this diverse selection, Tony, Ann and Chef Riley hold one-of-a-kind dinners, part of their monthly Northwest Winemakers' Dinner Series. Held in the off-season, the meals emphasize regional foods that enhance the characteristics of wines from a particular winery; the winemaker is also in attendance. It is well worth the effort to call ahead to find the schedule for these dinners.

We do not have many true country inns in western America. There is something very relaxing about a leisurely dining experience with wonderful wines, when concern about driving afterwards is removed.

Mardi and I were with Tony and Ann when the idea of creating *Special Places* was born. And it continues to be the discovery of exceptional places like the Shelburne Inn and the Shoalwater Restaurant which keeps us excited.

HERON & BEAVER PUB

Across the lobby is the Heron & Beaver Pub. The English stained-glass windows and dark, rich paneling contribute to its atmosphere. The pub has an exceptional collections of single-malt Scotches and fine Cognacs. They feature many Northwest microbrews on tap and all of the usual bar choices.

Lunch and light dinners are served in the pub throughout the year. We often take a lunch to go and enjoy the wonderful food as we are walking on the beach.

Both the Shoalwater Restaurant and the Heron & Beaver Pub have been featured in numerous national and international publications, including *Gourmet, Bon Appetit, Sunset Magazine* and the *Christian Science Monitor.* In 1995 the restaurant became one of only three in the state to be awarded the prestigious Four Stars in the *Mobil Travel Guide.*

GETTING THERE

From Seattle, take I-5 South to Olympia, then Highway 8 and 12 to Montesano. Follow Highway 101 south to Seaview. The restaurant is in the Shelburne Inn, on the left side of the road. From the Oregon coast, follow U.S. 101 across the Astoria bridge and turn left to Ilwaco. Head north for two miles until you reach Seaview.

INN AT THE MARKET
~ WASHINGTON ~

LOCATION: DOWNTOWN SEATTLE, IN PIKE PLACE MARKET
ADDRESS: 86 PINE STREET, SEATTLE, WA 98101
HOST: JOYCE WOODARD, GENERAL MANAGER
TELEPHONE: 206.443.3600
TOLL FREE: 800.954.8585, EXT. 5002
FAX: 206.448.0631
ROOMS: 65
RATES: $140 TO $210 DOUBLE; SUITES FROM $255; $15
    PER ADDITIONAL GUEST; SEASONAL RATES AVAILABLE
REMARKS: CHILDREN UNDER 16 STAY FREE IN PARENTS'
    ROOM. NON-SMOKING AND HANDICAPPED ROOMS AVAIL-
    ABLE.

Mardi and I celebrated our first anniversary here, in a room overlooking the majesty of the Olympic Mountains beyond Puget Sound and the eclectic energy of Pike Place Market below. The comfortable elegance of the Inn at the Market makes it an ideal spot from which to enjoy the environment of downtown Seattle. Guests enter from the street into a quiet brick-paved courtyard, decorated with large flower pots. The courtyard muffles the sounds of the city and prepares you for relaxing and enjoying the inn's comfortable atmosphere and personal service.

70

A LITTLE VILLAGE

Just beyond the courtyard and fountain is Pike Place Market, an historic farmers' market where fresh fish stalls, vegetable stands and delicatessens stand amidst a chorus of merchants calling out in a dozen languages. Our out-of-town friends often have fresh salmon, crabs and clams packed to go.

Surrounding the inn's courtyard are select shops and services. The Comfort Zone Relaxation Spa offers massage therapy, whirlpool, float tank and suntanning, all of which may be billed to your room. Room service for dinner is provided by Campagne, a wonderful French restaurant just across the brick courtyard. Bacco, an intimate bistro, offers room service breakfasts for guests of the inn.

IN THE INN

The inn combines European country decor with a host of amenities: downtown shuttle service, refrigerators, honor bars, coffee makers with fresh ground coffee delivered daily, and evening turn-down service with complimentary chocolates. A basket of luxury bath amenities is waiting in the spacious, tiled bathrooms.

Of the 65 guest rooms, 45 offer stunning views of Puget Sound, the Olympic Mountains, a garden courtyard or the market. All rooms feature floor to ceiling sliding-glass windows. Three parlor suites, two water-view townhouse suites and the deluxe rooms offer the best vantage points on Seattle surroundings.

A fifth-floor rooftop garden deck showcases a 180-degree view of Mount Rainier, Elliott Bay and the Pike Place Market below. This is where we begin and end each day. Relax in one of the comfortable Adirondack chairs that dot the deck, or watch the ferries make their way from island to island.

The inn's conference facility accommodates up to 20 people for boardroom-style meetings.

SEATTLE ON FOOT AND AFLOAT

The Inn at the Market is ideally situated for shopping or exploring downtown Seattle. Shops around the market, major downtown boutiques and department stores are all within six blocks, and business travelers will also find major office buildings within short walking distance. The symphony, repertory theater, cinemas, opera and ballet are all easily accessible. Neighboring art galleries display a variety of local and imported talent, and the Seattle Art Museum is just four blocks away from the Inn.

Descending the stairs from the market, known as the Pike Hill Climb, you will arrive on Seattle's waterfront. Seafood restaurants, marine supply stores, import stores, the Seattle Aquarium and Omni Dome Theater line the busy wharves. A tramway runs parallel to the water, offering easy access to the entire length of the district.

Washington state is proud of its ferry system. Take a ride from Pier 56 to Winslow, on Bainbridge Island, for a half-hour cruise. Winslow offers a selection of shops and restaurants, and makes a pleasant jaunt. Most Seattleites agree, there are few better spots from which to view the sunset over the Olympic Mountains than from the sundeck of the ferry.

GETTING THERE

From Interstate 5 south, follow Stewart Street west through downtown Seattle to First Avenue. Turn left onto First Avenue, travel one block to Pine Street and turn right. The Inn at the Market is on the right side of Pine Street. From Interstate 5 going north, take Seneca Street west through downtown Seattle to First Ave. Turn right, traveling north on First until you reach Pine Street. Turn left on Pine. Inn at the Market is on your right. Valet parking is available.

SORRENTO HOTEL
~ WASHINGTON ~

LOCATION: DOWNTOWN SEATTLE

ADDRESS: 900 MADISON STREET, SEATTLE, WA 98104

HOST: JIM TREADWAY, MANAGING DIRECTOR

TELEPHONE: 206.622.6400

TOLL FREE: 800.954.8585, EXT. 4007

FAX: 206.343.6159

ROOMS: 42 SUITES AND 34 ROOMS

RATES: $160 TO $1200

REMARKS: COMPLIMENTARY DOWNTOWN TRANSPORTA-
TION. VALET PARKING. 24-HOUR FITNESS CENTER. ON
SITE FLORIST, HAIRDRESSER, AND SHIATSU MASSAGE
PRACTITIONER. MOBIL FOUR STAR AND AAA FOUR DIA-
MOND AWARDS. ROOM SERVICE AVAILABLE.
WHEELCHAIR ACCESSIBLE.

Built in 1909, the Sorrento Hotel is Seattle's first grand hostelry and the oldest operating hotel in the city. From its birth, the Sorrento's goal has been to provide guests with "the very best obtainable" and with its successful blend of old-world European elegance and American efficiency, friendliness, and technology, this is a mission fulfilled. When you enter the rich warmth of the paneled Honduran Mahogany lobby and lounge, the luxurious Italian-Renaissance decor reminds you that in its early days the Sorrento was once the venue of choice for visiting Vanderbilts and

Guggenheims. With all of the modern conviences, the hotel continues to attract discerning guests from around the world. We were not at all surprised to discover that in a 1996 poll of *Conde Nast Traveler* magazine's readers, the Sorrento was listed among the top 25 Hotels in the United States.

STYLISH SOPHISTICATION

Intricate terra-cotta ornamentation and beautiful antiques enliven the rooms and suites whisking you back to the days when evening dress, pearls, and top hats were high fashion. Though this gem exudes classy indulgence, each room is modernized with every conceivable amenity. Dataports, fax machines, black-out curtains, color TVs, stereos, dual-line telephones, private mini-bars, hair dryers and ironing boards are provided in each room, as well as terry cloth bathrobes and complimentary shoeshines. Since the Sorrento Hotel sits on one of the hills which over look downtown Seattle, many of the rooms and suites possesses views of the skyline, the Olympic Mountains, the busy harbor and the famous Space Needle.

NORTHWEST SPECIALTIES

The Sorrento Hotel's dining room, the Hunt Club, long one of our favorites, is renowned for its romantic dining experience and was selected "Best Restaurant in Seattle" by *Seattle Magazine. Gourmet Magazine* recently rated the Hunt Club one of America's best restaurants.

Impeccable service and fabulous dishes of eclectic Northwest cuisine make the meals a truly elegant Seattle event. The Hunt Club chefs will astound your taste buds with Dungeness Crab Cakes with Sweet Corn and Bacon, Pan Roasted Breast of Northwest Pheasant, and Classic Braised Osso Buco with Red Pepper Polenta. The favorite Alderwood and Rosemary Smoked Rack of Lamb is a small taste of heaven. The wine list is substantial. The desserts are a

sinful way to finish off your evening. The Hunt Club always accommodates special diet requests and vegetarian selections are available at all times.

If the on-site fitness club, hairdresser, and Shiatsu massage practitioner don't keep you busy, the Sorrento Hotel offers transportation to the center of Seattle where you can explore the shops in Westlake Center or browse the bustling Pike Place Market.

SEATTLE'S SECRETS

Since Seattle is our home town, we are often asked about things to do while staying in downtown Seattle. First on our list is to walk down into the Pike Place Market and create a picnic lunch from among the many vendors and restaurants there. Then continue down the hillside stairs to the waterfront area along Elliott Bay. Board a Washington State ferry, with a walk-on ticket and enjoy your picnic as the ferry crosses the Sound to Bainbridge Island or Bremerton. Try to time your trip so that the sun in setting on Seattle when you return.

Another suggestion is to head over to the Seattle Center for an elevated view of the city from the top of the Space Needle and then drive to the Hiram Chittenden Locks to watch the working and pleasure boats as they are raised and lowered during their passage from the inland lakes out into Puget Sound. Whatever your interests, Seattle is full of possibilities!

GETTING THERE

From I-5 South: Take James Street exit, cross under the freeway and turn left onto 7th Avenue, make a right turn onto Madison Street, go up Madison and turn left onto Terry Street.

From I-5 North: Take Madison Street exit and turn right onto Madison Street, go up Madison and turn left onto Terry Street. The Sorrento is on the corner.

GARDENS →
HERB PLANTS →
← RESTAURANT
← RESTROOMS
← PARK

THE HERBFARM
~ WASHINGTON ~

LOCATION: 30 MINUTES EAST OF SEATTLE

ADDRESS: 32804 ISSAQUAH-FALL CITY ROAD, FALL CITY, WA 98024

HOSTS: THE ZIMMERMAN FAMILY

TELEPHONE: 425.784.2222

TOLL FREE: 800.954.8585, EXT. 8003

FAX: 206. 789.2279

CUISINE: FOCUS IS ON FRESH HERBS WITH THE SEASONAL, REGIONAL FOOD OF THE NORTHWEST

PRICES: SIX-COURSE LUNCHEON PROGRAM, $65 PER PERSON; NINE-COURSE, 4-HOUR DINNERS WITH FIVE WINES $100 TO $125 PER PERSON

HOURS: NURSERY AND GIFT SHOP, 9 A.M. TO 6 P.M. DAILY; WINTER HOURS 10 A.M. TO 5 P.M. LUNCHEON IS AT NOON; DINNERS BEGIN AT 7PM.

REMARKS: RESERVATIONS REQUIRED FOR RESTAURANT. FREE CLASS SCHEDULE AND CATALOG ON REQUEST.

No visit to the Pacific Northwest is complete without a few hours spent at The Herbfarm. Seventeen display gardens invite your wandering while the aromatic country store beckons with its large selection of books, dried wreaths, herbal soaps, herb seeds and teas. A good place to begin your visit to The Herbfarm is with a hosted tour of the walk-through gardens. The "Herbal Identification Garden" shows you herbs as they'll be when they mature at your home. At the "Shakespeare Garden," the Zimmermans have planted herbs mentioned in Shakespeare's plays. Each is marked with the appropriate quote from the bard. The "Good Cooks Garden" entices you to try fresh herbs in your cooking. An "Oregon Trail Garden" grows all the herbs considered essential by pioneering women of the early West.

A Devastating fire

Just as we were preparing this edition the Herbfarm restaurant was gutted by fire. Work began immediately to prepare to rebuild the renown restaurant. Ron and Carrie tell us that the wonderful dining experience will rise" Phoenix like" from the ashes of the old wooden home. Plans call for a slightly larger restaurant and the addition of a long awaited country inn.

In the meantime, the classes will continue and the store and gardens are open.

Knowing that the rebuilding is in process, we will describe for you the experiences you will soon have available once again.

Fresh From the Garden

If you've come for a luncheon, peek at the two-acre Restaurant Kitchen Garden, then proceed into the charming dining room. Tables are set with crocheted placemats and moss-green cabbage leaf underplates. Behind the tiled counter in the kitchen, Ron Zimmerman, chef Jerry Traunfeld and staff are ready to start you on a three-hour culinary adventure. As the six-course meal unfolds, Ron, Carrie and crew share culinary expertise and herbal lore, and generously divulge their recipes. Carrie weaves through tables with herbs, giving diners a chance to smell and taste various herbs in their purest forms.

Farm-grown Freshness

Menus are ever-changing as vegetables mature in the farm's gardens and as local fish and game come into season. Your meal might begin with herbal souffles in brown hen's eggs, to be followed by spring asparagus with wild morels and caraway greens. An intermezzo of palate-clearing rose geranium and sweet cicely sorbet might lead to herb-smoked salmon with carrot and arugula sauces, followed by The Herbfarm's "Salad From the Meadow's Edge" bursting with over 30 herbs, seasonal greens and edible flowers. The day's feast could conclude with a fanciful selection of herbally flavored desserts, coffee and your choice of over 17 herbal teas. In the old restaurant, a maximum of 36

lucky people were hosted Fridays, Saturdays and Sundays from late April through Valentine's Day in February. We are hopeful that the new restaurant will be larger so that more people can experience the wonders which emanate from the creativity of Jerry, Ron, Carrie and their talented staff.

Herbs to Go

A visit to The Herbfarm doesn't have to end when you leave; you can take plants with you and start your own garden at home. Herbs grown here are shipped all over the country, and are available for mail order, as are most of the gift shop's selections. Be sure to put your name on the mailing list. the catalogues which Ron creates are wonderfully informative. Their arrival in our home is eagerly awaited event for us both.

Over 300 Classes

The Herbfarm also presents over 300 classes each year on herbs for gardening, crafts and cooking. Father's Day weekend brings the annual Northwest Microbrewery Festival, featuring over 30 breweries.

Getting There

Take I-90 east from Seattle to Exit 22 (Preston-Fall City). Go through Preston and toward Fall City. At the "Y" in the road after three miles, go over the green bridge to 328th SE. Follow signs one-half mile farther.

BIRCHFIELD MANOR

~ WASHINGTON ~

LOCATION: IN WASHINGTON WINE GROWING REGION
ADDRESS: 2018 BIRCHFIELD ROAD, YAKIMA, WA 98901
HOSTS: WIL AND SANDY MASSET
TELEPHONE: 509.452.1960
TOLL FREE: 800.954.8585, EXT. 2001
FAX: 509.452.2334
ROOMS: 11
RATES: $80 TO $175
CUISINE: CLASSIC INTERNATIONAL, REGIONAL AND ORIGINAL SPECIALTIES.
PRICES: FROM $19.95 TO $29.95 PER PERSON. INCLUDES A FOUR-COURSE DINNER, WITH HOMEMADE BREAD AND AFTER-DINNER CHOCOLATE. WINE, COFFEE AND DESSERT ARE EXTRA. RESTAURANT SEATING IS AT 7 P.M. ON THURSDAY AND FRIDAY, 6 P.M. AND 9:00 P.M. ON SATURDAY.
REMARKS: RESERVATIONS REQUIRED.

Birchfield Manor was originally built in 1910 by a Yakima sheep rancher. In 1979, Wil and Sandy Masset purchased this 2-1/2 story Victorian home and, after some initial remodeling, began serving Birchfield Manor's memorable meals. After 10 years of popularity, the Massets decided to finish remodeling the main house and they added five guest rooms on the upper floor of the manor. Thist addition in services to their guests was so successful and warmly received that they continued on and have since added six new cottage rooms. This makes the Birchfield Manor one of the very few full country inns in Washington. When you combine exceptional food service and warm lodging hospitality and put this package right on the edge of the growing Washington wine area, you have a combination that is seldom matched.

ACCOMMODATING MORE THAN YOUR PALATE

Each of the rooms in the original manor house have a private bathroom, and the English country elegance of antique furniture. Jenny is a cozy sun-filled room with a queen bed. Annie, Victoria and Allison have queen-size brass beds. Elizabeth, our favorite of the original rooms has a king-size bed, sitting area and a separate dressing room.

The new guest cottage rooms contain all of the amenities you need for a relaxing visit to the high desert country around Yakima. Cottage #1 is wheelchair accessible and contains one of those roomy showers.

All of the cottage rooms have telephones, TVs and wonderful views out into the countryside. Rooms 5 and 6, the Penthouse Rooms are extra large with a Vaulted ceiling, king-size bed and an additional sofa pull out queen bed. The TVs come with VCR and the bath is equipped with a steam sauna shower.

After a day in the nearby wineries and a wonderful evening in the dining room, a stay at the manor completes the experience. A swimming pool behind the house is available to guests. Smoking is allowed only on the outside decks and patios.

A WORLD CLASS RESTAURANT

Chef Masset apprenticed at the Olympic Hotel (now the Four Seasons Olympic) in Seattle. He completed his training in Saint Moritz, Switzerland. Chef Wil combines regional specialties with classic, international flair, and the result is a wonderful blend of contemporary foods like loin of pork stuffed with eastern

Washington goat cheese, served with hazelnut sauce-prepared in classic style. We find the food to be exceptional. Every dish is prepared with only the freshest ingredients, selected by chef Wil.

Dining at the Birchfield Manor is like having your own dinner party with friends. The small and intimate atmosphere will make you and your friends feel special. And because dinner is by reservation only you won't feel rushed through your meal nor distracted by others coming and going.

Menus at Birchfield change weekly and each new menu offers a choice of five entrees, including fresh fish, steak, lamb, a chicken or pork dish and a special chef's selection. Each four-course dinner includes vegetables, manor-baked bread and chocolate. A recent menu offered an appetizer of chicken ravioli Florentine, maifun salad with almonds, Cajun-style sauteed pork tenderloin medallions with Cajun mushrooms and vegetable sauce, racks of Eastern Washington lamb, filet mignon, or breast of chicken with a red wine and raspberry vinegar sauce. The wine list features an extensive selection of Yakima Valley and Washington wines, as well as California and imported wines.

For a sweet ending, Chef Masset imports Callebaut chocolate from Belgium and makes the delicious truffles served at the end of every meal. He also sculpts chocolate, creating seasonal designs like sleighs and spring baskets. Fresh herbs grow in the manor's flower beds and their own hot house supplies the kitchen with tomatoes, pumpkins and other vegetables.

GETTING THERE

From Yakima, take Interstate 82 south to Exit 34. Take Exit 34 to State Highway 24, eastbound. Travel two miles. Turn right on Birchfield Road. The manor is the first house on the right.

RUN OF THE RIVER
~ WASHINGTON ~

LOCATION: ONE-HALF MILE EAST OF LEAVENWORTH, ONE MILE OFF HIGHWAY 2.

ADDRESS: 9308 E. LEAVENWORTH RD., LEAVENWORTH, WA 98826

HOSTS: MONTY AND KAREN TURNER

TELEPHONE: 509.548.71711

TOLL FREE: 800.954.8585, EXT. 1050

FAX: 509.548.7547

ROOMS: 6

RATES: $95 TO $150; INCLUDES FULL BREAKFAST. NO SMOKING. ADULTS ONLY. NO PETS.

REMARKS: RESERVATIONS RECOMMENDED. TWO-DAY MINIMUM WEEKENDS AND HOLIDAYS.

Run of the River is a rustic log inn constructed in 1978 and purchased by Monty and Karen Turner in 1986. Since then there have been several additions and remodels to accommodate returning guests and friends. The decor is natural, much of it hand-crafted by local artisans, and full of the bounty of this spectacular setting.

The inn stands adjacent to the confluence of the Icicle and the Wenatchee Rivers, a former rendezvous for the Native Americans of the Wenatchee tribe.

Plentiful fish, game and berries made the confluence area a favorite tribal village and hunting locale. All these resources are still in place as guests enjoy the wildlife and birdlife that call the river home. Set beside a secluded bend, Run of the River is surrounded on two sides by a wildlife refuge. From the rooms, guests enjoy vistas of Washington's Cascade Mountains, aptly named the Enchantments.

SEEKING A CHANGE

Before becoming the gracious innkeepers you will find during your visit, Monty and Karen were school teachers in Las Vegas. Wanting a change in their lifestyle, they began a search for a new home and occupation which would bring them closer to their love of the outdoors. Their quest ended with the discovery of their own " little piece of paradise at the secluded bend of the Icle River." As outdoor enthusiasts, they knew this would be their permanent home since it offered an abundance of hiking, biking and cross country skiing right from the inn.

Wanting to proceed slowly with their ability to consistently deliver a quality lodging experience, the Turners began with two rooms in 1986. They now offer six delightful rooms in the inn. All rooms have hand-hewn log beds and natural twig furniture, more on the artistic side than rustic. Three rooms have jetted tubs for two, and those on the lower level have glass fronted woodstoves for extra coziness. All of the rooms have private baths, refrigerators, cable TV and a log swing on the deck. The flower and herb gardens and the bounty of the Northwest supply a stream of seasonal adornments for the guest rooms, common areas and the kitchen.

From the beginning, Monty and Karen endeavor to make each guest's stay memorable, to "make it count. Time is so rare, it shouldn't be wasted during a getaway. We make sure we know what our guests need and how to meet those needs."

MOUNTAIN AIR AND CRACKLING FIRES

Run of the River's great room has massive windows that help bring the beauty of the area inside. Light knotty pine paneling and river rock hearth woodstove creates an inviting place and adds warmth to the great room. This is an inn any man will enjoy. The logs, river rocks, decks and views immediately relax even the most inn-resistant of the male guests.

HOMEMADE AND HEARTY

Breakfast is served family-style at 8:30 AM, although late risers can always mosey down later for a light beginning. Freshly ground coffee, fresh fruit smoothies and a basket of warm muffins start the day, and then comes breakfast. Typical might be a platter of cinnamon-swirl French Toast, or a vegetable frittata garnished with fresh herbs from the garden.

Run of the River is located in the heart of Washington's finest recreation country and bikes are available at the Inn for exploring the area's country roads. More challenging terrain is easily accessible from the Inn. Other adventure options include white water rafting, rock-climbing, cross country and downhill skiing, wind surfing and paragliding. For the lower-gear guest, golf, hiking, or shopping in the galleries and shops of Leavenworth are special treats. Leavenworth has many fine restaurants to choose from after a full day of outdoor activity.

GETTING THERE

From Seattle, take I-5 north to Hwy. 2. Follow Hwy. 2 east over Stevens Pass. One-half mile after leaving Leavenworth, just after the bridge, take a right onto East Leavenworth Road. Go exactly one mile and turn right. The inn's sign will direct you to turn right down a country lane towards the river.

DOMAINE MADELEINE
-WASHINGTON-

LOCATION: 7 MILES EAST OF PORT ANGELES

ADDRESS: 146 WILDFLOWER LANE, PORT ANGELES, WA 98362

HOSTS: MADELEINE AND JOHN CHAMBERS

TELEPHONE: 360.457.4174

TOLL FREE: 800.954.8585, EXT. 1055

FAX: 360.457.3037

ROOMS: 5

RATES: $135-$165

REMARKS: FRENCH, SPANISH, FARSI AND GERMAN SPOKEN. CHILDREN OVER 12 WELCOME. BREAKFAST INCLUDED. NO INDOOR SMOKING. NO PETS. RESERVATIONS RECOMMENDED. MOBIL 4 STARS AND AAA 3 DIAMONDS.

West from Seattle, across the great inland bay, the sun sets nightly over the imposing Olympic mountains. Much of this jutting peninsula is National Park and most all of it is wild and scenic. Sitting on top of the bluff at the northern end of this beautiful area is our favorite hideaway. Gazing out from a protective woodland over the straight of Juan de Fuca, nature itself pays tribute to the beauty and romance of Domaine Madeleine. The grandeur of the environment highlights the comfort and hospitality pervading this idyllic inn.

Innkeepers, Madeleine and John Chambers, warmly greet and welcome each guest with their kindness and enthusiasm. They have both admitted to being incurable romantics and they strive to make every stay a memorable experience.

Madeleine was reared and educated in France and has taught foreign languages at all levels. John is from Oklahoma and has been a biology professor for over 30 years. You will experience their flair for details throughout your visit.

The inn is comfortably furnished with Oriental antiques, accented by white walls, warm wood, and large picture windows overlooking the water below. A hand made harpsichord, crafted by John, rests in the corner of the living room, by the side of the Columbia River Basalt fireplace.

ROMANTIC LUXURY

The stylish home is furnished in an eclectic manner with Asian, European and American antiques and modern furniture. The five rooms have different themes and styles ranging from country French to contemporary. Three of the rooms have private entrances, three have kitchenettes, and four have private jacuzzi baths for two. all have romantic fireplaces, king or queen size beds, phones, T.V.s, VCRs, CD and cassette players, as well as courtesy robes, books and magazines. From every room, guests enjoy either a waterfront or mountain view, intimately absorbing the splendor of this special part of the world.

PLENTIFUL DELICACIES

The dining room has an informal, lively air in which guests visit with each other and their hosts as Madeleine generously serves an extravagant four-or five-course breakfast. A typical morning begins with fresh French bread and croissants, cheeses and fruits, followed by the house specialty such as chicken crepes, or gourmet seafood omelettes. All the while, enjoying custom-blended coffee, guests move on to dessert which may be chocolate mousse or fresh fruit tarts. This adds up to an amazing feast providing an energizing start to the day. Most all dietary requirements can be met.

THE GARDENS

The gardens at Domaine Madeleine are enchanting, for John has magically created replicas of Monet's "Petites Allees" and a scaled-down "Japanese Bridge and Lily Pond." You must ask John for a tour of his gardens. You will see his excitement and love for the flowers and shrubs come alive as he begins to tell you about his beloved gardens. It is then that you realize what a wonderful teacher he must be. I have rarely planted anything in our garden, yet was fascinated for the hour I was able to spend with John.

While some guests enjoy croquet, volleyball, badminton, horseshoes and boules on the property, we love to just sit out on the lawn and gaze North across the Strait of San Juan de Fuca and into Canada. For the more adventurous, you can explore the Dungeness Spit Wildlife Refuge, drive up from Port Angeles to Hurricane Ridge, or West to Lake Crescent/Marymere Falls. Adventure opportunities in the area include fishing, rock climbing, river rafting and sea kayaking or hiking in the Hoh rain forest and along the Pacific beaches which are two hours away.

GETTING THERE

From Seattle: Take Bainbridge ferry. Highway 305 to 3, to 104 to 101 through Sequim. Three miles past fifth traffic light, turn right onto Carlsborg (at signal) go 1.8 miles, turn left on Old Olympic. After 3.7 miles go right onto Matson for .8 mile. Turn left onto Finn Hall Rd. Go 1 mile to Domaine Madeleine sign and turn north on their gravel drive.

HOME BY THE SEA

~ WASHINGTON ~

LOCATION: 25 MILES NORTH OF SEATTLE, ON THE SOUTHWEST COAST OF WHIDBEY ISLAND

ADDRESS: 2388 EAST SUNLIGHT BEACH ROAD, CLINTON, WA 98236

HOSTS: LINDA DREW WALSH, SHARON FRITTS-DREW, HELEN FRITTS

TELEPHONE: 360.321.2964

TOLL FREE: 800.954.8585, EXT. 1016

FAX: 360.321.4378

ROOMS: ONE WATERFRONT SUITE AND TWO COTTAGES

RATES: NOVEMBER 1 - MARCH 31 $145 TO $155; APRIL 1 TO OCTOBER 31 $155 TO $175

REMARKS: THE CAPE COD COTTAGE ACCOMMODATES CHILDREN. COTTAGE RATES INCLUDE WELCOMING FIRST-MORNING BREAKFAST BASKETS PLACED IN THE KITCHENS.

Once, while traveling through Yugoslavia in the early 1970s with her two young daughters, Home by the Sea's Sharon Fritts-Drew emerged exhausted from a difficult bus ride. A kind woman gave them refuge in her home where hot showers, good food and warm beds more than made up for the language barrier. This memory inspired the creation of Sharon's inn a year later on Useless Bay in Washington, a place which she had summered at for the past 20 years. Sharon began innkeeping with her mother Helen Fritts. Today, Sharon's daughter, Linda Drew Walsh, encourages guests, "to take a pause from the hurried world," just as her mother would.

Conde Nast Traveler recently named French Road Farm (one of the inn's lodgings) among "The 50 All-American Getaways," calling the retreat a place where locals "searching for pre-cyberwealth simplicity appease their nostalgia."

YOUR CHOICE OF SETTING

Home by the Sea offers a two cottages: French Road Farm and the Cape Cod Cottage, shown in the photo. They have one very romantic suite, the Sandpiper.

French Road Farm is a restored 1920s farmhouse on 10 quiet, forested acres amid centenarian firs and youthful vineyards. It is located just 10 minutes inland and is decorated with French and American Country antiques. The light-filled bedroom holds a queen-size bed. The reading room has a comfortable couch that folds out into another queen-size bed. French doors in both rooms open out onto a spacious deck overlooking the vineyard. From the vantage point in the cottage's seven-foot whirlpool bath, you can watch deer, red foxes and eagles, or simply listen to the numerous songbirds.

Sandpiper Suite faces west toward the Olympic Mountains. Its sandy shore is the habitat of eagles, blue herons, geese, ducks and sandpipers. The suite is furnished with comfortable over-stuffed armchairs, antique quilts to snuggle up in, and many books. In the spacious suite are a complete kitchen, full bath, queen-size bed, hardwood floors, wood-burning stove and eight-foot picture windows to capture spectacular sunsets. Plush robes and herbal bath salts accompany the outdoor deep soaking Japanese hot tub.

Just down the road from Sandpiper Suite is the 1940s Cape Cod Cottage, a family retreat with a queen-size bed, a double bed, a child's single bed and a crib.

Furnishings include American antiques, a Japanese deep soaking tub and a large, wood-burning stove.

LOCAL BOUNTY

On your first morning, enjoy a complimentary breakfast basket filled with farm-fresh eggs, fruit, Smoked Salmon, home-baked breads and muffins; and Home by the Sea's private-label jam, cheese, milk, coffee and juice. And to the delight of gourmet cooks, cottage kitchens are well equipped to take advantage of the Pacific Northwest bounty.

WHIDBEY ISLAND

Whidbey is the longest continuous island in the United States. Useless Bay, located on the island's southwest corner, is tucked under Double Bluff which stretches for a mile and is a perfect spot for beachcombing.

Across the road from the farm cottage is Island Greens Golf Course, styled after a course in Scotland. This enchanting par 3, nine-hole course is open to the public. Players simply plunk green fees in the milk can chained to a nearby tree, and you can play all day. Merkerk Rhododendron Gardens is close enough to tempt all flower lovers. From spring through summer, grand bushes reaching 20 feet high display brilliant flowers of all shades.

Ten minutes away from each cottage is the seaside hamlet of Langley, with its antique stores, book shops, cafes and galleries.

GETTING THERE

Drive north on Interstate 5 from Seattle to the Whidbey Island Ferry, exit 189. Once on Whidbey head north on Highway 525 for six miles to Bayview Center. Immediately after the Center, turn left on Bayview Road. Continue one mile to Sunlight Beach Road and turn right. At the end of the road, on the left, is Home by the Sea.

INN AT SWIFTS BAY
~ WASHINGTON ~

LOCATION: IN THE AMERICAN SAN JUAN ISLANDS
ADDRESS: ROUTE 2, #3402, LOPEZ ISLAND, WA 98216
HOSTS: ROB ANEY AND MARK ADCOCK, OWNERS, DAN ZAWORSKI, CAROL & TIMOTHY ORTNER, INNKEEPERS.
TELEPHONE: 360.468.3636
TOLL FREE: 800.954.8585, EXT. 1041
FAX:360.468.3637
ROOMS: 5
RATES: $85 TO $175
REMARKS: RESERVATIONS RECOMMENDED. NO SMOKING OR PETS. ADULTS ONLY. RATES INCLUDE FULL BREAKFAST, GOLF AND TENNIS NEARBY.

Lopez Island is a short 45-minute ferry ride from the harbor town of Anacortes. This picturesque gateway to the San Juan Islands is within easy driving distance of both Vancouver, British Columbia and Seattle. Once westbound on a Washington State ferry, the stress of the day begins to fall away as the spectacular scenery glides by. The allure of these islands can be bicycling quiet country roads, kayaking crystal clear water, hiking along rugged trails, whale watching, fishing, beachcombing, or just plain relaxing with friends and family. The sheer physical beauty of this region includes majestic Mt. Baker to the north and the rugged Olympic Mountains on the southern horizon. In between are dozens of emerald islands, each with its distinct personality and charm.

At the Inn at Swifts Bay, comfort takes on an entirely new dimension. Hosts Rob Aney and Mark Adcock, while new to the inn, are committed to upholding the long standing tradition of helping each guest to have some good old-fashioned fun and relaxation. their philosophy, posted in the well-appointed kitchen reads, "Our mission is to provide the finest, most comfortable accommodations in the San Juan Islands, anticipate our guests needs before they know them and treat each guest with the utmost dignity and respect."

AT THE WATER'S EDGE

As a guest you have the island at your doorstep, or you can choose to remain on the three acres of wooded grounds during your entire stay. The gardens and the views to the water enhance the English country decor. Immerse yourself in the hot tub nestled at the edge of the woods (robes and slippers provided, of course), walk down to the private beach, or enjoy a vigorous workout in the exercise studio followed by a relaxing sauna. There is also an extensive collection of books to read in the elegantly appointed living room or in the comfort of your own room. You may also be surprised to encounter genuine heirloom photographs of Hollywood stars and starlets, calling to mind the grace and beauty of days gone by.

The rooms are individually decorated with charm and light airy colors. All rooms have queen-sized beds with white goose down comforters (or lambswool if you prefer) to snuggle under, and the three suites offer gas-log fireplaces, sitting areas and refrigerators. Two of the suites have a shared bath.

LEISURELY LUXURIOUS BREAKFASTS

At Inn at Swifts Bay, breakfasts are served "nine-ish," complementing the change of pace philosophy you'll find here. The breakfast room is bathed in warm sunlight, and the yellow hand-stenciled walls reflect the morning glow. Selections may include hazelnut waffles with fresh Lopez Island berries with creme fraiche, or crab cakes made with fresh Dungeness crab caught in the bay. Perhaps you'll enjoy our favorite, the light, airy Inn at Swift's Bay Mushroom and Pepper Frittata, combining a dozen different mushroom flavors into a delicious taste sensation and topped with a sun-dried tomato coulis. Muffins are all baked from scratch using original recipes developed at the inn. There is always plenty of fresh dark-roasted coffee, homemade jams and fresh juice.

EXPLORING LOPEZ ISLAND

Lopez Island is the most pastoral of all the islands. The 1,800 residents share a feeling of community and connection with the beautiful natural setting. Expect cool and wet weather during winter months, and warm, dry days during the summer. One of the greatest attractions of Lopez is the lack of "attractions." But for the curious and energetic, there are plenty of sights and activities ranging from kayaking trips, biking the island "loop," whale watching from nearby Friday Harbor, boating, fishing and serious beach walking. Herons, bald eagles, otters, seals, and the magnificent Orca (killer whale) are at home in these islands.

GETTING THERE

Take Interstate 5 to exit #230 to Anacortes and take the San Juan Islands Ferry to Lopez Island. When you disembark the ferry, drive one mile to Odlin Park. Turn left onto Port Stanley Road opposite park entrance. The Inn is one mile up the road on your right.

TURTLEBACK FARM INN
~ WASHINGTON ~

LOCATION: SIX MILES FROM ORCAS ISLAND FERRY LAND-
ING IN CROW VALLEY.
ADDRESS: ROUTE 1, BOX 650, EASTSOUND, WA 98245
HOSTS: BILL AND SUSAN FLETCHER
TELEPHONE: 360.376.4914
TOLL FREE: 800.954.8585, EXT. 1017
FAX: 360.376.5329
ROOMS: 7 IN FARMHOUSE, 4 IN ORCHARD
RATES: $80 TO $210
REMARKS: NO SMOKING INSIDE, NO PETS, NO INFANTS.
CHILDREN BY SPECIAL ARRANGEMENT.

Turtleback Mountain swells up from the west lobe of Orcas Island, one of nearly 172 islands in the San Juan archipelago. Orcas' interior is comprised of wide valleys bordered by deep forests and punctuated with shimmering ponds and lakes. It is overlooking one of these meadows that you'll find Turtleback Farm Inn. The setting is serene, complete with green pastures, a barn and outbuildings, 300-year-old maples and six fresh water ponds.

Susan and Bill Fletcher completely renovated a

100-year-old "folk national" style farmhouse into one of the most charming inns we have ever discovered. Turtleback Farm Inn has it all with its friendly hosts, great accommodations, superb breakfasts and a fresh, uncluttered decor. The work to maintain and improve the property is an ongoing effort as the inn looks as sparkling new today, as it did on our first visit.

Hanging on the wall inside the front door is an ad from the September 22, 1933, *Seattle Daily Times* featuring the film "Tarzan the Fearless." The ad reads, "Buster Crabbe, muscular Olympic swimming champion, whose latest screen appearance brings excitement aplenty to the Roxy Theater." The famous actor is Susan's father.

The living room is a cozy gathering place for inn guests. A welcoming fire warms you and guests are always invited to use the wet bar, which is always stocked with special teas, coffees and cocoa.

Each of Turtleback's seven individually decorated guest rooms reflect the Fletchers' careful attention to detail. All are special, from the Meadow Room with its expansive view, to the Nook, which is reminiscent of a ship's cabin. Spotless fir floors throughout the inn are softened by imported rugs. Floral print cottons envelope wooly comforters; the wool is directly from the backs of the sheep you see grazing outside.

FRESH START

Dining room tables are set with fresh white linens, fine china and silver, and a turtle-shaped trivet with a pot of freshly ground coffee or brewed tea. During the summer, there are fresh berries from the island, and the fall brings apples from the trees right on the farm. Next comes Susan's famed granola. The next course, may be ricotta pancakes with fresh berry sauce, eggs Benedict, or smoked salmon buckwheat crepe gateau. Celtic harp music wafts in from the kitchen as guests begin their Orcas day in fine fashion.

The Fletcher's are constructing four stunning new deluxe king-bedded rooms in the Orchard House, which will be ready for guests in July 1997. Bill and Susan live in a separate home on the farm, so in the evening when they retire, guests can experience having the entire farmhouse to themselves.

AN ORCAS FOR EVERYONE

You mustn't leave Turtleback Inn without the Fletchers' personal map and advice on what to see and do. Bicycling, sailing, canoeing, kayaking and golfing on the public course are common island activities. A walk along the beach at Obstruction Pass is a prime way to view soaring eagles or the dorsal fin of an Orca whale disappearing into the Sound. If fresh air and nature help work up an appetite, you'll have plenty of great restaurants to enjoy.

In addition to swimming, Cascade Lake at Moran State Park offers trout fishing from small rental boats, or a chance to try out the paddle boats. Hikers will enjoy the two-mile walk around Cascade Lake, and the more than 23 miles of trails in Moran State Park. An easy quarter-mile walk through the forest brings you to Rustic and Cascade Falls. For the more ambitious, Mt. Constitution awaits. Its 2,409 feet offer a challenging hike, or scenic drive to the highest point in the San Juan archipelago. The views from the stone tower on top of the mountain are spectacular.

GETTING THERE

Take the Washington State ferry from Anacortes to Orcas Island. Upon arrival on Orcas, drive 2.8 miles on Horseshoe Highway. Turn left at the road sign that indicates West Sound, Deer Harbor. Travel one mile and turn right on Crow Valley. Continue nearly 2.5 miles, the inn will be on your right.

ALASKA ADVENTURER
~ ALASKA~

LOCATION: MAY-SEPTEMBER, JUNEAU, SITKA & KETCHIKAN AND THE WATERS OF SOUTHEAST ALASKA

ADDRESS: 1860 58TH STREET, TACOMA, WA 98422

HOST: CAPTAIN BOB HORCHOVER

TELEPHONE: 253.927.7147

TOLL FREE: 800.954.8585, EXT.7000

FAX: 253.927.7232

RATES: SEVEN-DAY INSIDE PASSAGE SEGMENT FROM $993 PER PERSON.

REMARKS: INCLUDES GOURMET CUISINE, WINE, BEER, SOFT DRINKS AND SALTWATER FISHING TACKLE. PERSONAL CHECKS PREFERRED.

Few people have the opportunity to see the richness of the waters and rugged coast of Southeast Alaska. Most cruise the main channels at over 20 knots, cocooned in large cruise ships that offer only glimpses of this dramatic vibrant scenery. The real experience awaits those willing to slow down and go where the "locals" go.

Southeast Alaska is a long gnarly finger of land, dotted by a few cities and towns with even fewer cars and roads. Wildlife here lives largely free from the fear of man, and the waters are clear and teeming with life. Humpback whales sound alongside, porpoises ride the bow waves just beyond your touch, while bald eagles circle overhead.

EXPLORE IN COMFORT

The best way to discover the real Alaska is to cruise these waters with Captain Bob Horchover aboard his well-equipped, custom built 55-foot "Alaska Adventurer." Bob built the vessel with the sole purpose of taking groups of eight to 10 on custom cruises. Starting with a hull specifically designed for the Alaska waters, Bob created five comfortable staterooms and a spacious salon with large windows for perfect viewing. Video tapes, music and CDs are provided, along with a wide selection of books on Alaska. Fishing is just steps away under a covered and secure deck on the stern. An efficient heating system keeps you warm and dry. To get you even closer to nature, Bob has underwater microphones which let you listen in on conversations of the whales and porpoises.

The pilot house is equipped with high-tech navigation and communications electronics for your safety. Gyro stablizers take the bumps out of any wave action and make for a solid stable and comfortable ride. Bob carries a professional chef and a seasoned crew. I can personally guarantee you that the chef will wow you with each day's preparations. Fresh seafood and healthy fare is featured daily. Northwest and imported wines enhance the meals and the conversation. Dinners are casual, but elegant. Special diets can be accommodated with advance notice.

LOCAL KNOWLEDGE MAKES THE DIFFERENCE

Captain Bob is your host. He has logged over 40 years of commercial and personal boating in S.E. Alaska. The Alaska Adventurer is Bob's third custom-built boat. Each was originally equipped to provide

dental services to the remote villages, as an extension to his Juneau practice. Charter-boating began as a spare time hobby before any cruise ships discovered Alaska. Forty years of practical experience give Captain Bob unequalled local knowledge of waterways, harbors and weather patterns and enables him to provide you a superior quality experience. He knows the best spots to meet your expectations. When I wanted to see whales, he knew right where to go. As Bob says, "This is really fun, it's like taking friends and family to my favorite places."

EXPERIENCE OF A LIFETIME

Take advantage of Captain Bob's experience and let him show you the Alaska few will ever experience. The summer schedule is planned to catch nature's events at their prime. Scheduled trips focus on fishing, whale watching, or a combination of events. Book double occupancy or take the entire boat. Each day unfolds with new experiences which might include chipping thousand-year old ice cubes from a floating iceberg, photographing glaciers as skyscraper-size columns break off, cruising past 7,000 foot mountains or exploring a secluded harbor. It was after dinner, on just such a tranquil evening when our friend Bert hooked a 168-pound halibut off the stern of the boat. Two 15 foot Boston whalers provide access to tiny back waterways, streams and allow excellent beach combing. It is on a well-designed, smaller boat like this that Alaska can best be seen, experienced and shared.

After your cruise, you will have looked whales in the eye, caught salmon larger than your dog, and watched bears teach their cubs to fish. You'll also have had an opportunity to get reacquainted with someone special ~ yourself.

GETTING THERE

Southeast Alaska is served by Alaska Airlines.

OCEAN POINTE RESORT HOTEL & SPA

~ BRITISH COLUMBIA ~

LOCATION: DIRECTLY ON VICTORIA'S INNER HARBOUR

ADDRESS: ON THE HARBOURS, 45 SONGHEES RD., VICTORIA, B.C. V9A6T3

HOST: MR. F. ULRICH STOLLE

TELEPHONE: 250.360.2999

TOLL FREE: 800.954.8585, EXT. 4005

FAX: 250.360.5856

ROOMS: 250

RATES: $169 TO $279 (CANADIAN DOLLARS)

REMARKS: NO SMOKING IN RESTAURANTS AND MOST GUEST ROOMS. CONTINENTAL BREAKFAST INCLUDED IN EXECUTIVE CLUB CLASS ACCOMMODATIONS. FULL-SERVICE EUROPEAN SPA, SWIMMING AND TENNIS ON PREMISES. UNDERGROUND VALET PARKING. PETS ACCEPTED WITH ADDITIONAL $75 CHARGE. WHEELCHAIR ACCESSIBLE. GERMAN, JAPANESE, FRENCH, SPANISH, CHINESE, RUSSIAN AND HINDI SPOKEN. FOUR DIAMOND AWARD FROM AAA.

Located just 50 feet from Victoria's bustling Inner Harbour, *Ocean Pointe Resort Hotel & Spa* commands sweeping views of downtown Victoria, the stately government buildings and the fascinating harbour activities. From here, you view the entire Inner Harbour.

Rick and Kathy Stolle combine their friendly hospitality with Old World tradition befitting their international hotelier experience. The Stolles came to Victoria to build and operate their dream hotel. Their passion, style and determination is that is clearly reflected in the design of this stunning water front classic. We believe they found the best location for views into the Inner harbour.

The overall impression is one of casual elegance. Located in a park-like setting, and finished in muted and understated tones, the visitor's eye is immediately drawn to either the wonderful views from almost every room or to the extensive art collection assembled by the Stolles. At the hotel entrance, you are greeted by a spectacular carving of two Beluga whales rising from a sea of marble and granite. Carved from a single piece of Carrera marble this piece is aptly named "The Welcoming." Throughout the hotel, there are numerous commissioned and signed pieces by such artists as Umberto del Negro, Salvadore Dali, LeRoy Neiman, Claudine Armager and many others. Entering the lobby, you will see a vibrant tapestry by local artist Carole Sabiston. Here two wood-burning fireplaces flank a large two-story window which over-looks the Harbour.

PAMPERED AND PRIVATE

Ocean Pointe offers 250 deluxe rooms and suites, fur-nished in contemporary, tasteful fabrics and colors. Each room is equipped with minibar, phone with voice mail and fax capabilities, TV, spacious resort-size clos-ets. Some have kitchenettes. Almost all the rooms have harbour views. In 1997 *Conde Nast Traveler* voted Ocean Pointe onto their Gold List of the 500 Best hotels Worldwide. After your visit, you will know why.

The spa has a wide selection of packages and options available for men and women, ranging from full-day luxurious massage and body work, to spa hydrotherapies, herbal body wraps and cleansing facials. The fitness centre has professional fitness coor-dinators to help you maximize any workout, an indoor pool and whirlpool, two tennis courts, racquetball and squash courts and a sports shop. The resort's water-front location makes it a delightful place for walking and jogging, and golf can be easily arranged.

DINING ON THE BOARDWALK

The restaurants at Ocean Pointe are famous for using the finest local ingredients, preparation and ser-vice, and of course, for the spectacular views of the city and harbour. The elegant Victorian Restaurant offers fresh Pacific Northwest and Continental cuisine with such selections as Venison Carpaccio and Cinnamon Smoked Quail Breast, or Filet of B.C. Salmon and Scallop and Lobster Mousse.

The popular Boardwalk Restaurant also offers seasonal outdoor terrace dining. Choose from a full buffet or from the exceptional menu. The choices are healthy and imaginative, with lunch dishes such as Maple and Ginger-Glazed Beef or Smoked Salmon and Dungeness Crab Cakes. Dinner selections include appetizers, soups, salads and unusual pizzas like Smoked Chicken, or Caramelized Pear and Pecan with Stilton Cheese. Entrees range from Herb Crusted Baked Halibut and Sauteed Prawns or Grilled Lamb Chops. For relaxing over a drink at the end of the day, enjoy the fabulous views from Rick's Lounge.

EXPLORING VICTORIA

Whale-watching trips right from the Ocean Pointe dock via Sea Coast Expeditions are one of the most popular day trips. Try the harbour tours, visit the Royal B.C. Museum and enjoy great shopping in the quaint shops of old Victoria.

GETTING THERE

Ocean Pointe Resort is 30 minutes from the Victoria International Airport. OPR provides shuttle service from the Victoria Clipper which departs from Seattle twice a day.

ABIGAIL'S HOTEL
~ BRITISH COLUMBIA ~

LOCATION: THREE BLOCKS FROM THE HEART OF DOWN-TOWN VICTORIA

ADDRESS: 906 McCLURE STREET, VICTORIA, BC V8V 3E7

HOSTS: DANIEL AND FRAUKE BEHUNE

TELEPHONE: 250.388.5363

TOLL FREE: 1-800-954-8585, EXT. 1018

FAX: 250.388.7787

ROOMS: 16

RATES: $145 TO $299 (CANADIAN); $30 PER ADDITIONAL GUEST. SPECIAL WINTER RATES FROM NOVEMBER 1 THROUGH APRIL 30.

REMARKS: RATES INCLUDE FULL GOURMET BREAKFAST. NO PETS. NO SMOKING.

Abigail's Hotel, with its luxurious European style and colorful English gardens, evokes the true spirit of Victoria, a beautiful and sophisticated city on British Columbia's Vancouver Island. Not a lavish detail has been missed by owners/innkeepers Daniel and Frauke Behune. The inn has been operating since 1985.

UNIQUE PERSPECTIVES

Abigail's interior is a geometric masterpiece. Angled archways and vaulted ceilings create unique perspectives on the traditional Tudor design. Surprise nooks, notches and crannies evoke an atmosphere of discovery. Soft peach, rose, teal and ivory tones used throughout the inn are tastefully woven into a peaceful quilt of color.

Abigail's Hotel is set on a quiet residential cul-de-sac. Its four stories offer a broad selection of secluded rooms. Most of the rooms have fireplaces, and in two of these, the fireplace is double-sided and adjoins the bathroom and living area. Here, you can relax in a deep soaking tub while watching the crackling fire. Abigail's service-minded staff keeps rooms stocked with wood so you can easily light a fire on a chilly winter evening.

Extraordinary service and attention to detail are the benchmarks of this inn. Upon check-in, enjoy a complimentary glass of champagne as the innkeeper shows you through and introduces you to its various amenities. The knowledgeable staff has long tenure with the inn and you can rely on their recommendations for sites and dining choices.

The cozy library glows with warmth and beckons guests to gather in the comfortable leather loveseats. The bookshelves are filled with volumes of classic books to while away the time until hors d'oeuvres and sherry are served in the early evening. The library is also the ideal spot for small receptions and weddings. We often use the library as the meeting spot for arriving friends.

ELEGANT ADDITIONS

Eight of the 16 guest rooms offer both fireplaces and private Jacuzzis or deep-soaking tubs. The spacious ceramic-tiled bathrooms feature pedestal sinks and brass fixtures, establishing an elegance that is echoed in the crystal chandeliers, eyelet curtains and antiques in each room. Goosedown duvets and plush pillows accent the sumptuous beds. Our favorite room has a see-through fireplace in the wall between the bath and the bedroom.

ABIGAIL'S BREAKFAST

A gourmet breakfast is served from 7:30 a.m. to 9:30 a.m. in the sunny dining room, where fresh flowers adorn the oak tables. The big open kitchen is an inviting spot to watch the chef create the morning inspiration and to chat with other guests. Enjoy freshly brewed coffee, seasonal fruit, fresh orange juice and just-baked muffins and scones with homemade jams. Then the chef will prepare a special entree of the day using only the freshest and finest Northwest ingredients.

IN THE HEART OF VICTORIA

Whether you arrive by catamaran, ferry or plane, you'll be within an easy walk of almost anywhere you want to go. To the north, on Fort Street, you'll find the broad assortment of Victoria's famous antique shops. Auctions take place Tuesday and Thursday evenings, and can produce a real find for the collector. Government Street, near the Inner Harbor, is home to many of Victoria's shops, fine restaurants and bistros. The Royal British Columbia Museum, The Art Gallery of Victoria and the Parliament Buildings are all within minutes of Abigail's.

Outdoor activities abound as well. World class golf, wilderness hiking, mountain-and road-biking, are all accessible on the Pacific coastline and quiet beaches. Whale watching and great salt-water fishing are opportunities not to be missed. And don't forget to visit the world-famous Butchart Gardens.

GETTING THERE

From the Inner Harbour, head north on Government Street. Take an immediate right onto Humboldt Street. Continue four blocks to Vancouver Street. Turn left onto Vancouver and continue four blocks to McClure. Turn left. Abigail's is at the end of the cul-de-sac. Parking is in a lot behind the inn.

THE BEACONSFIELD INN

~BRITISH COLUMBIA ~

LOCATION: FOUR BLOCKS FROM THE INNER HARBOUR IN VICTORIA

ADDRESS: 998 HUMBOLDT STREET VICTORIA, B.C. V8V 2Z8

HOSTS: CON AND JUDI SOLLID

TELEPHONE: 250.384.4044

TOLL FREE: 800.954.8585, EXT. 1068

FAX: 250.384.4052

ROOMS: 6 AND 3 SUITES

RATES: $200 TO $395 CANADIAN, $145 TO $295 US

REMARKS: GOURMET BREAKFAST, AFTERNOON TEA AND EVENING SHERRY. NO SMOKING. NO CHILDREN OR PETS.

The Beaconsfield Inn is the first bed & breakfast that we ever stayed in and it's become the standard by which we judge all of the others. Located on a quiet street which leads to the Inner Harbour, this restored English manor was built in 1905 by millionaire R.P. Rithet as a wedding gift for his only daughter. Today, the inn has been restored to its former elegance and carefully appointed to evoke the feeling of the Edwardian era.

Innkeepers Con and Judi Sollid had long loved the

Beaconsfield Inn, and were frequent guests before purchasing it in 1993. They left their careers to devote their time and creative energy to providing a soothing and comfortable level of hospitality to their guests.

Grand double doors and stained glass windows mark the entrance to the inn, and open into a tiled sunroom with wicker furnishings and potted plants. Throughout the Beaconsfield, clean, balanced lines create an elegant simplicity, and stately decor reflects the tastes of the wealthy class that rejected the perceived frivolity of the earlier Victorian period.

REST, REFLECTION AND ROMANCE

Begin your introduction to the inn in the richly paneled library, where antique Persian rugs accent mahogany floors, and impressive leather couches invite you to sit and enjoy a book from the extensive collection that lines the shelves. Fill your cup from the silver tea service and enjoy the baked ginger shortbread and other sweets. Evening sherry is served under the beamed ceiling of this comfortable room.

On four levels of the inn, you'll find nine guest rooms in different sizes and with varying features. All have private baths, some with two-person Jacuzzi's. Many rooms have wood-burning fireplaces, which are especially appreciated on the cooler winter evenings, and some have hardwood floors, subdued Persian rugs and stained glass windows. Each room is decorated with period antiques that enhance the turn-of-the-century atmosphere. Goosedown comforters cover queen-sized canopy or partial canopy beds, and fresh flowers add to the pervasive air of romance.

EXCEPTIONAL BREAKFASTS

Judi has restored the inn's dining room back to its original elegance. The atmosphere is warm and light, with gleaning floors, magnificent moldings and windows overlooking the gardens and sun porch. The built in buffet is as exquisite today as it was a century ago. On winter mornings, you too might be able to enjoy your breakfast by flickering candlelight.

Con and Judi believe that a superb breakfast is essential to the continued enjoyment of the day. The gourmet affair may begin with fresh fruit juice, followed by a fruit dish such as toasted coconut sprinkled baked banana with French vanilla yogurt sauce. Your main course may be a garden medley quiche, or perhaps some French apple toast, with amaretto sauce and hot carmelized apple topping. This may be followed by homemade orange carrot muffins, or raspberry scones with preserves.

ENGLISH SEASIDE CHARM

Victoria possesses a fascinating array of sights to see and activities to pursue. Galleries and museums abound and the Beaconsfield is within an easy walk of all of them, including the Art Gallery of Greater Victoria and the Royal British Columbia Museum. Victoria is also a performance and fine arts center and is home to an excellent symphony and several theater groups.

There's also plenty of opportunity for a good round of golf, as Victoria has many top-notch courses. Con belongs to the royal Colwood Golf Club, and he will gladly arrange a tee time for you. For those who just want to take a stroll, oceanside Beacon Hill Park is just a block away.

GETTING THERE

From the ferry terminals at Swartz Bay or Sidney, take Hwy. 17 into Victoria. This becomes Blanshard Street; follow it to Humboldt Street, turn left and drive two blocks. From the Inner Harbor, go north on Government Street, turn right on Humboldt Street and continue for four blocks.

SOOKE HARBOUR HOUSE
~ BRITISH COLUMBIA ~

LOCATION: TWENTY-THREE MILES WEST OF VICTORIA

ADDRESS: 1528 WHIFFEN SPIT ROAD, RURAL ROUTE 4, SOOKE, BC V0S 1N0

HOSTS: FREDRICA AND SINCLAIR PHILIP

TELEPHONE: 250.642.3421

TOLL FREE: 800.954.8585, EXT. 2003

FAX: 250.642.6988

ROOMS: 13

RATES: $200 TO $270 (U.S.)

REMARKS: BREAKFAST AND LUNCH INCLUDED IN ROOM RATE SEASONALLY. RESERVATIONS RECOMMENDED. LUNCH SERVED TO HOTEL GUESTS ONLY. WHEELCHAIR ACCESSIBLE GUEST ROOM.

If ever an inn was created to lull one's life tempo back to a peaceful rhythm, it's Sooke Harbour House. This trim, white, elegant inn rests just above Sooke Harbour's Whiffen Spit, and through the inn's picture windows you'll have a sweeping view of the Strait of Juan de Fuca and Washington's Olympic Mountains. Look down, and you'll see an ever-changing landscape of tidal pools, kelp beds and natural driftwood sculptures that create a living mural.

Stitching the many fabrics of Sooke Harbour

House together are Fredrica and Sinclair Philip. Fredrica, born in Cannes, France, radiates a refined warmth. Dressed in her crisp French frocks, she graciously manages the workings of the inn. Sinclair is a native of Vancouver and holds a doctorate from the University of Grenoble, where he and Fredrica met. He is well-studied in wines and foods and an expert Northwest seafood chef.

PURE RELAXATION

With the lull of ocean waves, Sooke provides absolute respite from the outside world. Good food, good beds and long walks in nature erase schedules from your mind. Begin with a walk along Whiffen Spit. Bald eagles nest nearby, while herons, sandpipers, loons and cormorants frequent the area. Killer whales, seals and sea lions feed just offshore as well as the "resident" grey whale.

IDEAL FOR ROMANCE

Sooke Harbour House is an exquisite mingling of traditional North American country sensibilities and West Coast native design. The New House offers 10 distinctly different rooms. Each is named and decorated with a theme, and all have an expansive ocean view and private balcony or terrace. In each room, a comfortable sitting area faces a woodburning fireplace that's stocked and ready to light.

Our favorite is the Victor Newman Longhouse, named for the Sooke carver of its many Indian masks and a rare hand-hewn Chieftain's bench. This large room features a king-sized bed and bathtub for two. The tub is situated next to a see-through fireplace and lends a view of Sooke Bay and the mountains beyond. The Mermaid Room and the Underwater Orchard both have decks with outdoor whirlpools and stunning views through their own private gardens by the ocean.

The main house bears all the charm of an airy

French auberge. The three upstairs bedrooms are furnished with antiques, handmade flower wreaths and handsewn quilts. They also offer fireplaces and large whirlpool tubs.

WORLD CLASS DINING

Colorful gardens ring the inn: pansies, pineapple sage and Corsican mint are among the inn's 400 varieties of herbs, flowers, berries and fruit trees. I was initially surprised to see Sinclair snatch a crimson petal from a rose and take a bite out of it, until he explained that over 95 percent of the gardens on their grounds are edible, and most of it ends up on the menu. The ocean realm also offers a prodigious array of delicacies, from octopus, sea urchin and gooseneck barnacle to periwinkles and whelks. Under the spell of Sooke's masterful chefs, the land and sea gardens blend to create the freshest and most innovative cuisine in British Columbia.

DAILY SEA HARVEST

Here, when they say "seasonally," they mean "daily." Fredrica is a strong advocate of providing food only in its proper season. Sinclair is an avid scuba diver and often takes advantage of the rich bounties of their watery front yard for evening meals.

Fresh sea urchin roe may appear as appetizers. White Steamed Sablefish with an Anise-Hyssop Butter Sauce, or fresh skate sauteed with a Cranberry Vinegar Sauce may be among the choice of entrees.

GETTING THERE

From Victoria, take Highway 1 north to the Highway 14 intersection. Follow signs to Sooke. Approximately one mile from the stoplight in Sooke, turn left onto Whiffen Spit Road. Follow it to the water, where the Sooke Harbour House is on your right, at the ocean's edge.

THE AERIE
~ BRITISH COLUMBIA ~

LOCATION: 20 MILES NORTH OF VICTORIA ON SCENIC MALAHAT DRIVE

ADDRESS: P.O. BOX 108, MALAHAT, B.C., V0R 2L0

HOSTS: MARIA AND LEO SCHUSTER. MARKUS GRIESSER, GENERAL MANAGER.

TELEPHONE: 250.743.7115

TOLL FREE: 800.954.8585, EXT. 2004

FAX:250.743.4766

ROOMS: 23 ROOMS AND SUITES

RATES: $150 TO $395 (CANADIAN); INCLUDES FULL BREAKFAST.

REMARKS: NO SMOKING. NO PETS. CHILDREN NOT ENCOURAGED. RESTAURANT OPEN TO PUBLIC FOR SIX-COURSE DINNER NIGHTLY. RESERVATIONS ADVISED. DINING ROOM WHEELCHAIR ACCESSIBLE.

Like a falcon's aerie perched high on the cliffs, Maria and Leo Schuster's Aerie commands a bird's eye view of awe-inspiring fjords and the Canadian Gulf Islands. From the Aerie's window-lined dining room, you'll watch spectacular sunsets melt into darkness that's pierced only by the moon, stars and twinkling lights of Victoria and Port Angeles in the distance. The clean white stucco building–set off by its clay tile roof, bright blue awnings, romantic balconies and windows resembles a Mediterranean villa. The interior is elegant, featuring hand-carved furniture, original oil paintings and a collection of rugs from around the world.

You'll also enjoy The Aerie's large indoor or outdoor hot tub, sauna and sun deck. The latest additions include a tennis court and an indoor swimming pool. A handsome library offers good reading, and the inn has conference facilities that are ideal for executive gatherings. On an adjacent hilltop is The Aerie's helicopter pad; bring your own, or charter one from reliable local services. This inn also has a chapel for weddings and a large, partially covered deck for receptions and outdoor dining.

HEAVENLY HOSTS

Owners and innkeepers Maria and Leo Schuster, both originally from Austria, came to Victoria from the tropical Bahamas. When they discovered this property high above the Malahat, they knew this was where they would spend the rest of their lives. What started as an idea for a simple inn blossomed into a full-time labor of love. It took one full year to design and build the Aerie, with Leo's and Maria's hands-on expertise and dedication to perfection.

Maria and Leo are experienced in the hotel trade. Maria grew up in the hotel business and was the youngest female manager of a luxury hotel in Austria. In the Bahamas, she owned and operated an exclusive resort. Leo's culinary experience includes cooking in Europe, the Middle East and Canada. Leo left his job as executive chef at Donald Trump's Resort in the Bahamas to follow his and Maria's dream of building a world class resort in "heaven."

GRACE AND GRANDEUR

The Aerie's 23 rooms and suites reflect Maria's eye for decorating and details. Guests are greeted with a fruit basket in their rooms, which offer queen- or king-sized beds and private bathrooms. All of the rooms are individually decorated, many with hand-crafted Italian furniture, vaulted ceilings, private Jacuzzis, fireplaces and balconies with unbelievable views. Breakfast is served only to overnight guests. Omelets, eggs, smoked salmon, ham, bacon or sausages, fresh fruits and European style pastries are served in the dining room or dining room decks. Lunch is available to guests only.

A SEVEN-COURSE EXTRAVAGANZA

The inn is well known for the exquisite cuisine originally created by Chef Leo and now under the professional guidance of Chef Chris Jones. Dinner is a fabulous extravaganza. The dining room's white tablecloths, fine silver, china and crystal are crowned by an impressive 23-carat gold-leaf ceiling, and warm candlelight glows from each table. The atmosphere is casually elegant and intimate and the 180-degree view from the dining room offers the finishing touch.

The menus change frequently, as Chris buys only what is fresh and seasonal. The night we last dined, we began with Game and Pistachio Pate with Cranberry Relish, Herb Croutons Millefeuille of Smoked Salmon. This was followed by Shellfish and Fennel Bisque, Saffron Essence Garden Sorrel, Dungeness Crab Souffle. We shared a main course of Local Venison "Osso Bucco." Our dessert was port marinated strawberries with chocolate creme. Don't fail to choose a wine from the well-stocked cellar.

The Schusters have scattered tables and chairs along the nature trail that winds through the hotel's 10 beautiful acres.

GETTING THERE

Travel north from Victoria (or south from Duncan) on the Trans-Canada Highway to the Spectacle Lake Provincial Park turnoff. Take the first park turnoff, then follow the sign straight ahead to The Aerie. Or fly into The Aerie via chartered helicopter.

OCEANWOOD COUNTRY INN
~ BRITISH COLUMBIA ~

LOCATION: ON MAYNE ISLAND, AN EASY FERRY RIDE FROM VICTORIA OR VANCOUVER.

ADDRESS: 630 DINNER BAY ROAD, MAYNE ISLAND, BC V0N 2J0

HOSTS: MARILYN AND JONATHAN CHILVERS

TELEPHONE: 250.539.5074

TOLL FREE: 800.954.8585, EXT. 2005

FAX: 250.539.3002

ROOMS: 12

RATES: $120 TO $275 CANADIAN (OCTOBER THROUGH APRIL); $130 TO $295 (MAY THROUGH SEPTEMBER).

REMARKS: RATES INCLUDE BREAKFAST AND AFTERNOON TEA. CHILDREN 16 AND OVER WELCOME. TWO-NIGHT MINIMUM STAY ON WEEKENDS. SMOKING PERMITTED IN LIBRARY AND ON OUTSIDE DECKS. TENNIS, OCEAN KAYAKING, SAILBOAT CHARTER AND CRUISES AVAILABLE. NO PETS. MOORING BUOY AVAILABLE FOR BOATERS.

Geologically speaking, the Gulf Islands of Canada are a northward continuation of the American San Juans. Situated between Vancouver Island and the mainland of British Columbia, the chain includes several larger, inhabited islands, and some just big enough for a beach chair. Somewhere in between is Mayne Island, a quiet rural community with a permanent population of less than 800 people.

For years Marilyn and Jonathan Chilvers spent the holidays in their waterfront cottage on Mayne Island, taking a break from demanding advertising and public relations careers. In 1989, they came upon a large Tudor house for sale overlooking Navy Channel. Gradually, the idea of opening an inn took hold and soon the house was transformed into Oceanwood Country Inn, complete with a full-service restaurant.

HEARTHSIDE

After a warm greeting from Marilyn and Jonathan, you can settle down by the fireplace in your room or wander into the living room for some conversation, music and books. Take a deep breath, as the Chilvers maintain, "Stress is a word that is forever banished from our lexicon."

If you have business to attend to, a fully equipped boardroom accommodates meetings of up to 12. The games room features over 25 games. Marilyn and Jonathan maintain a diverse collection of books and magazines, and the comfortable sofas in the library offer quiet places to read. Ask Jonathan for a personal tour of the garden, which supplies fresh herbs and vegetables to the restaurant.

A NATURALISTS PARADISE

Of the inn's 12 guest rooms, 11 have queen-sized beds; one offers two twins. Each room has a private bath and a wonderful water or garden view. The Wisteria Room is one of the most stunning rooms, with a sunken living room with fireplace and a private soaking tub on a sunny view deck. From two of this room's three decks, you'll have a clear view of the channel where you will probably see eagles fishing. There is also a large outdoor hot tub for the use of all guests which has a stunning view down the channel.

FRESHLY SEASONED

Included with your night's stay is your morning repast served in the inn's water-view dining room.

You'll find a variety of cold cereals, yogurt, fruit, fresh coffee, tea and juices. Oceanwood's fresh baking includes delicious coffeecake, scones, croissants and muffins, and the hot entree changes daily. Our favorite is the scrambled eggs with gravlax. Tea is served at four o'clock in the garden room, with a variety of cakes and cookies to hold you over until dinner.

The restaurant at Oceanwood seats 30 and is open to the public for dinner. This is an exceptional four-course, prix fixe meal that Jonathan says, "changes endlessly and upon the whims of Chef Ed Sodke." Tomato Dungeness crab soup may start off your meal, followed by an appetizer of mushroom and goat cheese ravioli au gratin. Herb and Garlic Pork Loin with Rhubarb and Lemon Confit leaves just enough room for a Chocolate Almond Cake with Raspberry Coulis. Choose from a wide array of fine wines to complement dinner.

SPACE TO COLLECT YOUR THOUGHTS

Mayne Island is not well-known for its entertainment industry. Marilyn notes, "People come here to wind down. A big day might involve going for a bike ride along country lanes (the inn provides six bikes for its guests), walking on the beach before tea, then settling down for a nap." You might also want to allow time for a sauna in your busy schedule. It is a pleasant 45-minute walk from Oceanwood to the local market, craft shops, or the island pub if you're up for some fish and chips or a pint of ale.

GETTING THERE

Oceanwood Country Inn is served daily by B.C. Ferries from Tsawwassen and Swartz Bay, and by a scheduled float plane service from Vancouver. Arrangements can be made to have the island taxi meet guests at the Mayne Island ferry terminal.

YELLOW POINT LODGE
~ BRITISH COLUMBIA ~

LOCATION: ON THE WATER EIGHT MILES NORTH OF LADYSMITH ON VANCOUVER ISLAND.

ADDRESS: RURAL ROUTE 3, LADYSMITH, BC V0R 2E0

HOST: RICHARD HILL

TELEPHONE: 250.245.7422

TOLL FREE: 800.954.8585, EXT. 2006

FAX: 250.245.7411

ROOMS: 30 IN WINTER AND 54 IN SUMMER

RATES: $61 SINGLE TO $117 DOUBLE (CANADIAN); $61 PER ADDITIONAL GUEST. MID-WEEK REDUCTIONS OF 20 PERCENT, OCTOBER THROUGH APRIL. AMERICAN PLAN.

REMARKS: NO PETS. GUESTS 16 AND OVER WELCOME. TWO-DAY MINIMUM STAY ON WEEKENDS, THREE-DAY MINIMUM ON HOLIDAYS. RATES INCLUDE ALL MEALS, EXTRA SNACKS, HOMEMADE COOKIES, AND MUFFINS.

On the eastern coast of Vancouver Island is a promontory known as Yellow Point There, over 65 years ago, Gerry Hill built a lodge and created a refuge from the stress of city life. He built his log dream lodge right where he wanted it to be- out on the granite rocks overlooking the water. You see, Gerry had honed his dream for years while a Prisoner of War in World War I. When the locals tried to get him to be more conservative and build the lodge back among the massive trees, they soon realized that you can not easily change a man with a well-crafted dream. Gerry created Yellow

Point lodge and he was the inspiration behind the many services offerred to the guests.

When his lodge burned down in 1985, Gerry was in his 90's and was training his son Richard in the fine arts of running the lodge. The new lodge was rebuilt, in time for Gerry to welcome back his beloved favorite guests. The new structure has a similarly impressive design as the original log lodge. Richard and his wife Sandi are carrying on the dream.

Yellow Point lodge is one of the very few we have ever discovered where guests develop such an intense loyalty to the place and the spirit that they annually volunteer to assist with maintaince and grounds work. In fact, the "Friends of Yellow Point" help to make sure you're visit is memorable.

SECLUDED SANCTUARY

At capacity, in the summer, Yellow Point Lodge never has more than 100 guests, which means you'll never feel crowded. You are free to enjoy all 180 acres and explore over one and a half miles of beach that make up the property. Simplicity and hospitality are the driving forces behind the popularity of this eccentric resort. Hill intended his home to be a sanctuary, for friends and strangers, for the wildlife and the trees. Richard and sandi carry on this tradition, personally attending to guests, the lodge and property.

OFF-SEASON ATTRACTIONS

In the summer, the lodge fills up early, but midweek and off-season accommodations are more easily arranged. Although the summer months provide weather conducive to a wide range of outdoor activities, we prefer the off-season. In the fall, dozens of different migratory birds arrive in the area, and as the winter rolls in, sea lions, gulls, and killer whales are easily visible just offshore. Our favorite time to visit is in March. If you hit it just right, you can catch the time when the spawning herring are chased close to shore by the salmon, who in turn are chased by the Sea lions. Not far behind are the forging Orcas. This complete spectical of nature can be viewed from the rocks in front of the lodge.

AT HOME WITH MANY STYLES

Of the resort's accommodations, nine private rooms in the lodge and five new cabins have the most modern conveniences. Several cottages offer separate bedrooms and private baths, while others are geared for more adventurous experiences, with no running water and camp-style communal washrooms. Richard Hill says, "Yellow Point is comfortable but not fancy. It's not for everyone, but if you like meeting friendly people and feeling at home in a natural and beautiful place, you'll like it here."

FISHERMAN'S CHOICE

In addition to muffins just out of the oven, breakfast includes a buffet of fresh fruit, cereals, juices, yogurt and granola, followed by a full breakfast with eggs any style, bacon, sausages and pancakes. Lunch is served buffet-style, and may be turkey in puffed pastry or chilled salmon. Homemade soups and a variety of salads accompany homemade breads and rolls. For dinner, a fisherman, may pull up to the dock and unload the day's catch of salmon. Barbecues are also frequent dinner events.

GETTING THERE

From Vancouver, take the ferry route from Tsawwassen to Nanaimo or the Horseshoe Bay ferry to Nanaimo, then drive south on Route 1 about five miles to Cedar Road. Follow the signs through Cedar to Yellow Point, about 10 miles. From Victoria, drive north on Route 1 and proceed toward Ladysmith, Three miles beyond Ladysmith, turn right on Cedar Road and follow the signs to Yellow Point Lodge.

MIDDLE BEACH LODGE
~ BRITISH COLUMBIA ~

LOCATION: ON THE WEST COAST OF VANCOUVER ISLAND.
A FIVE-HOUR SCENIC DRIVE FROM VICTORIA.

ADDRESS: 400 MCKENZIE BEACH ROAD, TOFINO,
BRITISH COLUMBIA V0R 2Z0

HOST: CHRIS LEFEVRE, PROPRIETOR

TELEPHONE: 250.725.2900

TOLL FREE: 800.954.8585, EXT.1031

FAX: 250.725.2901

ROOMS: 52

RATES: $72 TO $210 (CANADIAN); INCLUDES
CONTINENTAL BREAKFAST.

REMARKS: RESERVATIONS RECOMMENDED. NO SMOKING,
NO PETS. WHEELCHAIR ACCESSIBLE. THE LODGE AT
THE HEADLANDS IS OPEN ALL YEAR ROUND. FRENCH,
SPANISH AND PORTUGUESE SPOKEN.

The west coast of Vancouver Island is a wild and beautiful place. The fresh Pacific winds, secluded beaches, forested mountains and abundant wildlife all combine to make this a very spiritual place. This coast was not such a hospitable place to the early survivors of shipwrecks. Without the survival skills of the hardy native peoples, those cast ashore soon perished, until a life-saving trail was hewn through the forest and along the coast. Once you have arrived and viewed the wild and rugged coast, you will understand the perils of being cast ashore here a hundred or so years ago. For those of us lucky enough to land here today, the perils have been replaced with pleasures.

The West Coast still retains its wildness and beauty, but the ability to survive and to appreciate the wonders of the area have been greatly improved with the opening of the Middle Beach Lodge. Travelers today reach the once isolated coastline of Long Beach, Tofino and Clayoquot Sound (pronounced "Klak-wit") after a spectacular three-hour drive from Nanaimo through the coastal mountains of Vancouver Island.

Middle Beach Lodge is the inspiration and creation of Chris LeFevre. He built the lodge to nestle along the coast and to face the private Middle Beach, just a few miles south of the small village of Tofino. The lodge is one of the best examples of rustic West Coast architecture that we have discovered. The magnificent lounges which overlook the Pacific Ocean have massive stone fireplaces with crackling fires to warm you after a brisk beach walk. The open-beamed ceilings and overstuffed couches make this a prime destination for relaxing. A visit here is a mandatory annual experience for us. It is a time to relax with nature, walk in the rugged beauty and shift our priorities back into place.

A HANDCRAFTED FEEL

The 1996 addition to Middle Beach Lodge included a new lodge and cabins at the rugged headlands. The new buildings, known as "The Headlands," are separated from the original lodge, which is referred to as "At the Beach," by several hundred feet. Although new, the rustic construction glows with the depth and character of the recycled timbers and marine fittings which were used throughout the lodge. These features include teak doors, fir floors and antique pine furnishings in the "Mission" country style.

All of the rooms, suites and cabins are equipped

with private baths, striking handmade furniture and large comfortable beds with warm duvet comforters. The bathroom doors were salvaged from a coastal freighter. All cabins and most suites have kitchenettes. Almost every lodging choice here has a spectacular view of the ocean, and the cabins also have wood-burning fireplaces.

FRESH FROM THE SEA

The lodge dining room overlooks the ocean, and has a choice of communal tables or small intimate ones. Breakfast is a continental affair, with a fine selection of cereals, fruit, freshly baked goods and homemade jams. Coffee, teas and hot chocolate are always available. West Coast dinners and barbecues served daily in peak season, include fresh crab, salmon and just-caught ocean fish.

Once beyond the pleasures of the lodge, you will find a host of activities available. The West Coast of Vancouver Island is a wild and beautiful place; fresh ocean air, secluded beaches, forested mountains all invite the outdoor enthusiast. Whales come close to the coast here and boats are available to take you out to greet them. Play golf, sea kayak, explore isolated beaches, bask in the nearby hot springs or hike in the temperate rain forest. At every turn, you will be in some of the most photogenic country in the world. For those who prefer curling up in front of a crackling fireplace, watching the waves and the sparkling blue water, this could be heaven on earth.

GETTING THERE

Middle Beach Lodge is a two-hour drive from Port Alberni, three hours from Nanaimo and five hours from Victoria, B.C. Fifteen minutes north of Long Beach and three kilometers before the small town of Tofino, look for the Bella Pacifica/Middle Beach Lodge sign on the left.

SHIPS POINT BEACH HOUSE

~ BRITISH COLUMBIA ~

LOCATION: 2 1/2 HOURS NORTH FROM VICTORIA, 45 MIN-
UTES NORTH OF NANAIMO.

ADDRESS: 7584 SHIPS POINT ROAD, FANNY BAY, B.C.
VOR 1WO

HOSTS: DAVID AND LORINDA RAWLINGS

TELEPHONE: 250.335.2200

TOLL FREE: 800.954.8585, EXT. 1061

FAX: 250.335.2214

ROOMS: 6

RATES: $135 TO $195 HIGH SEASON; $100 TO $160
LOW SEASON (CANADIAN). RATES INCLUDE FULL
BREAKFAST.

REMARKS: RESERVATIONS RECOMMENDED FOR DINNER.
SMOKING ON OUTSIDE DECKS. NO PETS. SWIMMING ON
PREMISES. EXECUTIVE RETREATS FOR UP TO 12 PER-
SONS. WEDDINGS AND RECEPTIONS FOR UP TO 60 PER-
SONS. FOUR-STAR RATED CANADA SELECT;

When Ships Point Beach House arrived on a barge from a distant logging camp, a rich and colorful history accompanied the one-time bunkhouse. It became a fishing and hunting lodge in the 1950s. Later it was remodeled to served as a home for special needs residents for the next 20 years.

In 1994, David and Lorinda Rawlings began to realize their dream of creating an up-scale Bed and Breakfast on the northern reaches of Vancouver Island. After 16 months of energetic labor, they transformed the home into the only luxury bed and breakfast inn north of Nanaimo.

CAPTAIN VANCOUVER SLEPT HERE

The resort is located only 30 feet from the shore of Fanny Bay, where, according to local folklore, Captain Vancouver dropped anchor in 1792. He named this secluded spot Fanny Bay and declared the location where the inn would later be built as the Ships Point Peninsula. Today guests can sample the oysters for which the bay is famous, relax over one of Lorinda's innovative breakfasts, or just enjoy the view from the award-winning hot tub deck. The vista encompasses nearby Denman Island, north to Baynes Sound and up the forested island to Mt. Washington.

The Inn has six ensuite rooms, five of which are queen-size and one twin-size. All enjoy ocean views and each is designed and named for the special touches. The Rose Garden Room is decorated with a Japanese styles and overlooks part of the rose garden, which has over 100 rose bushes. The Executive Suite has a fireplace, his and her bathrooms and a shower. It is on the ground floor with its own private entrance. The decor has an eastern art motif and blends in with the nearby ocean which is only 30 feet away.

The four rooms upstairs include the Teddy Bear Room, which in addition to the bears has a view into the forest where eagles nest. The Periwinkle Room is named for the sea shell and the soft ground cover. The Tequila sunset Room offers prime views of the wonderful sunsets. Our favorite is the Captain Vancouver Room, which offers two extra long antique twin beds.

The inn is decorated with an elegant yet casual flair with comfortable antiques. During our visits, I can usually be found curling up on the down sofa in front of a roaring fire in the late afternoon. Lorinda keeps the fridge stocked with complimentary beverages, and homemade baked goodies and hot beverages are always available. The sun deck even has two heat lamps for your comfort during the early spring mornings or for late night star gazing.

A GREAT START TO THE DAY

Lorinda serves a wickedly good French press coffee and a selection of teas to begin the morning breakfast ritual. She provides home-made breads and muffins to accompany the full country breakfast. Don't miss the opportunity to include a dinner in the inn during your visit. Reserve your spot when you call for reservations, we guarantee that the meal will be a highlight of your visit.

We use the relaxing time in the hot tub, under the spreading branches of the 100 year old cherry tree to plan excursions to many area attractions. To the west, remote and rugged Barclay Sound offers fishing and wildlife charters for many of the Inn guests. Majestic old growth forests of Cathedral Grove are only 45 minutes away, and delightful Qualicum Beach is where you will find shops, art galleries and wonderful antique stores. On nearby Hornby Island the many renowned resident artists draw on the rugged natural beauty of their island home for inspiration. A drive up Mount Washington is a must do experience. The drive up the coast to Campbell River takes a little over an hour.

Without straying far from the inn, you can use the double and single sea kayaks to paddle over to Denman Island or skim out among the nearby seals. David keeps a 21-foot boat available for salmon fishing. For a real thrill try fly fishing for salmon.

GETTING THERE

From Nanaimo, drive north on Highway #19 through Parksville to Fanny Bay. Turn right at Ships Point Rd and drive east for three kilometers to the inn.

DURLACHER HOF
~ BRITISH COLUMBIA ~

LOCATION: ONE HALF MILE NORTH OF WHISTLER VILLAGE, 75 MILES NORTH OF VANCOUVER

ADDRESS: 7055 NESTERS ROAD, WHISTLER, BRITISH COLUMBIA V0N 1B0

HOSTS: ERIKA AND PETER DURLACHER

TELEPHONE: 604.932.1924

TOLL FREE: 800.954.8585, EXT. 1019

FAX: 604.938.1980

ROOMS: 8

RATES: WINTER $130 TO $255 (DOUBLE, CANADIAN); SUMMER $110 TO $175. SKI, GOLF, HONEYMOON, ADVENTURE AND SUMMER PACKAGES AVAILABLE.

REMARKS: RATES INCLUDE FULL COUNTRY BREAKFAST AND AFTERNOON TEA. NOT SUITABLE FOR SMALL CHILDREN. TWO-NIGHT MINIMUM ON WEEKENDS. MAIN FLOOR IS WHEELCHAIR ACCESSIBLE. NO SMOKING. NO PETS. GERMAN SPOKEN.

Only a short hop from the two highest alpine skiing mountains in North America is a quaint pension built in traditional Austrian fashion. Originally from Austria themselves, Erika and Peter Durlacher have designed and decorated their Durlacher Hof after the farm houses that dot their native Alps. Every detail is authentic, from Edelweiss in bloom to the farmhouse Kachelofen (fireplace/oven). In fact, *The Los Angeles Times* wrote, it's "difficult to tell whether you're in Innsbruck, St. Anton or Lech."

Whistler Resort has become one of the most popular year-round mountain resorts in the world. It is rated No. 1 in the U.S. and Canada. Known best for its alpine skiing, the resort is home to Whistler and Blackcomb mountains, and impressive peaks with record vertical drops of 5,280 feet and 5,006 feet, respectively. Come summer, Whistler Resort is an outdoor lover's recreational paradise.

PERSONAL SLIPPERS

Since opening, the bed-and-breakfast has practiced a fun tradition. A tidy basket of Austrian Hut shoes, located in the entry, awaits each new arrival. As you enter, you kick off your shoes and slip into one of the inn's alternatives. The slippers are then yours for the remainder of your stay. This clever custom is just one example of the comfortable, homey atmosphere that owners and innkeepers Peter & Erika Durlacher create. Erika, with a strong streak of perfectionism and a level of energy that would power a small city and a will to pamper, ensures that you get the most out of your stay.

A TOUCH OF THE TYROL

The spacious Durlacher Hof offers eight guest rooms, each named for a mountain in the Austrian Alps. As we expected, the rooms are warm and welcoming with hand-carved pine furniture, and extra-long queen and twin beds, which are draped with thick goose down duvets and pillows. Private baths with Jacuzzi tubs or shower are ideal after a full day of skiing or golfing. Most of the guest rooms have a balcony, complete with superb views of Whistler, Blackcomb or Wedge Mountain.

A charming European styled guest lounge, with wood floors, handcrafted furnishings and leather wing chairs, provides cozy warmth and fellowship in the evenings. A brick patio makes a perfect spot for morning coffee, afternoon tea or a few chapters of that bestseller you're reading. The Durlachers have included a

sauna, a roomy outdoor whirlpool, not to mention ski storage, daily maid service and ample free parking.

AUSTRIAN CUISINE

Each morning guests enjoy a now legendary bountiful old country breakfast with hot coffee, tea, juices, home-baked breads and European specialties. Afternoon tea with goodies is also served, for those who stay behind or come in early. On selected evenings, the Durlacher Hof serves dinner for its guests, featuring the mouth-watering works of guest chefs or Erika's own Veal Roasts with Spatzle, Robust Dumpling Soups, Linzer Torte and Strudel.

ALL SEASONS

Some say Whistler offers skiers the most exciting high alpine experience on the continent. You be the judge as you choose from 96 runs on Whistler and 85 runs on Blackcomb.

With an average annual snowfall of 30 feet, there is ample opportunity for cross-country skiing, snowshoeing and snowmobiling. Summer and fall in Whistler are breathtaking, with alpine meadows, colorful wildflowers and azure mountain lakes for sailing, fishing, biking, hiking, horseback riding, and paragliding. There are four golf courses, if golf is your game, and Erika can keep you informed about the full schedule of events, including classical, jazz and bluegrass music festivals.

GETTING THERE

From Vancouver, travel 75 miles (125 km) north on Highway 99 into Whistler. After the fourth traffic light in Whistler, take the first left, which is Nesters Road. The Durlacher Hof will be on your immediate left. Transportation to the inn from the Vancouver International Airport may be arranged via bus, helicopter, rental car or train.

TYAX MOUNTAIN LAKE RESORT
~ BRITISH COLUMBIA ~

LOCATION: 125 AIR MILES NORTH OF VANCOUVER; 60 MILES WEST OF LILLOOET.

ADDRESS: TYAUGHTON LAKE ROAD, GOLD BRIDGE, B.C. V0K 1P0

HOSTS: GUS ABEL

TELEPHONE: 250.238.2221

TOLL FREE: 800.954.8585, EXT.3003

FAX: 250.238.2528

ROOMS: 34

RATES: $70 TO $90 (U.S.) CHALETS $180 TO $300

REMARKS: CHILDREN WELCOME. NO SMOKING, NO PETS. RESERVATIONS RECOMMENDED. WHEELCHAIR ACCESSIBLE. FRENCH AND GERMAN SPOKEN. TENNIS, SWIMMING ON SITE.

Tucked away in the heart of south-central British Columbia, Tyax Mountain Lake Resort blends the isolation of a beautifully remote setting with the first-class facilities of a top-rated resort. The lodge is on the shore of Tyaughton Lake in the Chilcotin Range about 60 miles by gravel road northwest of Lillooet. The resort covers over 275 acres and includes 7,000 feet of lake front.

Tyaughton Lake, which means "lake of the jumping fish," still retains that reputation today for pan-size Rainbow Trout. We were delighted to land a five-pound Rainbow during our first visit.

The remote four-seasons lodge is the creation of Gus Abel. Gus was born in Africa, raised in Germany, became a sea captain and emigrated to Canada in 1976. Gus built the resort in 1986 as the largest log structure on the North America west coast. The stunning peeled spruce building is fully 35,000 square feet, and the vaulted ceilings in the lounge/dining room soar to over 30 feet. Tyax Mountain Lake Resort offers all the amenities of a luxury hotel in the midst of some of the most beautiful and stunning wilderness in North America.

SOLID COMFORT

There are 30 large guest rooms, 24 of which have private balconies. Most of these rooms have sweeping views of the lake and up into the 9,000 foot high mountains. The rooms are accented with solid pine furniture and have wonderful eider-down comforters on the queen-size beds. Each of the seven log chalets has its own beach, fireplace and three to six bedrooms. The rooms have televisions and phones, but these are not available in the chalets.

INTERNATIONAL FLAIR IN THE REMOTE MOUNTAINS

The restaurant is elegant and the food is delicious. It must be because over half of the guests are repeat visitors. The people at the tables around us on our most recent visit were from Sweden, Germany or Japan, as the reputation of the resort is spread by happy and tired guests.

Did we say tired guests? Most likely because there are more activities than most of us have energy for. In the summer you can go fishing, swimming, hiking, canoeing, sailing, riding trail-wise horses, mountain bike the miles of trails, play tennis or try your hand at gold panning. The most popular day trip for is hiking in the alpine meadows. One of the most romantic activities might include paddling a canoe on the lake as an eagle catches a fish right off your bow, or watching a beaver family construct their own lodge. A popular attraction is the ghost town of Bralorne and the abandoned Pioneer Mine.

The resort owns a DHC-2 Beaver float plane for flightseeing over mountain wilderness and giant glaciers. Avid fishermen or hikers can be set gently down on a remote alpine lake for a memorable day of fishing or exploring. We did the fly-in trip to Spruce Lake and stayed overnight in the well- equiped tent, complete with all the cooking facilities we needed for a wonderful time together.

During the winter when snow blankets the ground, guests often play hockey on the frozen surface of the lake, use the 20 kilomeyers of groomed trails for cross-country skiing, snowmobile along the lake or snow shoe along the quiet mountain paths. The resort is nestled in the foothills of some of the best power snow mountains in North America. With all of the past mining activities in the area, there are miles of old trails to take you high above the tree line into snow covered alpine meadows. Here you can gaze out on miles and miles of untracked power snow. You will think you're on top of the world with breath taking views of huge glaciers. The resort can provide all the equipment, gloves and even an experienced guide.

GETTING THERE

Float plane pick up from Vancouver or Whistler British Columbia can be arranged in advance. By car from Vancouver take Highway 1 to Lytton, north 50 miles on Highway 12B to Lillooet along the mighty Fraser River. Take Highway 40 from Lillooet 60 miles to Gold Bridge. BC Rail provides a daily service from North vancouver, via Whistler, to Lillooet.

PARK ROYAL HOTEL
~ BRITISH COLUMBIA ~

LOCATION: IN WEST VANCOUVER, JUST NORTH OF THE LION'S GATE BRIDGE

ADDRESS: 540 CLYDE AVENUE, WEST VANCOUVER, B.C. V7T 2J7

TELEPHONE: 604.926.5511

TOLL FREE: 800.954.8585, EXT 4001

FAX: 604.926.6082

HOST: MARIO CORSI, OWNER/ MANAGER

ROOMS: 30

RATES: $95 TO $225 (CANADIAN)

REMARKS: COFFEE OR TEA AND MORNING NEWSPAPER DELIVERED TO ROOM, COMPLIMENTARY. FREE PARKING.

The Park Royal is a country style inn found in a busy metropolis," says host Mario Corsi. "It's cozy, and has a staff who really cares about the comfort of the guests." Mario should know; after all, most of his staff have been with him for a good part of his 25 years as manager of the hotel. Mario's European upbringing and hotel training have led him to create a high standard of service and quality reminiscent of a Continental hotel. "Nothing phony or glitzy," he says proudly. "Just a good feeling, like being in a little village." That philosophy and Mario's enthusiasm are what make the Park Royal such a rare find in a city of more than 1.7 million.

ON THE RIVER BANK

Located on the north side of Vancouver's harbor, just minutes from the bustling downtown area, the Tudor style, ivy-festooned hotel provides a quiet retreat. The two-story building is surrounded by trimmed lawns and flower beds. The Capilano River flows along the back. Twelve of the inn's 30 rooms face the river and overlook the gardens. On quiet nights you can open the window and be lulled to sleep by the sounds of rushing water. Most rooms offer queen or double beds. All rooms have private baths, and are individually decorated with floral print wallpapers, antique oak furniture and leaded glass windows. A large suite offers a jacuzzi, VCR, plush terry robes and a wet bar. Plans are underway to upgrade and remodel some of the older rooms. Because of the constant demand by guests, it is difficult to take rooms out of service. The quietest and newest rooms are on the water side, so ask for the second floor, riverside rooms.

A LIVELY PUB

An authentic English pub downstairs offers lively piano entertainment Monday through Saturday evenings. Light meals can also be taken there. We have spent many a winter evening in front of the big stone fireplace, warmed by the crackling fire, enjoying the music and eating the great homemade potato chips. A note of caution, most Canadian pubs do not have a separate "no smoking" area, so be forewarned.

DINING IN STYLE

The Tudor Room restaurant is regarded as one of the top dining spots in the city. One of the sure signs this acclaim is real is that the room is often full of locals. Regional specialties and old standards combine to create a diverse menu. Chef Richard Palfanier, is quite proud of the freshness and consistency of his menu. The dining room, which overlooks the garden, and is warmly appointed with tapestry-covered chairs, vintage prints and stained glass. Dinner entrees include breast of pheasant with red currants and brandy, black pasta with smoked salmon, red caviar and cream, and traditional favorites such as Chateaubriand and beef Wellington. A resident professional baker supplies fresh breads and stunning desserts.

Breakfast and lunch selections are as noteworthy as dinner. Begin the day with huevos rancheros or "Eggs Park Royal" (poached eggs, smoked salmon, salmon caviar and Hollandaise sauce). Lunch offers a steak and kidney pie, scallops in a fresh basil cream or veal scaloppine.

EXPLORING THE 'OTHER' VANCOUVERS

Park Royal is just a few minutes walk from the Park Royal Shopping Center. Ambleside Park stretches along the shore and may be reached by following a trail outside the hotel. North Vancouver offers additional opportunities for exploration. Grouse Mountain is a favorite destination of ours. Aerial tramways depart for the top every 15 minutes, offering spectacular views of the city and environs. En route to the mountain, walk the Capilano Suspension Bridge which stretches 450 feet across the canyon, some 230 feet above the river.

GETTING THERE

Follow Georgia Street through Vancouver and cross the Lion's Gate Bridge. Take the West Vancouver Exit and turn right on Taylor Way, then right onto Clyde Avenue. Go one block, turn right. The hotel is on the left. From Trans-Canada 1, turn off at Exit 13 (Taylor Way Vancouver), go downhill to Clyde Avenue and turn left at the Park Royal sign.

TEAHOUSE RESTAURANT

~ BRITISH COLUMBIA~

LOCATION: ON THE MOST WESTERLY POINT OF STANLEY PARK, OVERLOOKING THE OCEAN.

ADDRESS: FERGUSON POINT IN STANLEY PARK

HOSTS: JUDY FOSTER, GENERAL MANAGER; BRENT DAVIES, OWNER

TELEPHONE: 604.669.3281

TOLL FREE: 800.954.8585, EXT.8005

CUISINE: WEST COAST

PRICES: BRUNCH ENTREES $8.95 TO $17.95;

LUNCH ENTREES $8.95 TO $17.95; DINNER ENTREES $14.95 TO $24.95 (CANADIAN)

HOURS: LUNCH 11:30 A.M. TO 2:30 P.M. MONDAY - FRIDAY; DINNER 5:30 P.M. TO CLOSING DAILY; SATURDAY BRUNCH 11:30 A.M. TO 2:30 P.M.; SUNDAY BRUNCH 10:30 A.M. TO 2:30 P.M. OPEN DAILY EXCEPT CHRISTMAS DAY. LOUNGE OPEN THROUGH OUT THE AFTERNOON. ALL DAY DINING ON PATIO IN SUMMER.

Situated in the midst of Stanley Park (rated one of the world's finest parks-within-a-city by National Geographic magazine), the Teahouse Restaurant combines elegance and nature in a most comfortable way. A recent poll named the Teahouse the most romantic restaurant in Vancouver. More people tell the staff that they proposed to their spouses here: Valentine's Day was booked over a month in advance, but to date there's no official count of engagements that took place that evening.

Ferguson Point was a military installation during World War II, and the present-day Teahouse served as a garrison and officers' mess. Following the war, the building was used as a private residence, then as a small-scale summer teahouse. In 1978, present owner and Vancouver native, Brent Davies, leased the house from the Parks Board, renovated and opened it as a restaurant. So you're not misled, the name was kept for historical purposes. The Teahouse does not serve high tea in the afternoon, but does serve lunch and dinner throughout the week and a terrific weekend brunch. We particularly enjoy the outdoor all day dining on the patio during the summer months.

A GARDEN WITHIN A GARDEN

The Teahouse is a beautiful old building. Facing the front of the restaurant, you'll see the glass-enclosed "greenhouse" environment, which Brent added to the original structure. Brent calls this "the Conservatory." Inside, trees reach to the sky under a glass roof, which warms the room in the winter and keeps you cool under the summer sun. Filled with a profusion of green plants and flowers, the Conservatory is a garden within the larger garden that surrounds the restaurant. On the opposite side of the restaurant is the Drawing Room. As the name suggests, this is a more intimate setting than the Conservatory, with walls of windows and a large tree growing in the center of the room. This is the place we love to linger over a really decadent dinner and a bottle of wine from the excellent cellar.

MORE THAN SIMPLY TEA

The Teahouse Restaurant serves weekend brunches as well as daily lunches and dinners. The cuisine far surpasses the connotation of a "teahouse," and rarely do you find a staff with the degree of professionalism and friendliness that characterizes the people who work here. Ask for their recommendation on wine to accompany your appetizer of Steamed Mussels, done in an anchovy broth, or Seared Scallops, served with potato gnocchi, red pepper coulis and parsley oil. Mardi's favorite selection is the Cured Salmon and wild Mushroom Roulade with basil oil and marinated fennel. As an entree, consider the Chermoula marinated Salmon, couscous and lentil vinaigrette, or the Roasted Scallops and Prawns, with sweet potato roesti and sherry butter sauce.

Dinner's menu is an expanded version of the luncheon menu, with specialty items such as rack of lamb, roast duck, veal, venison, salmon, prawns and fresh fish of the day. Perhaps my favorite is the Grilled Rare Tuna in a spicy tomato broth with artichoke and fennel ragout. The Teahouse offers a truly international selection of wines on three individual wine lists to complement your meal. The restaurant creates all of its desserts on the premises, which range from light coups de grace to thundering chocolate crescendos. A selection of dessert wines, Teahouse coffees and tea provides a balanced accompaniment to any selection.

The Teahouse strikes the balance between elegant and casual that allows patrons to come in for a meal after cycling around the park, or before an engagement at the theatre. Come as you are and enjoy.

GETTING THERE

The Teahouse Restaurant is located at Ferguson Point in Stanley Park, between Second and Third beaches. From north and west Vancouver, take the Lion's Gate Bridge south. Immediately after the bridge, take the Prospect Point/Park Drive Exit and continue two kilometers (1.5 miles) to the restaurant at Ferguson Point. From downtown Vancouver, take Georgia Street to the same exit.

THE WEDGEWOOD HOTEL
~ BRITISH COLUMBIA ~

LOCATION: IN THE HEART OF DOWNTOWN VANCOUVER, ACROSS FROM THE GARDENS AND WATERFALL OF THE ROBSON SQUARE CONFERENCE CENTRE

ADDRESS: 845 HORNBY STREET, VANCOUVER, B.C. V6Z 1V1

HOSTS: ELENI SKALBANIA

PHONE: 604.689.7777

TOLL FREE: 800.954.8585, EXT. 4011

FAX: 604.608.5348

ROOMS: 87

RATES: $200-$520 CANADIAN

REMARKS: RESERVATIONS RECOMMENDED. CHILDREN WELCOME. NO PETS. WHEELCHAIR ACCESSIBLE. SPA AND FITNESS CENTER, MEETING AND EVENT FACILITIES ON-SITE. SPANISH, CHINESE, FRENCH, PERSIAN AND GREEK SPOKEN. COMPLIMENTARY COFFEE AND TEA. IN-ROOM SAFETY DEPOSIT BOX.

An elegant and world-class structure, set in the center of Vancouver's thriving and cosmopolitan downtown, the Wedgewood Hotel has been a well-kept secret to visitors of Vancouver since it opened in 1984. While the secret is definitely out, the elegance and charm remain. The 13-story, 87-room complex is the work of its owner and general manager Eleni Skalbania, who purchased the old Mayfair hotel and turned it into the luxurious Wedgewood. After personally supervising all construction, Skalbania handled the interior decorating, too, moving her personal antiques and works of art to accent the Wedgewood's public areas. She continues to be the heart and soul of the Wedgewood, which was named for Lord Wedgwood of London. Skalbania pays the same attention to her hotel's guests. That personal touch is paying off by the continued rise in popularity, both in return customers and recommended visitors.

STYLE THAT BESPEAKS CULTURE

Guests of the Wedgewood include a strong mix of weekday business travelers and weekend tourists, who flock to Vancouver's bustling downtown scene. Skalbania, who grew up in Greece and moved to Vancouver in 1960, renovated and refurbished the hotel using traditional European decor, including many original antiques, fine tapestries, and other pieces of art. That decor spills over into the nearly 90 rooms: singles, doubles, suites and penthouse suites. All rooms feature balconies, while the penthouse suite has a fireplace, wetbar and scenic garden terrace. The front rooms overlook the gardens and waterfalls of nearby Robson Square. In-room safes, iron and ironing board, full mini-bars and TVs are standard. Relax in the solitude of Skalbania's comfortable oasis, then venture out into the city, to the Vancouver Art Gallery or the smorgasbord of shopping options.

CULINARY DELIGHTS, CULTURAL WONDERS

The Wedgewood's intimate, full-service restaurant, Bacchus, cooks up breakfast, lunch, dinner, afternoon teas and weekend brunch. The room offers a romantic and cozy atmosphere, with firelit room and warm and romantic surroundings featuring authentic Murano stained glass, Cherrywood furnishings and rich velvet accents. A piano bar offers a complementary ambiance. Led by the culinary leadership of a silver medalist from the Torquay International Gastronomic Festival,

house specialties include house-smoked hickory salmon, Chilean sea bass and homemade Tuscany pizza. All fresh ingredients are purchased daily from a nearby Vancouver market. Twenty-four room service is available for those interested in in-room business or more romantic dining.

The Wedgewood Hotel provides personal and thorough service to any business group or individual. The helpful staff with assist with private meeting rooms, telephone conferencing, faxing, copying services or other requirements.

VANCOUVER TO EXPLORE

For the tourist, or the business person with time to spare, the activities found by foot or car are unlimited. Explore all downtown Vancouver has to offer—shopping, restaurants and entertainment—on safe, easy-to-follow streets. The colorful city offers a flavor often found only in Europe, with unique art galleries and theatres. We always make the time for a stroll up one side of Robson Street and down the other. Don't miss Stanley Park and include a stop at the Teahouse Restaurant.

North of Vancouver after a stunning drive you will arrive in Whistler and discover some of the best downhill and nordic skiing in North America.

A popular day trip is nearby Vancouver Island. The capital city of Victoria is on the southern tip of the island. You can reach the island by ferry, or best yet, take a float plane over and land in the bustling Inner Harbour of Victoria.

GETTING THERE

Two and one-half hours north of Seattle, Washington, on Interstate 5. From 99, cross the Granville Bridge and immediately exit onto Seymour. Take Seymour to Smythe, turn left, then turn right onto Hornby to the hotel.

SEASONS IN THE PARK RESTAURANT
~ BRITISH COLUMBIA ~

LOCATION: ON LITTLE MOUNTAIN IN QUEEN ELIZABETH PARK

ADDRESS: 33TH AVE. AND CAMBIE STREET

HOSTS: MEGAN BUCKLEY, GENERAL MANAGER; BRENT DAVIES, OWNER

TELEPHONE: 604.874.8008

TOLL FREE: 800.954.8585, EXT. 8004

FAX: 604.874.7101

CUISINE: PACIFIC NORTHWEST

PRICES: BRUNCH ENTREES $8.95 TO $13.95; LUNCH ENTREES $9.95 TO $14.95; DINNER ENTREES $12.95 TO $21.95 (CANADIAN)

HOURS: LUNCH 11:30 A.M. TO 2:30 P.M. MONDAY - FRIDAY; DINNER 5:30 P.M. TO CLOSING DAILY; SATURDAY BRUNCH 11:30 A.M. TO 2:30 P.M.; SUNDAY BRUNCH 10:30 A.M. TO 2:30 P.M. OPEN DAILY EXCEPT CHRISTMAS DAY. ALL DAY DINING ON SUMMER PATIO.

Queen Elizabeth Park is set on Little Mountain and affords a phenomenal view of Vancouver. From this lofty vantage point, Seasons in the Park restaurant provides a panoramic view of the city below. From your table you can see Grouse Mountain, Vancouver Island and the city skyline. Many local people don't even know how wonderful the view is from here.

A ROOM WITH A VIEW

The main dining room seats 110 people, and features wall-to-wall windows and tiered seating from front to back so that your view won't be obstructed.

The Gazebo, built onto the main structure, is reminiscent of the Conservatory in the Teahouse Restaurant (see Teahouse in this section.) The Gazebo is situated at the edge of what used to be a deep quarry. If the glass walls opened you could literally drop 100 feet. Flowering shrubs and gardens are etched into the hillsides of the quarry; a pond at the quarry bottom with weeping willows at pond's edge resounds with a chorus of frog songs and conversations. Above the gardens outside the Gazebo you see the Vancouver cityscape. Beyond this dramatic skyline lies the picturesque North Shore Mountains.

Lunch at Seasons in the Park begins with fresh, seasonal appetizers such as smoked sockeye salmon with wild rice cake and horseradish cream, or smoked goose salad with mango and beetroot, served with grilled chicory. We never miss the savory Pacific oyster stew. Seasonal soups and a choice of salad complement a full selection of main course items such as smoked black Alaska cod poached in milk and served with a light mustard dill sauce. Or try the ravioli dish that was served to Presidents Clinton and Yeltsin on their visit to Seasons.

A ROOM WITH A VIEW

For a complete romantic evening, arrive early enough to watch the sun set behind the mountains and the lights of the city begin to sparkle. Start your dinner with cold peppered salmon poached in a terrine and a trio of peppercorns with a dill dressing. This will lead nicely into your entree, whether it's prawns and scallops seared with Pernod and a light tomato tarragon and green peppercorn dressing, or glazed pork rib chop, pan-roasted on the bone and glazed with sage and served with prune relish.

A WINE LIST TO REMEMBER

Seasons in the Park's wine selection is the same outstanding list you'll find at its sister restaurant, The Teahouse. Three separate lists include a full range of international wines: Argentina, New Zealand and Greece are included in the wine selections, as well as the more familiar European and West Coast vineyards. A fine cellar reserve list and ever-changing wine-by-the-glass add to the choices each diner must make, or leave the selection to the capable and enthusiastic wait staff.

All of Seasons' desserts are prepared on the premises. For a light finish, try a trio of sorbets–three seasonal fruit sherbets with fresh fruits and almond lace wafer, or the sunburned lemon pie. The Belgian chocolate terrine, with white and dark Callebaut chocolate served with raspberry coulis is memorable.

The waitstaff at Seasons is young, vibrant and fun-loving. They help create the refreshing environment that is elegant without being stuffy, casual without being slick.

Before or after dining, we always take the time to walk up the hill a little from Seasons to the Bloedel Conservatory, where tropical plants, tropical fish and tropical birds are housed. The beautiful glass-domed building offers the same great view as the restaurant. Just beyond are the Quarry Gardens. Also in the park are quiet spots to read and a whole hillside to explore. Little Mountain is the highest point in Vancouver.

GETTING THERE

From downtown Vancouver, travel south on Cambie Street until you reach 33rd Avenue. Turn left at the stop sign and follow Queen Elizabeth Park Drive up the winding road through the park. It's at the top of Little Mountain. There is free parking by the restaurant and the Bloedel Conservatory.

EMERALD LAKE LODGE
~ BRITISH COLUMBIA ~

LOCATION: ON THE SHORE OF EMERALD LAKE, ONE HOUR FROM BANFF, ALBERTA

ADDRESS: P.O. BOX 10, FIELD, B.C. VOA 1G0

HOSTS: DIETER WINN, GENERAL MANAGER, PAT AND CONNIE O'CONNOR, PROPRIETORS

TELEPHONE: 250.343.6321

TOLL FREE: 800.954.8585, EXT. 2007

FAX: 250.343.6724

ROOMS: 85 GUEST UNITS IN 24 CABIN STYLE BUILDINGS

RATES: (CANADIAN): SUPERIOR ROOMS: LOW SEASON, $165; HIGH SEASON, $275. DELUXE ROOMS: LOW SEASON, $195; HIGH SEASON, $315. EXECUTIVE SUITES: LOW SEASON, $230; HIGH SEASON, $340.

REMARKS: CHILDREN UNDER 12 FREE WITH PARENTS. NO PETS.

Built by the Canadian Pacific Railway in 1902 as one of a series of camps erected to encourage travel and thus recoup the cost of the expensive rail line, the Emerald Lake Chalet was the *creme de la creme*. The majestic lodge of handhewn timber and massive stone fireplaces offered the very latest in modern conveniences–electricity, wood stoves and hardwood floors. The rate, even with the added amenity of a full orchestra to entertain the guests, was still exorbitant–$5 per day. The chalet became the private retreat of only the affluent and the adventurous of spirit.

Calgary resident Pat O'Connor had watched the sun set on the grandeur of the Emerald Lake Chalet, and he was concerned over its steady decline. In 1980, Pat purchased the chalet and its surrounding 13 acres, beginning a process, he recalls, that "I would never have dreamed could be so difficult." The property took six years and $8.5 million to restore.

The renovation of Emerald Lake Lodge reflects O'Connor's respect for the delicate balance between commercial and environmental concerns. To ensure the peaceful quiet of the site, the parking lot is located five minutes away from the lodge. Guests unload and park their cars and are quickly delivered to the lodge by shuttle.

SPIRIT OF THE CANADIAN ROCKIES

"We cater to people who want to spend time in the mountains, for people who want all the advantages of the Rockies without roughing it," says Pat. Emerald Lake Lodge does its best to fulfill the promise of the great outdoors. The tour desk has information on such seasonal activities as alpine and nordic skiing, snowshoeing, horseback riding, canoeing, fishing, white water rafting and sightseeing. For ambitious hikers, the lodge staff can arrange overnight stays at remote hiking huts. Burgess fossil beds is a strenuous but rewarding two-hour hike. Takkakkaw Falls, the third-highest waterfall in Canada, is easily reachable by car.

In the winter, you can enjoy some of the best heli-skiing in the world from here. For cross-country skiers, there are 50 miles of trails where deer, elk and other wildlife roam. You can also take a dog sled ride, try snow shoeing or take a romantic moonlit sleigh ride. For downhill skiers, the lodge is just 20 minutes from Louise, the largest ski area in the Canadian Rockies. A free ski shuttle operates between the lodge and Lake Louise throughout the season.

RUSTIC ELEGANCE

The lodge's 24 new buildings were built 25 feet off the ground so that the surrounding vegetation would be able to regenerate. The 85 guest units are spread over three hillsides, each with a water view. The studios and the suites contain queen-sized beds covered with comforters, and the homey feel of antiques and wicker. All rooms have stone hearth fireplaces, private entrances, full baths and telephones.

The property is on a finger of land that reaches into Emerald Lake, and is reachable only by crossing a wooden bridge. The building's two massive stone fireplaces remain the focal point for the Emerald Lounge and lobby. And the Kicking Horse Bar's 1882 oak bar adds a grand reminder of the Yukon's lively Gold Rush days.

There's a Club House with an outdoor 14-foot hot tub, and sauna and sundeck, both with wonderful views down into the lake. Sitting in the warm waters of the hot tub and watching the color of the lake change at dusk is our special way of celebrating each visit to the lodge.

ROCKY MOUNTAIN CUISINE

An old-fashioned veranda shades the dining room's spectacular views. Elegant in chintzes of dusty rose, gray and hunter green, the rustic room has a comfortable coziness. The lodge is gaining a well earned reputation for its new regional Rocky Mountain Cuisine, featuring outstanding presentations of game and award-winning regional wines.

GETTING THERE

From Calgary, drive east to Banff and north past Lake Louise. Turn west on Trans-Canada Highway 1 and go to Field. Follow the signs five miles north to Emerald Lake. The parking lot will be on your left. Call the lodge for a shuttle when you arrive.

DEER LODGE

-ALBERTA-

LOCATION: TWO AND ONE-HALF HOURS WEST OF CALGARY, AND FOUR KILOMETERS OFF THE TRANS-CANADA HIGHWAY, DEER LODGE IS A SHORT WALKING DISTANCE FROM LAKE LOUISE.

ADDRESS: P.O. BOX 100, LAKE LOUISE, ALBERTA T0L 1E0

HOST: MARTAIN CLOUTIER

PHONE: 403-522-3991

TOLL FREE: 800.954.8585, EXT. 2036

FAX: 403. 522.3883

ROOMS: 73

RATES: REGULAR SEASON $95-$160 CANADIAN
PEAK SEASON $145 TO $210

REMARKS: RESERVATIONS RECOMMENDED. CHILDREN WELCOME. NO PETS. FREE PARKING. ROOFTOP HOT TUB AND INDOOR SAUNA. MEETING AND EVENT FACILITIES ON-SITE. FULL-SERVICE RESTAURANT.

With an absolute postcard setting in Alberta's Banff National Park, Deer Lodge is the ideal destination for an individual, couple or family looking for a quiet retreat, excellent, innovative cuisine and an attentive staff. Whether you desire quite, tranquil winter nights or strenuous, fast-paced summer days, the scenery will suit you.

The rustic lodge has a storied past, first taking shape in 1921 as a log teahouse when it was opened by one of the early guiding families just behind the Chateau Lake Louise. Just a few minutes from the lake, it became a popular destination for visitors and guides. Four years later the guest rooms were built, the lodge's rich heritage reflected in the architect's traditional mountain decor, and the house took turns as a lodge, drug store and residence before joining together to become Deer Lodge.

Since 1988 the lodge has undergone three renovations, keeping the architectural features by emphasizing the original stone and log incorporated into the structure. With a unique mixture of nineties comfort and roaring twenties charm, the Deer Lodge turns off all modern distractions and takes its visitors into another more relaxing world.

As the travel writer for Canada's newspaper, *The Globe and Mail* wrote: "Think quaint, cozy, quirky and rustic. Think scalding open-air hot tubs...Think crackling fireplaces, good wine and hearty plates of garnished game. Think atmosphere with a capital A."

TWENTIES DECOR NINETIES STYLE

Guests of Deer Lodge experience true mountain hospitality—both in service and beauty. With magnificent Lake Louise only a stroll away, and breathtaking mountain views from the rooftop hot tub, your hectic daily routine will be a distant memory. The 1920s heritage is reflected and honored in the Lodge's antiques and furnishings throughout its three-story structure of log, brick and stone.

Following a full day of skiing in Lake Louise or Banff, or hiking and rock climbing in the nearby hills, put your feet up, inside the fireplace sitting room or in the magnificent outdoors, enjoy a cup of mountain tea and take in the views.

Deer Lodge features three heritage buildings connected by newer structures. All single and double rooms are equipped with private baths, cozy feather comforters and teahouse-era antiques. To keep with the rustic feel of yesteryear, in-room telephones are few and none of the rooms have TVs. Entertainment consists of quiet music, historical area lectures and walks with the innkeeper. Like to read? There are plenty of natural nooks and crannies to enjoy the privacy you deserve.

NORTH OF THE BORDER FARE

Deer Lodge features one of the best dining rooms in the Canadian Rockies, the Mount Fairview Dining Room, which offers a unique and outstanding menu and an extensive wine list in a much appreciated smoke-free environment.

The chefs are making headlines with their concentration on a fare called Rocky Mountain Cuisine. This type of cooking relies on a principle that foods should be served together only if they grow together, and served only in the season when they are grown. When you dine at Mount Fairview, or at its sister properties, Emerald Lake Lodge in British Columbia and Buffalo Mountain Lodge in Banff, you may experience a dish such as guinea fowl with birch bark or ravioli with dandelions. Another popular item is the Game Platter: sliced, peppered and smoked duck breast, venison mini salami, air-dried buffalo, game pate, venison ham, mustard melons and cranberry relish. Others include a wonton stuffed with caribou or a sun-dried cranberry sauced smothering a local pork tendorloin.

If a simpler fare is more your style, check out the Caribou Lounge. It is open for breakfast and lunch and offers magnificent views of the Victoria Glacier.

GETTING THERE

Two and one-half hours west of Calgary via the Trans Canada Highway. Follow the signs to Lake Louise. Deer Lodge is a 10 kilometer drive north of Field, British Columbia.

BUFFALO MOUNTAIN LODGE
~ ALBERTA ~

LOCATION: ON NINE WOODED ACRES ON TUNNEL MOUNTAIN, ABOVE THE TOWN OF BANFF

ADDRESS: P.O. BOX 1326, BANFF, ALBERTA TOL 0C0

HOSTS: BRENT POLLOCK MANAGER; PAT AND CONNIE O'CONNOR, PROPRIETORS

TELEPHONE: 403.762.2400

TOLL FREE: 800.954.8585, EXT. 2008

FAX: 403.762.4495

ROOMS: 108

RATES: REGULAR SEASON $165 TO $210 (CANADIAN) PEAK SEASON $225 TO $265 (CANADIAN)

REMARKS: COMPLIMENTARY PARKING, STEAM ROOM AND HOT TUBS, NO PETS. SMOKE-FREE DINING ROOM.

The Rocky Mountains have long been an area of great significance to Canada's native people. Buffalo Mountain Lodge lies on the gentle slopes of Tunnel Mountain which early visitors knew as "Sleeping Buffalo." Rising above the scenic, historic town of Banff Tunnel Mountain has witnessed a great deal of geologic and human history. Bordered by the granite spires of Cascade Mountain and Mount Rundle, rock formations called "hoodoos" rose out of the sweeping Bow Valley, where moose, elk, deer and bison were plentiful. Here, the earth's hot mineral baths provided rejuvenation. It was a peaceful life for the Indians–a life of ceremony and celebration. Today people from around the world continue to celebrate the beauty of this area.

RESPECT FOR THE PAST

With a spirit of veneration for the past, for unspoiled nature and life's simple pleasures, Pat O'Connor and his wife, Connie, have created Buffalo Mountain Lodge. Above the town of Banff, the lodge's forested setting offers privacy and pure mountain air. It's the kind of place that compels you to slow down and enjoy the moment.

Opened in 1988 and set amidst nine acres of tall pines, the Lodge offers seclusion and privacy the architectural style is simple elegance with hand hewn construction. "We were drawing from the past respect for things built properly and built with heart," says Connie." High, open-beamed ceilings display a massive stone fireplace. The custom-made cherry front desk and bar are beautifully accented with pine and bent-willow and cherry furnishings. A magnificent buffalo head is mounted above the crackling fireplace.

The lodge's cheerful, professional staff go out of their way to please. Guests have access to the property's outdoor spa facilities, which include a 14-foot hot tub and a steam room.

CUSTOM ACCOMMODATIONS

Of the 108 guest accommodations, 48 new units were added in July, 1997. These units feature either two queen-size or one king-size bed and "stickley" style chairs in front of the wood-burning fireplace. Each has a large bathtub, a separate shower stall and a pedestal sink in the spacious bathrooms. The other units feature a gas or wood-burning fireplace, private baths, feather and down duvets, with one queen-size bed or two double beds. All guest units have cable television, telephones and in-room coffee makers. The exteriors of the new buildings compliment the existing structures and grounds.

ROCKY MOUNTAIN FARE

The simple elegance of the lodge's design extends to the elegance of the restaurants. The dining room has a well-founded reputation for providing the finest of the Rocky Mountain Cuisine. Blending the best of classical French cooking with innovative California ideas, they create delicious menus that feature hearty soups and breads, superb entrees and freshly baked pastries and desserts. The *Wine Spectator* recently awarded their Award of Merit to the Lodge's wine list. Cilantro Cafe, open from mid-May until mid-October offers innovative California cuisine.

BANFF: BACKCOUNTRY AND BACKSTAGE

The lodge can provide picnic lunches for a day of fishing at Lake Minnewanka. For winter guests, there's the featherlight powder of the Canadian Rockies. Banff is located near four world-class ski mountains. You can also take off on cross-country skis to experience the thrill of untracked powder snow.

Banff, known the world over for its beauty and soothing hot mineral springs, provides the perfect base camp for exploring the outlying areas. Banff is also recognized for the excellence of Banff Centre's music, theatre and dance performance. The Whyte Museum of the Canadian Rockies and the Luxton Museum do an outstanding job of reproducing the colorful history of Banff National Park and its native people.

GETTING THERE

The Lodge is located on Tunnel Mountain Road just off the Trans-Canada Highway. The Calgary International Airport is 1.5 hours away.

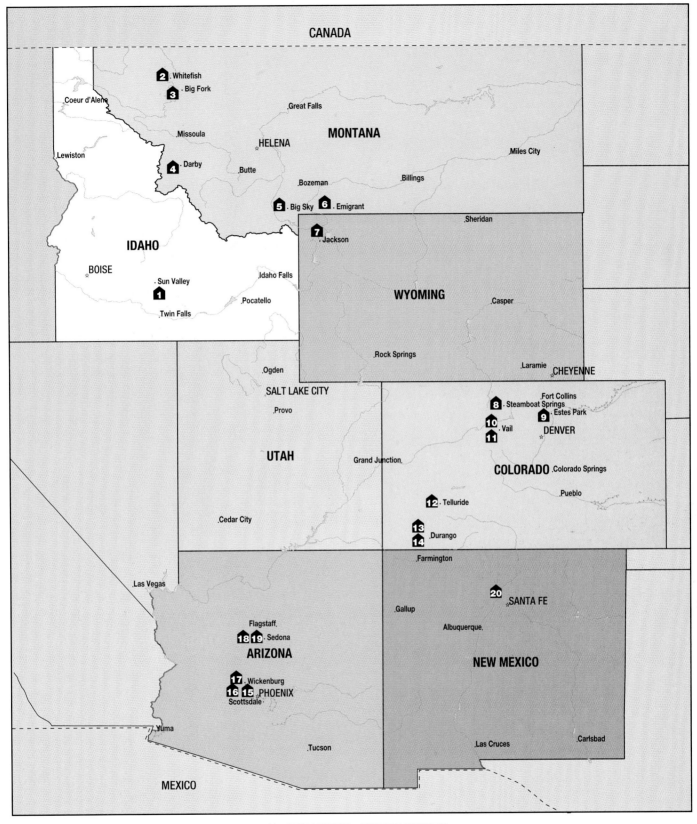

MOUNTAIN WEST - UNITED STATES

1. RIVER STREET INN - Sun Valley, ID
2. KANDAHAR LODGE - Whitefish, MT
3. FLATHEAD LAKE LODGE - Bigfork, MT
4. TRIPLE CREEK RANCH - Darby, MT
5. LONE MOUNTAIN RANCH - Big Sky, MT
6. MT. SKY GUEST RANCH - Emigrant, MT
7. TETON PINES RESORT - Jackson, WY

8. VISTA VERDE RANCH - Steamboat Springs, CO
9. ROMANTIC RIVERSONG - Estes Park, CO
10. TRAPPER'S CABIN - Beaver Creek, CO
11. SADDLERIDGE - Beaver Creek, CO
12. SAN SOPHIA - Telluride, CO
13. LIGHTNER CREEK INN - Durango, CO
14. BLUE LAKE RANCH - Durango, CO

15. HERMOSA INN - Phoenix, AZ
16. WIGWAM RESORT - Litchfield Park, AZ
17. RANCHO DE LOS CABALLEROS - Wickenburg, AZ
18. CANYON VILLA - Sedona, AZ
19. CASA SEDONA - Sedona, AZ
20. TERRITORIAL INN - Santa Fe, NM

RIVER STREET INN
~ IDAHO ~

LOCATION: ON TRAIL CREEK IN SOUTH KETCHUM, NEAR RIVER RUN BASE LODGE.

ADDRESS: 100 RIVERS STREET W, KETCHUM, ID 83340

FOR MAIL USE PO BOX 182, SUN VALLEY, ID 83353

HOSTS: SCOTT AND AMY SMITH

TELEPHONE: 208.726.3611

TOLL FREE: 800.954.8585, EXT.1020

FAX: 208.726.2439

ROOMS: 8

RATES: $130 TO $185 DOUBLE

REMARKS: INCLUDES FULL BREAKFAST. NO SMOKING.

Sun Valley's first bed and breakfast inn, The River Street Inn is neatly tucked away on a quiet street just blocks from the center of Ketchum. The inn is a pleasing blend of friendly warmth and respectful privacy. Its innovative architecture weaves the charm of Victorian sensibilities with the open spaces of contemporary Western design.

In the spacious living room with sage green carpets and white-washed oak trim, comfortable couches invite you to enjoy the warmth emanating from the natural brick fireplace. From the living room, French doors open onto the deck. Cottonwoods and aspens border Trail Creek, which runs below.

River Street Inn's secret for a memorable stay is simple: let the guests set the tone. If you'd like to visit over a cup of coffee in the kitchen, the more the merrier. If you prefer privacy, it is always respected. Scott and Amy Smith and their attentive staff are available for conversation or to help with any arrangements you may need to enhance your stay.

CLEAR VIEWS

The eight guest rooms are really more like suites. Decorated in soft prints and pastels, they feature televisions, king-and queen-sized beds, big walk-in showers, small refrigerators and our favorite amenity, Japanese-style soaking tubs, which accommodate two. Five of the suites face the Trail Creek, and three suites offer clear mountain views. Breakfast at the River Street Inn is an indulgent feast that will carry you well through lunchtime. River Street's "no rules" apply here as well–breakfast is from 8 a.m. to 10 a.m., unless you want it earlier or later

or served in your room. Begin with fresh fruits, juices, coffee or tea. Then get ready for one of the homemade baked Danish rolls or some coffeecake. To accommodate health-conscious guests, there are low-fat substitutions, such as making pancakes with cottage cheese.

DOWN IN THE VALLEY

Ketchum and Sun Valley are situated in the beautiful Wood River Valley. Sun Valley, long noted as a skier's haven also offers a wide variety of other activities and sports. Bald Mountain hovers over the town, offering some of the most challenging downhill skiing in the country, yet it has terrain for the less adventuresome as well. A shuttle runs the five blocks from River Street Inn to the award-winning River Run Lodge at the base of Baldy. Cross-country skiing has also become increasingly popular in the area, and groomed

trails begin virtually outside your door.

SUMMER AND FALL

Mardi lived for six years in Ketchum. She came for the skiing, but it was the summer and fall which kept her here and which keep us coming back. The summer climate is warm and dry. The bright, clear days are perfect for enjoying rounds of golf at one of the many courses in the area. North of town is the incomparable Salmon River, where thrilling white water adventures await you if you dare. The inn has bicycles to rent, allowing unlimited access to the network of bicycle trails which wind through the valley, and many shops in town rent mountain bikes for off-road cycling. The crisp fall days are brilliantly colored, enhancing hiking and horseback riding expeditions in this less-crowded season.

FAMOUS AND FIT

North of town is a cemetery where a simple slab marks Ernest Hemingway's grave. Farther out on Trail Creek, you'll find his memorial. On it is written, "Best of all he loved the fall; the leaves yellow on the cottonwoods, leaves floating on the trout streams and above the hills the high blue windless skies."

You can walk anywhere in Ketchum from River Street Inn. The area supports art galleries, summer theater and symphony productions, and a wide variety of great restaurants, breweries and night spots. We always reserve one night out for dinner in the historic Pioneer Salon and Restaurant

GETTING THERE

Fly into Hailey Airport, south of Ketchum and head north on U.S. 75, turn left at River Street, just beyond the Trail Creek Bridge. The inn is two blocks toward the mountains, on your left. There is plenty of parking in front of the inn.

KANDAHAR LODGE
~ MONTANA ~

LOCATION: ON BIG MOUNTAIN, EIGHT MILES NORTH OF WHITEFISH.

ADDRESS: BIG MOUNTAIN SKI RESORT VILLAGE, P.O. BOX 1659, WHITEFISH, MT 59937

HOSTS: BUCK AND MARY PAT LOVE

TELEPHONE: 406.862.6098

TOLL FREE: 800.954.8585, EXT. 6001

FAX: 406.862.6095

ROOMS: 48

RATES: $99 SINGLE, $109 DOUBLE, $179 SUITES (SUMMER); $100 TO $160 ROOMS, $132 TO $170 LOFTS, $220 TWO-ROOM SUITES (WINTER). WEEKLY RATES, SEASON PACKAGES ARE AVAILABLE.

REMARKS: CHILDREN UNDER 12 STAY FREE.

Buck and Mary Pat Love are ski devotees with an admiration for the grand style of European ski lodges. They are also the owners and managers of Kandahar Lodge, and bring their love of people and skiing together in this mountaintop retreat.

Mary Pat and Buck wanted to create the entire package: great skiing, beautiful scenery, and first class lodging and dining. As Mary Pat explains, "We decided our first priority was to spend as much time as possible with our guests; we are both committed to making them feel comfortable, relaxed and at home." To put their philosophy to work, they built their home as part of the lodge and live there with their daughters, Lindsay and Hailey. They are, in the best sense of the word, innkeepers.

Their "inn" is a warm and inviting three-story wooden lodge built around a central sunken lobby with an immense rock fireplace, an array of comfortable sofas and chairs flanked by reading lamps, period antiques and original art. The entrance to the lodge has window arches and side panels of etched glass that display mountain and forest scenes by renown local Whitefish artist Myni Ferguson.

FLEXIBILITY AND FUN

On either side of the lobby, wide carpeted staircases lead guests to their second- and third-floor rooms, suites or lofts. You can choose from rooms designed for one to eight people. Sixteen of the 48 units have small fully stocked kitchens. The rooms have cedar paneling, pine furniture and down comforters on the beds. In the summer of 1997 two new meeting and retreat rooms will be ready for use. The beautiful Board Room will comfortably seat 12, while the larger Conference Room will seat up to 50.

CAFE KANDAHAR

Nestled into the flank of the lodge is the compact Cafe Kandahar. In the morning, guests can take their breakfast at the sturdy wooden tables. It is in the evening when the Cafe takes on a special warm glow. Your host might suggest your meal start with "Oysters Kandahar," served Cajun-style. In addition to the two nightly specials, you can always count on entrees such as the marinated chicken breasts, done with Montana hothouse tomatoes and artichokes; or fresh sea scallop fettuccini with a garlic-basil pesto. The cafe does not sell liquor, but guests can bring in their own bottle during dinner.

YEAR-ROUND ENJOYMENT

Kandahar Lodge is open year-round and offers guests an assortment of activities. In summer (May to October), guests make the lodge their base and take day trips to majestic Glacier National Park, hike in the rugged Mission Mountains, sail on Flathead Lake or shop in the nearby towns of Whitefish and Kalispell. For the outdoor enthusiast, there is boating, waterskiing and fishing on Whitefish Lake, and several million acres of designated wilderness to explore. The lodge has golf packages at seven nearby courses, and the gondola lift to the top of Big Mountain is a must-do activity while you're there. In October eagle-watchers flock to West Glacier to catch sight of the majestic birds.

Buck and Mary Pat are avid sailors as well as skiers. Each April, you will find them participating in the North American Ski/Yachting Championships, which take place on Big Mountain and Flathead Lake.

In the winter months (November to April), snow comes early and stays late. Big Mountain and the Kandahar Lodge are often blessed with fresh, powdery snow. *Ski Magazine* called 7,000-foot Big Mountain "one of the best ski areas in the world." The mountain receives over 300 inches of snowfall annually; you can ski 3,000 acres on 50 marked trails using eight lifts, including a high speed quad and gondola.

There is a ski trail from the mountain to the lodge, making the return trip especially easy. Once there, guests enter the warm boot room, lock up their gear and walk in stocking feet directly to one of the two saunas or to the Jacuzzi for a relaxing slow soak in the 102 degree water.

GETTING THERE

From Whitefish, turn right onto Wisconsin Avenue (Highway 487) and follow the signs to Big Mountain.

FLATHEAD LAKE LODGE
~ MONTANA ~

LOCATION: HIGHWAY 35, ONE MILE SOUTH OF BIGFORK; 35 MILES SOUTH OF GLACIER NATIONAL PARK.

ADDRESS: P.O. BOX 248, BIGFORK, MT 59911

HOSTS: DOUG AND MAUREEN AVERILL

TELEPHONE: 406.837.4391

TOLL FREE: 800.954.8585, EXT 6002

FAX: 406.837.6977

ROOMS: 38

RATES: WEEKLY: ADULTS $1,694, TEENAGERS $1,253, CHILDREN 6-12 $1,064, CHILDREN 3-5 $833, INFANTS $96. RATES INCLUDE ALL MEALS AND ARE SUNDAY TO SUNDAY.

REMARKS: NO PETS. OPEN MAY THROUGH SEPTEMBER. RESERVATIONS REQUIRED.

Since 1945, the Averill family's Flathead Lake Lodge and Dude Ranch has been offering guests one full week of lodging, meals and activities on this 2,000-acre ranch on the east shore of Flathead Lake. The lodge caters to families with children of all ages, and the 100 guests are limited only by their inability to do everything at once.

The unique combination of the lodge, its setting and recreational activities give the Averills an almost unheard-of repeat visitor rate. Over 60 percent of Flathead Lake Lodge's guests come back. Mr. George

Wood holds the record, he has come every summer for 48 years. Known as Grandpa George he even gave Doug's wife, Maureen Averill, away at their wedding.

THE WRANGLERS

"People come here for the horses," says Doug Averill, an ex-rodeo rider who became manager of the ranch when his dad, Les Averill, retired in 1975. "We have horses for the inexperienced riders and quarter horses for those who know how to handle that kind of horse. A lot of our guests are simply nuts about horses." So the Averills give them horses–morning, noon and night. Guests can sign up for breakfast rides, group rides, family rides or fast rides. The wranglers start their day at 5:30, and even at that hour there are kids down at the stable, eager to help them brush and feed the horses.

At the end of the week there is a kid's rodeo and children of all ages participate in the barrel races, pole bending contests, three-legged races and the water balloon challenge. Once a week, a roping club comes to the ranch to put on a performance, and Buck, a longtime ranch hand, entertains guests with stories and demonstrations of old-time skills.

As much as guests love the horses, we can't forget the lake. The clear blue waters of Flathead lap at the shore of the ranch, and guests are encouraged to take out the sailboats, fishing boats, canoes and windsurfers. There's waterskiing every day at 1 p.m., and an experienced waterfront hand (referred to as a water wimp by the wranglers) is nearby to handle the powerboat and to give lessons.

THE LODGE

The Civilian Conservation Corps built the Main Lodge and the South Lodge in 1932, and both two-story Western structures have large lobbies with huge river rock fireplaces. The Main Lodge houses the office, Saddle Sore Saloon (guests bring their own liquor), kitchen and family-style dining room.

The 25 to 30 families that arrive at the ranch each Sunday are housed in 20 cabins which accommodate 2-7 guests, and 18 lodge rooms suitable for 2-4 people. Ranch buildings are constructed of native larch logs, and most cottages also have log furnishings. Each unit has its own bath, two or three bedrooms, a comfortable living room and Western-style comforts. Most of the accommodations look out on spectacular Flathead Lake or off to the Rocky Mountains.

FAMILY STYLE DINING

Everything is prepared fresh each day at Flathead Lake, including all the breads and pastries from the in-house bakery. Breakfast might consist of huckleberry pancakes and bacon and eggs one day and omelets the next. Coffee is always served first thing in the morning, so you can have that essential cup while standing next to a crackling fire in the Main Lodge. Lunch is light: Salads and quiche or food that the kids like—hamburgers and soups. Lunch is usually served outside on the deck overlooking the lake. Dinner might be a steak fry, fresh salmon, chicken, prime rib or a whole roasted pig.

If the horses and the lake don't take up all of your free time, there is tennis, volleyball or basketball, swimming and nightly beach fires and sing-alongs. There are, in fact, only two things that guests can't do on the ranch: watch television and play video games.

GETTING THERE

From Polson, take Highway 35 north. The sign for the ranch is about one mile south of Bigfork. From Glacier National Park, take Highway 2 toward Columbia Falls, turn onto 206, heading south. It will join with Highway 35, go past Bigfork one mile south to the ranch.

TRIPLE CREEK RANCH
~ MONTANA ~

LOCATION: 72 MILES SOUTH OF MISSOULA INTERNATIONAL AIRPORT.

ADDRESS: 5551 WEST FORK STAGE ROUTE, DARBY, MT 59829

HOSTS: WAYNE AND JUDY KILPATRICK

TELEPHONE: 406.821.4600

TOLL FREE: 800.954.8585, EXT. 3007

FAX: 406.821.4666

ROOMS: 18 CABINS

RATES: $475 - $995 PER NIGHT, PER COUPLE, ALL INCLUSIVE.

REMARKS: ALL MEALS, SNACKS, BEVERAGES AND ON-RANCH ACTIVITIES INCLUDED. CHILDREN 16 AND OLDER WELCOMED. 18 INDIVIDUAL CABINS. WHEELCHAIR ACCESSIBLE. TRANSPORTATION AVAILABLE. TENNIS COURTS, SWIMMING POOL, AND PUTTING GREEN ON-SITE. NO PETS.

Triple Creek Ranch is a Montana Hideaway, designed for adults. Originally intended as a private retreat, the ranch was carved out of the side of majestic Trapper Peak, the highest peak in the region. Triple Creek is a year round destination resort for professional people and discerning travelers who desire a small world class facility and spectacular outdoor activities.

In 1986, Wayne and Judy Kilpatrick opened the resort to the public, setting the standard for luxury in a ranch environment. Surrounded by the pristine

Bitterroot National Forest, Triple Creek imitates its surroundings with log and cedar cabins. The library/conference room, lounge and dining room in the main lodge offer a chance to meet and greet fellow guests before luxuriating in the seclusion of your own cabin.

ALPINE WARMTH

There are 18 individual cabins displaying a modern, elegant mountain decor. Extensive use of leather, brass and glass give the rooms a wide-open warmth, bringing the outdoors right to you. Features available in the cabins range from fireplaces, steam showers, stocked wet bars to hot tubs. Each cabin contains a King-or Queen-sized bed, TV and VCR, and a telephone with a data port. We loved the daily delivery of fresh baked cookies to our cabin. As the ranch is nestled in the forest, outstanding views of the Bitterroot Mountain Range, Ponderosa pines, Piquette Mountain and Baker Point are accessible from every cabin. Mardi loved our cabin immediately and suggested that we cancel the rest of our two-week trip and stay here the entire time.

REGIONAL SPICE

At Triple Creek Ranch all meals, snacks, and drinks are inclusive and served in either the central dining room or in the intimacy of your own cabin. Spend the evening feasting on world class cuisine with entrees such as Chef Martha's Rack of Ellensburg Lamb followed by a lemon tartlet with raspberry sauce. One evening we participated in a special ranch ritual and went out to the stocked trout pond, where we personally caught the trout we wanted for dinner. The staff prepared it just the way we wanted. This was a wonderful option. Another distinctive feature of Triple Creek is that all alcoholic beverages are included. While remote, the eager-to-please staff can accommodate and most dietary requirements, given notice.

HEAVEN OUTDOORS

Just step outside to find your own beautiful playground. The possibilities are endless. Enjoy fly fishing, hiking, horseback riding, tennis, and bird or wildlife viewing or photography. Relax in the outside pool or hot tub or polish your putting skills on the green. They provide mountain bikes and ATVs for an exhilarating afternoon's ride. One afternoon, we enjoyed a champagne and salmon pate lunch served at the top of Baker Point. Nearby day adventures include guided fly-fishing float trips on the Bitterroot River, or white water rafting on the Salmon River. You can also go heli-hiking, heli-fishing and flight-seeing over the majestic Bitterroot Mountains. When it is time to wind down, enjoy this natural paradise in your own secluded hot tub perched on your deck, nestled in the woods.

YEAR ROUND ACTIVITIES

Winter excursions support a number of inspiring activities. After a fresh early morning snowfall, go on a brisk horseback ride or take an invigorating snowmobile expedition through the glistening winter scenery. If you crave some great downhill skiing, try some runs in the deep Montana power snow at Lost Trail power mountain, just 28 miles away. We had a great time exploring the ranch on snowshoes and on cross-county skis. For trail skiing, try Chief Joseph Cross country Ski Area, which features groomed and ungroomed trails for all ski levels.

GETTING THERE

The International Airport in Missoula, Montana, receives Delta, Horizon and Northwest jet service. Take Highway 93 South to Darby. Five miles past Darby, turn right on Route 473 (West Fork Road). Just past the seven mile marker, the driveway to Triple Creek Ranch will be on your right. Triple Creek Ranch is also helicopter accessible.

LONE MOUNTAIN RANCH

~ MONTANA ~

LOCATION: FOUR AND ONE-HALF MILES WEST OF HIGHWAY 191 AND WEST OF YELLOWSTONE.

ADDRESS: P.O. BOX 160069, BIG SKY, MT 59716

HOSTS: BOB AND VIVIAN SCHAAP

TELEPHONE: 406.995.4644

TOLL FREE: 800.954.8585, EXT. 6003

FAX: 406.995.4670

ROOMS: 30

RATES: PER PERSON, PER WEEK; DISCOVERY PACKAGE $1,525 INCLUDES THREE MEALS A DAY, GRATUITIES AND AIRPORT TRANSPORTATION. SPECIAL FLY FISHING PACKAGE AVAILABLE. REDUCED RATES FOR FAMILIES WITH SMALL CHILDREN. WINTER RATES PER PERSON, PER WEEK; INCLUDING 3 MEALS A DAY, GRATIUITIES, 7-DAY TRAIL PASS AND TRANSPORTATION $1,230.

REMARKS: OPEN LATE MAY THROUGH OCTOBER; DECEMBER THROUGH EARLY APRIL. RESERVATIONS REQUIRED.

Nestled in its own secluded valley next to a clear mountain stream, Lone Mountain Ranch is a dream destination for lovers of the outdoors. Summer family fun, spectacular fly-fishing, horseback riding, children's program, naturalist-guided hikes and Yellowstone tours, and winter cross-country skiing adventures are all packaged to include comfortable Western lodging and ranch meals in a friendly, informal atmosphere.

With its close proximity (20 miles) to the natural wonders of Yellowstone National Park, Lone Mountain

Ranch provides guests with enough activities to keep them happy for much longer than a week's visit.

SUMMER FAMILY FUN

The ranch successfully integrates activities for guests of all ages. Children can choose from a variety of interesting adventures including campouts in an authentic teepee, horseback rides, rodeos, nature walks, games, orienteering and llama hikes. Activities are available for kids ages four and older.

Horseback rides are a favorite activity. Sunday is reserved for matching guests with horses. Monday through Saturday you can saddle up for a half-day ride to the Spanish Peaks or an all-day trip into Yellowstone National Park. Wranglers accompany small groups and are quick to point out the backcountry wildlife, flowers and natural features.

We particularly like the ranch's popular naturalist program. Yellowstone interpretive trips offer opportunities to explore the park's famous features as well as its better-kept secrets. Naturalist-guided nature walks are offered several times a week. We believe the best time to go is during the fall, when the lack of crowds draw the Yellowstone wildlife down from the high country for easier viewing.

PRETTIEST SPOT ON EARTH

The original ranch buildings were built in 1926 using hand-hewn logs. Bob and Vivian Schaap took over the ranch in 1977 to create a cross-country ski center and summer guest ranch. The 24 immaculate cabins and the newly constructed six bedroom Ridgetop Lodge accommodate guests, with all the comforts a cozy fireplace, electric heat, private baths and spacious front porches. The cabins are furnished with lodgepole pine furniture and each possesses its own character.

RANCH COOKING WITH GOURMET FLAIR

We know that an active day builds hearty appetites. Guests are treated to nationally-acclaimed ranch cuisine. The three meals are served daily in the relaxed, smoke-free, atmosphere of the ranch's beautiful log dining room. Delicious sack lunches are available for guests who choose to be out and about at lunch time. In the summer, there are special weekly meals; two outdoor barbecues and campfire sing-alongs. Special diet requests are easily accommodated.

FLY FISHING AND CROSS-COUNTRY SKIER'S PARADISE

Lone Mountain Ranch fly-fishing program is included in the Orvis-endorsed list. Fishing adventures can include wading, float-tubing or fishing from a drift boat. Fall is our favorite time to wander the nearby blue-ribbon trout streams.

The ranch has 45 miles of professionally groomed cross-country ski trails that begin right outside the cabin doors, while first-track telemarkers can anticipate miles of backcountry trails blanketed by virgin snow. Many guests also enjoy snowshoeing on nearby trails.The ranch has a full-service ski shop, with rental and demo equipment, and professional instructors. All-day naturalist guided ski trips to Yellowstone and the Spanish Peaks are available. We have found nothing to compare to the thrill of skiing through geyser basins, past snow-ghosted trees, frozen waterfalls and wintering herds of elk and bison.

GETTING THERE

From Bozeman, go south on Highway 191 through the Gallatin Canyon for 40 miles. Turn right at the Big Sky Resort turnoff. Proceed up the Big Sky Spur Road 4.5 miles to the Lone Mountain Ranch sign. From Yellowstone, exit the west entrance and drive 48 miles north on Highway 191 to the Big Sky Resort turnoff. Turn left and proceed as above.

MOUNTAIN SKY GUEST RANCH
~ MONTANA ~

LOCATION: FOUR AND ONE-HALF MILES UP BIG CREEK ROAD, OFF HIGHWAY 89, NORTH OF YELLOWSTONE PARK

ADDRESS: BIG CREEK ROAD, EMIGRANT, MT (RANCH), OR P.O. BOX 1128, BOZEMAN, MT 59715 (OFFICE)

HOSTS: SHIRLEY ARSENAULT, MANAGER; ALAN AND MARY BRUTGER, PROPRIETORS

TELEPHONE: 406.587.1244

TOLL FREE: 800.954.8585, EXT. 6004

FAX: 406.587.3977 (WINTER) 406.333.4911 (SUMMER)

ROOMS: 27

RATES: WEEKLY: ADULTS $1925 TO $2345, CHILDREN 7-12 $1,680 TO $1,890, SIX AND UNDER $1,330 TO $1,505

REMARKS: OPEN LATE MAY TO OCTOBER. RESERVATIONS REQUIRED.

One of the most remarkable things about Mountain Sky Guest Ranch is the number of familiar faces we see each time we visit. From the seasonal kids' counselors and ranch-hands to the growing and changing faces of the children who return each year with their families, people just can't seem to get enough of this place.

Mountain Sky was built in the 1930s; the old cabins, the lodge and their furniture were crafted with wood taken right off the property. The original cabins and split-log furniture are still in use, but are blended today with new furnishings to provide a warm, relaxed setting for a family vacation.

The week at Mountain Sky begins on Sunday. Guests can use the afternoon to freshen up, unpack, walk down to the stable or tennis courts, or enjoy a complimentary drink poolside while getting to know their neighbors.

Although this is a family-oriented ranch, Alan, Mary and Shirley and the friendly staff know very well that parents need a vacation, too. Experienced counselors supervise nature walks, swimming, games and fishing. A children's wrangler gives guidance and instruction on horsemanship and special "Kids' Dinners" are prepared, followed by activities such as a hayride, Indian pow wow or softball. This allows the adults to fully enjoy the gourmet cuisine. Mountain Sky Ranch has the best developed children's program we have ever experienced.

CABINS: RUSTIC AND CONTEMPORARY

The main lodge has three massive rock fireplaces, braided rugs over wooden floors and a piano made from rough-hewn lodgepole pine. It houses a comfortable great room, the lounge and bar, two dining rooms, a meeting room and the office.

The original log cabins have been remodeled to include all the modern conveniences. These one-, two- and three-bedroom cabins have a rock fireplace or wood burning stove and Western hand-hewn furniture. Newer cabins feature spacious sitting rooms and comfortable furniture. There are also small refrigerators, coffee makers, private baths and generous closets. These cabins sleep two to six.

WRANGLER'S BELL

Mountain air and activity work up mighty appetites. Long before you rise, the staff is busy setting

up the buffet tables, laden with pastries, cinnamon rolls, croissants and muffins, all freshly baked each morning. Soon after you hear the ring of the Wrangler's Bell, you can choose from made-to-order omelets, ham and eggs, fresh fruit, granola or blueberry pancakes. Lunch offers a casual buffet, with a choice of ethnic specialty foods, such as Tex-Mex, pasta selections or Cajun fish. Dinners at Mountain Sky are exceptional. Fresh seafood is flown in from the coast, and the best of Montana produce and beef are served. Hors d'oeuvres are served in the warmth of the Mountain View Lounge before dinner. Dinner may feature Fresh Salmon or Mesquite Grilled Rack of Lamb. The ranch has an extensive wine collection to complement any selection.

For horse lovers there are breakfast, morning and afternoon rides over miles of trails on the ranch and adjacent Gallatin National Forest. Riders often spot deer, elk and moose amid the rock cliffs, grassy meadows and forested slopes of the ranch.

IT'S ALL IN THE WRIST

Fly-fishing is another major attraction at the ranch. There is an instructor on staff to teach the basics. You can practice your casting at the private trout pond or try your luck in Big Creek.

Whether your favorite vacation pursuit is hiking, playing tennis on championship courts, or just relaxing in the hot tub, heated pool or sauna, Mountain Sky provides the arena.

GETTING THERE

Turn off I-90 at Livingston and head south on Highway 89 for 30 miles. Look on the right side of the road for the sign for Mountain Sky Guest Ranch at the Big Creek Road turn-off. The 4.5 miles to the ranch are slow. From Yellowstone, the Mountain Sky turn-off will be on the left-hand side of Highway 89, 30 miles north of Gardiner.

TETON PINES RESORT
- WYOMING-

LOCATION: JACKSON HOLE AT THE BASE OF THE TETON MOUNTAINS

ADDRESS: 3450 NORTH CLUBHOUSE DRIVE, JACKSON, WY 83001

HOSTS: JEFF HEILBRUN, GENERAL MANAGER

TELEPHONE: 307.733.1005

TOLL FREE: 800.954.8585, EXT.3002

FAX: 307.733.2860

ROOMS: 16

RATES: $160 - $355 DOUBLE DURING WINTER, $325 - $695 DOUBLE IN SUMMER.

REMARKS: ARNOLD PALMER GOLF COURSE ON PROPERTY. SWIMMING POOL, TENNIS COURTS, HOT TUB. RATES INCLUDE CONTINENTAL BREAKFAST SERVED IN ROOM, TENNIS AND HEALTH CLUB PRIVILEGES, AIRPORT AND SKI SHUTTLE SERVICE. NO PETS. WHEELCHAIR ACCESSIBLE. RESERVATIONS RECOMMENDED.

If the name Jackson Hole conjures up visions of strikingly vertical mountains, lush valleys and herds of elk, then you will be pleased to know that your vision and modern reality are in harmony. The Jackson area is startlingly beautiful. The Teton Mountains majestically create the western wall of the valley. Throughout the year, you can see more wildlife here than perhaps anywhere else in the country.

An ideal place to stay while exploring Jackson is the Teton Pines Resort and Country Club. Here the philosophy is to treat every guest like a golf club member.

This makes it easy to feel included in all the activities and gives you immediate access to others who share your attraction to the area and to the lifestyle.

YEAR AROUND RESORT

Teton Pines Resort and Country Club is located about seven miles west of the busy center of Jackson and toward the ski area. Teton Pines has been receiving great reviews since opening in 1987. The raves have come for three reasons, the fine golf, the spacious rooms and the fine dining. With each of our visits, we have yet to discover an off season in Jackson. During the summer, you can hike, play golf and explore the nearby Grand Teton National Park, or Yellowstone. During the winter, you can downhill ski at Jackson Hole, Grand Targhee or Snow King, some of the best slopes in America. Cross-country skiing begins just out your front door. The golf course is transformed into a scenic and rolling 14K groomed trail and skate track. Lessons are available and they will arrange a memorable tour into the scenic Grand Teton National Park. This is another "can't miss" experience.

ARNOLD PALMER DESIGNED GOLF

The golf course is one of Arnold Palmer's finest designs. To ensure that the course is enjoyable to all players, they have four sets of tees ranging from 5,500 to 7,412 yards. This is a "must-play" course for any avid golfer. The scenery is spectacular, the golf challenging and the memories lasting. Best yet, as a guest, you will receive a discount on the green fees.

If tennis is your game, you can enjoy playing on seven outdoor courts in the summer and three indoor courts in the winter. Tennis professional Dave Luebbe and his staff are available for lessons and clinics. They have a well equipped pro shop.

Another favorite activity is fly fishing in the pristine streams, rivers and lakes in the area. The clear mountain stream which runs beside the accommodations, runs into a fully stocked trout pond where fly fishing clinics are held during the summer months.

The newly remodeled lodging facilities at Teton Pines are impressive. The interior designs use an elegant western decor. Each room is actually a "junior suite" with two full bathrooms, wet bar, refrigerator, microwave, coffee maker, cable television, outdoor deck with tremendous views of the Tetons and the golf course. One and two bedroom suites are available adding a living room with fireplace, plenty of space and another deck. A continental breakfast is served to you in the comfort of your own room.

The resort clubhouse building, in addition to the reception area and some fine shops, is home to the Grille at The Pines restaurant. Chef Michael Gallivan's tasty creations will draw you back over and over again. Our selection of Tiger eye Ahi tuna appetizer and Artic Char had been flown in that day.

In addition to the daily specials, Chef Michael changes his eclectic fare seasonally and pairs menu selections with carefully chosen wines to complement each entree. Several signature chocolate desserts are available to tempt even the hardiest resisters. Sunset through the 30-feet high windows is not to be missed. The view is north at the Tetons as the setting sun dances among the craggy peaks. During the summer months, a country breakfast is served on Sundays.

GETTING THERE

From the town of Jackson, follow Hwy. 22 west for four miles. Cross the Snake River and turn right on Hwy. 390. The Teton Pines Resort is two miles down the road and on your left.

VISTA VERDE
~ COLORADO ~

LOCATION: 25 MILES NORTH OF STEAMBOAT SPRINGS

ADDRESS: P.O. BOX 465, STEAMBOAT SPRINGS, CO 80477

HOSTS: JOHN AND SUZANNE MUNN

TELEPHONE: 970.879.3858

TOLL FREE: 800.954.8585, EXT. 6006

FAX: 970.879.1413

ROOMS: 8 CABINS, 3 LODGE ROOMS

RATES: WEEKLY: JUNE-SEPTEMBER $1,450 TO $1,750 PER ADULT, LOWER RATES FOR CHILDREN, AND IN WINTER.

REMARKS: RATES INCLUDE MEALS, LODGING AND ACTIVITIES. MINIMUM STAY OF SEVEN NIGHTS IN SUMMER, THREE TO FIVE NIGHTS IN WINTER, MOBIL FOUR STAR AWARD. PERSONAL CHECKS ONLY.

Everyone who comes to Steamboat Springs wants to leave with a cowboy hat. They get caught up in the town's friendly, true western atmosphere, and they want to take a part of it with them. Some decide to forget the hat and make Steamboat their home instead. This proved to be the case for John and Suzanne Munn of South Bend, Indiana, who traversed the wilds of Colorado in search of something expansive and free. They found it in the 500 acres of forest, meadow and pasture just north of Steamboat known as the Vista Verde. They have spent the last several years sharing the romance and adventure of cowboy living with up to 25 guests at a time.

LOG CABIN LIVING

Originally built in the 1930s, Vista Verde has maintained its small and special feeling. The latest addition to the ranch is a 5,000 square foot log lodge that John and Suzanne have recently completed. With large windows overlooking the wide open spaces outside, this handsomely crafted lodge serves as a roomy and warm gathering spot for Vista Verde's guests.

Vista Verde offers activities for the entire family, plus special children's programs give parents and kids some time on their own. These include panning for gold, riding lessons and nature hikes. Sweetheart's Parlor is the spot for indoor activities on chilly or rainy days. A fun finale to each week is the rodeo, in which the dudes demonstrate their new found skills in roping and riding.

RUSTIC AMENITIES

Upstairs in the main lodge are the Gilpin, Pearl and Mica guest rooms, each named for a lake of the nearby Zirkel Wilderness Area. The comfortable rooms have log bedframes and chairs and beautiful antique dressers.

Every year, the Munns upgrade their eight guest cabins, complementing the rustic log exteriors with indoor amenities for your comfort. Named for the mountain peaks surrounding the ranch, these one-two- or three bedroom cabins are fully carpeted, furnished with antiques and big easy chairs, and have living rooms, snack bars and full baths. The cabins are immaculate and well designed to make you feel at home during your stay. You'll find an array of interesting books for your enjoyment as you relax on your large front porch, unwind in your private hot-tub or read by the fire before retiring for the night under warm down comforters.

THREE FABULOUS MEALS

Country gourmet meals are served in the wood-paneled lodge dining room, where guests gather around smooth pine tables to enjoy the fine cuisine prepared by Culinary Institute-trained chefs. Breakfast begins with fruit and fresh bakery items, cold cereal and granola. Then enjoy an Omelette Vista Verde, with fresh herbs, green chili and Monterey Jack cheese, served with special western homefries.

After an active morning, refuel at lunch with a steaming bowl of Navy Bean soup, or a large slice of Shepherd's Pie. At dinner, the ranch chefs put their skills to work with delicious results. Appetizers such as mini Seafood Brochette prepare you for the main course, which may be Roast Rack of Veal Escoffier with fresh Tarragon and Shallots, or Duck Breast Nantucket with Cranberry Wine Sauce.

MOUNTAIN ADVENTURES

In winter, Vista Verde maintains more than 30 kilometers of groomed Nordic ski trails with skating lanes and double tracks for side-by-side skiing, plus horseback riding, sleigh rides and snowshoeing for non-skiers. Vista Verde can also arrange for dogsledding or snowmobiling. Expert guides lead ice-climbing expeditions up frozen mountain waterfalls, teaching you skills and use of equipment. In the summer, horseback riding, mountain biking and hiking are the preferred pastimes. Wranglers provide one-on-one riding instruction and lead trail rides through forests of pine and aspen.

GETTING THERE

Take U.S. 40 west through Steamboat, turn north on County Road 129 for about 18 miles through the "town" of Clark. Turn east on CR 64, Seed House Road, and go about five miles until you see the sign for Vista Verde. The ranch road is 1.5 miles long.

ROMANTIC RIVERSONG INN
~ COLORADO ~

LOCATION: 1.5 MILES SOUTHWEST OF ESTES PARK

ADDRESS: P.O. BOX 1910, ESTES PARK, CO 80517

HOSTS: GARY AND SUE MANSFIELD

TELEPHONE: 970.586.4666

TOLL FREE: 800.954.8585, EXT. 1022

FAX: 970.577.1961

ROOMS: 9

RATES: $135 TO $225, DOUBLE OCCUPANCY; LESS $10 FOR SINGLE RATE

REMARKS: NON-SMOKING. THREE ROOMS ARE WHEELCHAIR ACCESSIBLE.

The small mountain village of Estes Park draws many visitors in the summer and fall, but is often overlooked in the winter and spring–the seasons we find to be most inviting. Not far away along the winding road that follows the Big Thompson River, you will discover our reason for returning each year, the Romantic RiverSong Inn

Built in the 1920s as a summer estate, this lovely Craftsman-style inn is surrounded by extensive formal gardens, canals, ponds and countless hiking trails through a well-populated wildlife habitat. The 27-acre property abuts the Roosevelt National Forest on the side of Giant Track Mountain. Nine years ago Gary and Sue Mansfield acquired the inn, and left their consuming real estate and travel careers behind to bring new life to the RiverSong.

ROMANTIC RIVERSONG

The Mansfields are full-blown romantics, and it shows in every aspect of the inn's operations. The two have conspired in engagements and fostered elopements. On Valentine's Day the RiverSong is awash in hearts and flowers.

The gathering room is an inviting spot for relaxing or conversing with other guests. A roaring fire in the floor-to-ceiling rock fireplace warms chilly mountain days, and a wall of windows opens onto the snow-covered mountains beyond. It's our afternoon tradition to stop in for tea and fresh-baked cookies.

DIVERSE DECOR

The nine guest rooms at the RiverSong Inn are among the most romantic we've seen in the last 12 years. Guest room decor in the main house, Carriage House and duplex cottage range from elegant Victorian to Colorado mountain log-style to Southwestern-style. There are no phones or televisions to disturb your serenity. The Mansfields have invested a great deal of care in the design of the inn, right down to the radiant heated floors you'll find in many of the rooms and in showers and baths. Plush terry robes are provided for your comfort.

The new cottage houses two rooms, including Meadow Bright, an authentic, western-styled room built from rock and log. It has a giant log canopy bed, a fireplace and a waterfall shower that cascades over river rock next to a whirlpool tub for two. Indian Paintbrush is one of our favorite rooms, where, after a

bath in the two-person tub, we can climb into the room's suspended bed and be rocked to sleep before the warmth of the fire. Chiming Bells has a queen-sized brass bed, a redwood shower, sunken tub and a large fireplace. Forget-Me-Not and the marble-floor bathroom. The bedroom has a jetted tub for two in front of the fireplace. Pasqueflower, Shooting Star and Mountain Rose are each appointed with antique furnishings and romantic amenities.

ROCKY MOUNTAIN MORNINGS

Guests gather for breakfast near the fireplace in the inn's circular dining room. Pecan and sweet rolls or other fresh-baked breads start off the meal, followed by steaming Iowa Corn Fritters with fresh Maple Syrup or my special favorite, the infamous John Wayne Casserole, a delicious concoction of chili, cheese and corn. Berry Cobblers are a specialty of RiverSong.

Be sure to have at least one dinner at RiverSong, when the 150 year-old, three-board pine table is set with white lace, Sue's heirloom silver and her sparkling china.

Rocky Mountain National Park is 1-1/2 miles from the inn, and offers hiking and rock climbing. The wildlife viewing is fantastic. We've run across mule deer and elk grazing in the inn's meadows. Big horn sheep, coyotes and raccoons are abundant, and there's great birdwatching also. Winter activities include cross-country skiing, snowshoe hikes and ice skating on the village pond.

GETTING THERE

From Denver, take I-25 north then follow Highway 36 to Estes Park. In town, #36 turns left to Rocky Mountain Natl. Park, at the light at Mary's Lake Road, turn left, cross the bridge and immediately turn right on the little country road. The road ends at RiverSong.

TRAPPER'S CABIN

~ COLORADO ~

LOCATION: 110 MILES WEST OF DENVER, AT BEAVER CREEK RESORT.

ADDRESS: P.O. BOX 5788, AVON CO 81620

HOSTS: R.G. JACOBS, KENT MASON

TELEPHONE: 970.845.5788

TOLL FREE: 800.954.8585, EXT. 6009

FAX: 970.845.6204

ROOMS: 1 COMPLETE CABIN

RATES: $400-$600 PER PERSON PER NIGHT FOR A FOUR-BEDROOM, FOUR-BATH CABIN.

REMARKS: ALL MEALS INCLUDED. DAILY SKI PASS IN WINTER AND YOUR OWN HORSE IN SUMMER MONTHS.

Trapper's Cabin is truly a one-of-a-kind property, surrounded by high alpine meadows, aspen and pine forests, and stunning views. This high mountain hideaway brings guests close to the history of the early Western pioneers who homesteaded the area, attracted by the sheer magnificence of the surrounding peaks and the promise of striking it rich in gold or silver. This is, as host Kent Mason describes it, "A wonderful spot in "God's country" with abundant wildlife, summer wildflowers and winter splendor." These hosts pride themselves on providing their guests the ultimate personalized ranch experience."

AN ELEGANT RETREAT

Trapper's Cabin is situated at an elevation of 9,500 feet, adjoining the White River National Forest. Here, on this peaceful and secluded mountainside, wildlife roams freely, including black bear, elk, deer and mountain lions. The cabin is located within the boundaries of Beaver Creek Resort ski area, on top of Beaver Creek's western hillside, a site which allows maximum privacy and relaxation. In summer, great fields of wild flowers bloom with vibrant color, while winter offers the romantic seclusion of ski-in/ski-out or snowcat-access only. Don't worry about lugging your luggage in on skis. All of your belongings are delivered by the cabinkeeper in the snowcat. Winter is our favorite time to stay at Trappers Cabin for a few days of seclusion, wonderful vistas and superior skiing. All this and a chef too!

ROOM FOR RELAXATION

The pine-log cabin is available exclusively to one party or family at a time. There is only an emergency phone, no TV, and no planned activities or reservations to be made. As R.G. aptly puts it, "We've taken away normal distractions and hassles of your vacation itinerary." There are four large bedrooms in the cabin, each with queen or king bed and private bath. Every bedroom has a spectacular view of the rugged country just outside. For a family or initmate group of friends, Trappers Cabin is the ideal retreat.

The decor is authentic American West, from the pine dining table for 10, to the large rock fireplace in the living room. The spacious deck offers "top of the world views" and a welcome outdoor Jacuzzi for those tired muscles. The cabin is blissfully remote, and safely self-sufficient, with a full kitchen for late-night snacks. For the time you are here it's all yours.

DINING UNDER (ALMOST IN) THE STARS

The cuisine at Trapper's Cabin cannot possibly be confused with traditional ranch or cabin fare. The host has a five-star background and the resulting meals can simply be described as fabulous. During our visit, our Chef Kent started the evening by presenting a tray of hors d' oeuvres featuring cavier, smoked trout and duck, and a variety of French cheese.

The house dinner specialty might be wild game combinations like Elk and Salmon and special-order fresh herbs. Signature desserts include Peach Cobbler, Wild Berries (in season) or a decadent Chocolate Mousse. An extensive wine list and well-stocked bar provide perfect accompaniment to your meal after a full day of physical activity, romantic seclusion or (Yes, it's possible!) both.

Perhaps Mardi's favorite aspect of the evening came when we returned from a snowshoeing walk after dinner and she realized that the spotless cabin was all ours again for the rest of the romantic evening.

DELIGHTFUL DAYS

After a hearty breakfast, you can choose from adventure opportunities that are literally right outside your door. You can go any direction from the cabin–on foot, horseback, bike, skis or snowshoes, and never have to get in a car.! We have never been to a place like this before where your entire day literally lays out before and below you. Other nearby adventure opportunities include: golf, river rafting, rock climbing and hot-air ballooning.

GETTING THERE:

Approximately 110 miles west of Denver on I-70. Three miles south up to Bear Creek Resort Village at the Avon exit. Nearby Eagle County Regional Airport operates all year-round. From there it's a short 30-minute drive east on I-70 from Eagle.

SADDLERIDGE AT BEAVER CREEK
~ COLORADO ~

LOCATION: 115 MILES FROM DENVER INTERNATIONAL AIRPORT AND 48 MILES FROM EAGLE-VAIL AIRPORT.

ADDRESS: 44 MEADOW LANE, BEAVER CREEK, CO 81620

HOSTS: BETH SCHBOT, GENERAL MANAGER.

TELEPHONE: 970.845.5450

TOLL FREE: 800.954.8585, EXT. 6008

FAX: 970.845.5459

ROOMS: TWO VILLAS

RATES: $350-$1,350 NIGHTLY. ACCOMMODATIONS ARE TWO-BEDROOM, TWO-3/4 BATH VILLAS.

REMARKS: RESERVATIONS RECOMMENDED. RESTAURANT IS OPEN DAILY AND IS WHEELCHAIR ACCESSIBLE. NO PETS. DAILY MAID SERVICE. COVERED HEATED PARKING.

SaddleRidge is Beaver Creek's premiere slopeside resort, offering privacy and spectacular views of Beaver Creek Village and ski slopes. Here, no expense was spared to create an atmosphere of quality and pampered comfort. Host and general manager Beth Schbot describes it best when she says, "At SaddleRidge, we treat our guests as if they were in our own home."

AUTHENTIC ATMOSPHERE

This world-class resort was built in 1987 as a private executive retreat. Naomi Leff, one of designer Ralph Lauren's award-winning interior designers, was asked to create at SaddleRidge the ambiance of a living museum of the American West.

Twenty-seven million dollars later, and under Naomi's creative direction, SaddleRidge has one of the finest collections of American Western artifacts and art in the United States. Just a few of the notable pieces that guests will find in the resort's library and restaurant include Buffalo Bill's desk, General George Armstrong Custer's parade issue hat and canteen, ceremonial moccasins dating back to 1870, and Annie Oakley's gun. There are also several original portraits by photographers Edward Curtis and Roland Reed, and a fine collection of Native American jewelry and beaded pouches.

SLOPESIDE LUXURY

All the villas at SaddleRidge are individually decorated in various Western themes such as an old-time stage depot or trading post. Allof the linens are from the Ralph Lauren Home Collection, reflecting the special attention to detail that makes this luxury resort so distinctive.

The villas have hardwood floors throughout, floor to ceiling windows in the living area with views of the village and ski slopes, a large fireplace and private balcony. All the fully equipped kitchens have top-of-the-line appliances, including gas stove and trash compactor. We find that everything has been carefully thought out, from the tastefully appointed dining room, to the amenities in the laundry rooms.

Each master bedroom has a king-sized bed with crisp linens and a European-style goose-down comforter. The rooms are equipped with a humidifier, in-room safe, walk-in closet and a master bath with whirlpool tub, shower/steam and terry robes. The second bedroom has twin-sized beds and the same luxurious amenities as the master suite.

IMAGINATIVE DINING

SaddleRidge Restaurant is a dining experience that is not to be missed. Executive Chef Dave Corbin has created a menu of seasonal Colorado cuisine, such as Grilled Pheasant with Mushroom Risotto, Venison Rack with Vegetable Enchilada and Corn Bread, Grilled Duck with Asian Marinade and Chinese Mashed Potatoes. The restaurant serves dinner daily from 6:00 PM to 10:00 PM, offering the atmosphere of a well-equipped hunting lodge from a bygone era. Although there is no room service, arrangements can be made for dinner to be served in guests' villas. We find that having a glass of a vintage port on a cozy couch in front of the 40-foot high river rock fireplace is the perfect way to end the day.

AT YOUR FINGERTIPS

At SaddleRidge there are numerous activities, none of which require a drive, unless of course, it's during your golf game. On the premises you can enjoy indoor/outdoor heated pool, exercise room, Skiing (downhill, Nordic or snowboarding), snowshoeing, golf, tennis and mountain biking. The concierge is available to help with any of these, as well as with off-site excursions such as river rafting, hot air balloon rides, hiking, and horseback riding in the high Colorado Rockies.

GETTING THERE

From Denver, follow I-70 west 115 miles to the Avon exit (#167). Turn left at the bottom of the exit and continue straight through three stop lights. Stop at the Beaver Creek Resort Welcome Gate for your access pass. Once through the gate, follow Village Road to the end of the golf course and turn left onto Offerson Road. Follow Offerson and turn left onto Meadow Lane, and continue through the SaddleRidge gate. Concierge is in the clubhouse at top of main stairs.

SAN SOPHIA
~ COLORADO ~

LOCATION: IN THE TELLURIDE HISTORIC DISTRICT, ONE BLOCK OFF THE MAIN STREET.

ADDRESS: 330 WEST PACIFIC STREET, TELLURIDE, CO 81435

HOSTS: KEITH HAMPTON AND ALICIA BIXBY

TELEPHONE: 970.728.3001

TOLL FREE: 800.9954.8585, EXT. 1023

FAX: 970.728.6226

ROOMS: 16

RATES: $130 TO $260 DOUBLE FOR WINTER AND HOLIDAYS; $114 TO $200 DOUBLE FOR SUMMER AND FESTIVALS.

REMARKS: NO SMOKING. COMPLIMENTARY AFTERNOON HAPPY HOUR/APRES SKI.

In 1988 the San Sophia, a romantic bed and breakfast inn offering western hospitality and great food opened for business in the pristine surroundings of the Colorado Rockies. After sending their visiting friends and relatives to the inn, local business people, Keith Hampton and Alicia Bixby made a change in their lifestyle and became the owners and innkeepers of this beautiful inn. What a successful combination that has become. Former directors of the renown Telluride Wine Festival, Keith and Alicia seem to know everyone in town. With their love of fine wines, foods and hospitality, you two will soon feel right at home in this well-appointed inn. Their hands on management of the inn is supported by the fledgling assistance of their children Ryan and Rachel.

A History of its Own

Although the San Sophia is fairly new, it has a solid foundation of history. During construction, more than 200 horseshoes were uncovered at the inn's site, which was occupied by the Telluride Livery Stable at the turn of the century.

The Victorian-style building was designed and built to be an inn. The large bay windows and elaborate stained glass windows provide an abundance of light. One of our favorite features of the inn is the classical turret observatory on top of the building. from here you will have an incredible 360 degree view of Telluride and the surrounding San Juan Mountains.

Inside the inn, soft desert pastels and period antiques set the tone for a decor that is informal and comfortable, encouraging guests to gather for conversation before the fireplace in the library.

To the Mountains and Beyond

The inn's 16 rooms are named after former gold and silver mines in the local area. No two rooms are alike. Each is designed for maximum space and comfort. Private baths have an outstanding array of bath amenities, including bubble bath, herbal soaps and shampoos, and two-person whirlpool tubs. Rooms have plush carpeting, brass queen beds covered with handmade quilts and armoires with cable television. More deluxe accommodations have VCR's, even bigger tubs and bay windows with views to the surrounding mountain ranges.

Breakfast Fits the Day

The start of the day in the San Sophia is stunning. the large windows in the dining room focus your view up the valley toward the 12,000 foot peaks of Ajax and Telluride Mountains. When we last visited in the summer, we could sit and watch the water cascading down Ingram Falls, the second highest waterfall in the state. This view is also available if you want to dine out on the East Dining deck.

The San Sophia's buffet-style breakfasts are not only delicious fuel for your day's activities, they are events in themselves. A variety of fruit juices, fresh fruit and yogurt are followed by your favorite hot and cold cereals. While you're here try our favorite, the great frittata with chorizo sausage and perfectly seasoned home fries-one of the true measure of a good breakfast. And don't miss the chocolate chip coffee cake, and the freshly baked yeast breads which are available.

The inn is within 1/2 block of mountain biking, fly fishing, downhill and cross-country skiing; incomparable hiking begins at the front door. Horseback riding and golf are within seven miles of the San Sophia. Visit the Anasazi Ruins or investigate the area's history at the Telluride Museum. After a day of skiing, park in the inn's underground garage, and leave your skis in individual storage lockers and let the boot warmers dry your boots by the next day. Then drop yourself into the sunken Jacuzzi under the gazebo outside, and make plans for your next outing in Telluride.

Getting There

Turn west onto Highway 145 at the town of Ridgeway, and continue for 37 miles to Telluride. As you enter Telluride on Colorado Ave., proceed four block to the beginning of the downtown business district. Turn right for one block and the inn is on the corner of Aspen and Pacific.

THE LIGHTNER CREEK INN
~ COLORADO ~

LOCATION: IN A BEAUTIFUL CANYON, 4 MILES WEST OF
   DURANGO.

ADDRESS: 999 CR 207, DURANGO, CO, 81301

HOSTS: RICHARD AND JULIE HOUSTON

TELEPHONE: 970.259.1226

TOLL FREE: 800.954.8585, EXT.1030

FAX: 970.259.9526

ROOMS: 8

RATES: $95 TO $150 SINGLE OR DOUBLE, INCLUDES
   FULL, GOURMET BREAKFAST.

REMARKS: NO PETS. NO SMOKING. CHILDREN OVER 10
WELCOME.

The setting for The Lightner Creek Inn is beautiful any time of year. To the north are impressive mountains offering down hill and cross-country skiing in the winter and riding and hiking in the summer. To the south and west is open, high desert country. The famous Indian cliff dwellings of Mesa Verde are less than an hour's drive away. Taos and Santa Fe are both within an easy day's drive into New Mexico.

It was the beauty of this canyon just outside of Durango, that captured the spirit and dreams of Richard and Julie Houston. This energetic couple knew they wanted to leave their professional careers in property management and systems engineering and create a new lifestyle. When they discovered the Lightner Creek area, they knew their search for a new home was over. Taking the 20 private acres of meadows and woodlands and a 1903 farm house as the raw materials, they transformed the site into a bed and breakfast with beautifully manicured lawns and professionally landscaped flower gardens overlooking a pond and stream that flows through the grounds. They built an inviting gazebo which has become our favorite place to come and relax. And because the inn is located next to a Wildlife Preserve, don't be surprised to see bald eagles, coyotes, falcons or elk just outside the inn's doors.

COUNTRY CHARM

The main house resembles a French country manor house with large, comfortable common rooms and a kitchen Mardi would kill to have.

Each of the well-appointed bedrooms are named after significant women in Richard and Julie's life. The Svea Elen Room is done in soft blues, pinks and yellows. A hand made quilt and down comforter cover the queen-size Lexington sleigh bed. The view is out to the brick courtyard, gazebo and creek. This spacious room has a handicap-equipped bathroom. The Vicki Lynn Room is highlighted with white roses, warm peach, cool blues and greens. The room has a private bath and separate entrance. The Kimberly Jane Room is the original living room of the main house. The Victorian decor includes a tapestry covered fainting sofa. This beautifully decorated room shares a bath with the Eleanor Lucy Room, which is named after Richard's mother and feels like a step back in time with its 100 year old English Oak furniture. The room has a private entrance and opens up to a huge second story balcony overlooking the pond and stream. The Kelly Kay Room is named after Richard's daughter. This is the smallest but perhaps the cutest of the rooms with its queen-size mission style pine bed, 100 year old german pine marble topped dresser and 24-caret gold and crystal ceiling light. The Karen Olivia Room is a favorite for honeymooners with the floral paper, white batenberg lace down comforter and pillows. It was Julie's aunt Karen who designed and planted the beautiful perennial gardens on the property. The Bonnie Joan Room is named for Julie's mother. The Lexington replica bed is accented by the pine floor. The private bath has a spacious tile shower.

Next to the main house is the 700-square-foot Carriage House. The Carriage House's second floor has a very private and romantic room with a king-size featherbed, private bath, and an outdoor deck overlooking the grounds.

SUNSHINE BREAKFASTS

Breakfast is served in the cheerful, inviting sun room. Guests can request that the full, gourmet breakfast be served in time to catch an early morning scenic train. Or, for those who find their warm beds just a little too difficult to leave, guests may enter the sun room more leisurely and linger over breakfast. Either way, the food and sunny room are a wonderful way to start the day.

IN DURANGO

Each morning, during the season, the narrow gauge steam train leaves Durango for the incredibly scenic trip to Silverton and back. Near the inn are golf and tennis facilities, and the Houstons are happy to make these arrangements for guests.

GETTING THERE

From Durango, go west on Highway 160 for three miles. Turn right on CR 207, the inn is one mile up the road on the left.

BLUE LAKE RANCH

~ COLORADO ~

LOCATION: 15 MINUTES WEST OF DURANGO
ADDRESS: 16000 HWY. 140, HESPERUS, CO 81326
HOSTS: DAVID ALFORD AND SHIRLEY ISGAR
TELEPHONE: 970.385.4537
TOLL FREE: 800.954.8585 EXT. 1034
FAX: 970.385.4088
ROOMS: 4 ROOMS IN MAIN INN, A 3-BEDROOM LOG CABIN ON THE LAKE AND A 1-BEDROOM COTTAGE IN THE WOODS, TWO SUITES IN RENOVATED BARN AND A HOMESTEAD HOUSE ON THE RIVER.
RATES: $65-$180 WINTER, $85-$225 SUMMER.
REMARKS: NO SMOKING. NO PETS. GOLF, SKIING, AND TENNIS NEARBY.

Back in 1977, when David Alford first told his local Durango friends that he planned to buy a run-down 100 acre farm in Hesperus, they thought he was crazed. They patiently explained to the ex-New Yorker that 100 acres at 7,500 feet elevation is not enough land to run cattle or plant enough of a crop. Besides, they knew the place was over grazed and stripped of good soil years ago by the homesteaders. Nevertheless, David bought the place and quietly began the process of creating his own Eden of the West.

An avid gardener, David hauled in hundreds of

truckloads of manure and began to till it into the tired soil. The rocks were his only crop at first. With these, he made raised planting beds, lined walkways around the property and created patios. David's philosophy was "If I plant and care for them, they will grow." David's own field of dreams is now available for you to see. And he and his wife Shirley do hope that you will come.

FRAGRANCE IN THE FAMILY

In all the years that Mardi and I have been staying in wonderful inns, The Blue Lake Ranch has the most spectacular gardens we have ever seen. As you enter the ranch property, you begin to pick up little hints that this place is special. Andthen there is the fragrance. The enticing perfume is rising from thousands and thousands of flowers. Even non-gardeners are captured by the masses of color, peacocks parading through the yard and the European ambiance of the stylish inn which has also grown and matured to full bloom.

David married his favorite next door neighbor a few years back. Shirley has taken a break from her medical practice to join in at the inn. It is a family operation, complete with Shirley's mom doing lots of the baking for inn guests.

COMPLETE PRIVACY

The main house has four spacious rooms. The three-bedroom, three-bath log cabin (our favorite) is built next to a three acre spring fed lake. It has a large wrap around deck providing great views of the lake and the mountains. I found it a great spot for casting into the lake in hopes of landing one of the monster trout you can see cruising past. Handmade Pine furniture and Navajo rugs complement the two stone fireplaces. There are two suites in the Ranch's renovated barn: The Mountain View Suite and the Pinon Suite. Both have views of the La Plata Mountains. The Mountain View Suite also looks out onto a beautiful garden surrounding a private flagstone patio with comfortable chaise lounge chairs and a grill. Inside, the suite features a cozy kiva fireplace in the living room, a dining area and kitchen. Upstairs, the hayloft has been transformed into two spacious bedrooms. The Pinon Suite is nestled in two private gardens and has a covered portal on the south side for outdoor relaxing. The comfortable living room has a small kitchen and a bedroom with three French doors leading out into the gardens. The Cottage in the Woods is secluded in the pines and surrounded by a rose, iris and wildflower garden. It has a gas-burning fireplace a large bay window, king-size bed, kitchen and bath with a jacuzzi. The secluded River House is located on the La Plata River, one mile from the inn. It is a small country house with a gas burning fireplace, kitchen and two bedrooms.

MOUNTAIN AIR APPETITES

The dining room is a sunny atrium overlooking the lake and the gardens. Breakfast is a full buffet, and offers special homemade treats such as tamales and huge cinnamon rolls. We rarely leave without begging for some of their homemade jams, jellies and honeys which they gather.

Activities in the area include hiking, fishing, breathing the crystal clear mountain air, and soaking in welcome seclusion of this 100-acre "Eden." Popular day trips are outings to the Mesa Verde archeological sites. And a ride on the Durango-Silverton narrow gauge railway train, up a rugged, spectacular canyon.

GETTING THERE

From the north, east or west, take Hwy. 160 to Hesperus. Then Hwy. 140 south for 6.5 miles. The unmarked driveway is on the right. From the South take Hwy. 140 north. The driveway is 1.3 miles beyond the junction with Hwy. 141.

THE HERMOSA INN
~ ARIZONA ~

LOCATION: 2 BLOCKS NORTH OF CAMELBACK ROAD, 2 MILES NORTHEAST OF THE BILTMORE CORRIDOR SHOPPING AND ENTERTAINMENT CENTER.

ADDRESS: 5532 NORTH PALO CRISTI ROAD, PARADISE VALLEY, AZ 85253

HOSTS: JUNE BENTLEY

TELEPHONE: 602.955.8614

TOLL FREE: 800.954.8585, EXT 2037

FAX: 602.955.8299

ROOMS: 35

RATES: $89 TO $575, INCLUDING CONTINENTAL BREAKFAST BUFFET

REMARKS: RESERVATIONS RECOMMENDED. NO SMOKING INDOORS. CHILDREN WELCOME. NO CHARGE FOR AGE 6 AND UNDER IN EXISTING BEDDING IN PARENT'S ROOM. NO PETS. NOT FULLY WHEELCHAIR ACCESSIBLE. MEETING AND EVENT FACILITIES ON-SITE. SPANISH SPOKEN.

An authentic Southwestern-style hacienda oasis set in Arizona's peaceful Paradise Valley, the Hermosa Inn combines a quaint, quiet charm with a comfortable, secluded ambiance. The Inn is bordered by beauty on all sides: the majestic Squaw Peak to the north, a picturesque canal to the south, the awesome Camelback Mountain to the east and the desert to the west. Exquisite green lawns and stone walkways lined with blooming flowers link the various dwellings and invite Hermosa Inn guests to stroll among the desert gardens. The single-story adobe construction features individually decorated casitas, each offering a unique character that leaves every guest with the luxury of being away combined with the comforts of home. As the story goes, a woman named June Bentley came to visit the Hermosa Inn one day....and never left. She is now the hotel manager. June learned the hotel business by watching and following in the steps of her mother and grandfather in England.

THE CHARM OF THE OLD SOUTHWEST

The Hermosa was originally built by Lon Megargee in the 1930s, a transplanted Philadelphian and cowboy-artist who drew inspiration from the architecture he studied in Mexico and Spain. He initially took the isolated plot of land in the open desert and added a simple one-room studio to call home. After adding other buildings to the main house, he converted his hacienda into a guest ranch. Taking a few years to create the structure, Megargee dubbed his Southwestern home "Casa Hermosa," which means "beautiful house." Reopened in 1994 after a substantial restoration, the Inn is scattered over six acres of desert gardens, marked by gracious olive and mesquite trees, towering palms and brilliant flowers.

We enjoyed the fact that at the Hermosa Inn, there is no "standard" room. Guest rooms come in six types of accommodations, from the Adobe Casitas, a hand-built guest room with a bedroom and sitting area, to the Villa 1,700 square-feet two-bedroom, two bathroom, full-kitchen luxury. All rooms feature hand-painted Mexican tile and private patios, vaulted ceilings, luxurious Southwestern decor, wet bars or kitchenettes and TVs and telephones. Most rooms also have charming beehive fireplaces.

SAVE ROOM FOR AWARD-WINNING CUISINE

Inspired by the talents of the creator of the Hermosa Inn, Lon Megargee, the Inn's critically acclaimed restaurant is known as LON's at the Hermosa. One of the area's most popular dining hotspots, the 190-seat restaurant is cared for by Executive Chef Michael DeMaria, an award-winning former member of the U.S. Culinary Olympic Team. LON's authentic, rustic Southwestern furnishings and artifacts are the perfect complement to DeMaria's mouth-watering meals, which are grilled over mesquite and pecan woods. Our favorites for the evening were the Grilled Pork Chop with Apple Mashes Potatoes and Wood Grilled Swordfish with Pineapple Risotto. Paintings and photos of Megargee decorate the walls, and visitors are welcome to dine indoors or out. The sunday brunch out on the patio was a highlight of our visit.

AN INTIMATE MEETING PLACE

The Hermosa Inn is the perfect place for an important business meeting or retreat. The front office will assist you with arranging for a meeting room, such as the Stetson, a 60-capacity private quarters within LON's, or many private villas and haciendas. Fax machines and copiers are always available for your use. The Stetson is a popular place for weddings and larger private dinner parties.

Three tennis courts are expertly maintained at the Hermosa, and those needing lessons can take tips from a tennis professional. Golfers may make arrangements for a round at one of several neighboring championship courses. Guests of the Inn may work out at "The Q," one of the area's most exclusive clubs, which features a swimming pool and jacuzzi.

GETTING THERE

From the Sky Harbor Airport, drive north on 24th Street to Stanford. Turn right on Stanford to N. Palo Christi Road. The inn is on the left.

THE WIGWAM RESORT
~ ARIZONA ~

LOCATION: 17 MILES WEST OF CENTRAL PHOENIX.

ADDRESS: 300 WIGWAM BLVD. LITCHFIELD PARK, AZ 85340

HOST: CECIL RAVENSWOOD

TELEPHONE: 602.935.3811

TOLL FREE: 800.954.8585, EXT. 3004

FAX: 602.935.3737

ROOMS: 331

RATES: $126 TO $446 PER NIGHT

REMARKS: THREE CHAMPIONSHIP GOLF COURSES. TENNIS COURTS. TWO HEATED POOLS. CHILDREN WELCOME. SMALL PETS WELCOME (DEPOSIT REQUIRED). WHEELCHAIR ACCESSIBLE. FITNESS CENTER. ROOM SERVICE. CONFERENCE/BANQUET FACILITIES.

Opened to the public in 1929, The Wigwam Resort has become known for quiet elegance and style in a genuine Arizonan setting. Low-rise adobe-style buildings rest on verdant manicured grounds, protected by the nearby mountain range. The architecture is definitely Southwest territorial, and though it is frequently renovated and remodeled for comfort, the old-style flavor remains. The original building is part of the main lodge in which the library, cozy fireplaces and two of the three award-winning restaurants make their home. Southwestern art and furnishings decorate the main lodge and all of the guest rooms providing a true regional feel.

HIGHLY RATED

The Wigwam Resort has been rated as one of only 11 Mobil five Star Resorts for the past 22 years. This ranking is mainly due to the courtesy and service that seems to flow from every staff person we have ever met. From the moment of your arrival you can feel the warmth of the staff. Remarkably, the Wigwam has a staff of over 700, giving it a ratio of two staff members for each room. We find it is very easy to become caught up in the comfort and charm of this desert resort, making it very difficult to leave.

AUTHENTIC ARIZONA

All of the private rooms exemplify contemporary comfort, embellished by natural fibers and a palette of desert hues. Private baths, patios, two phones, private bars, cable TV and spectravision, air conditioning, and one king-size or two double beds furnish each room. The garden rooms have about 480 well-designed square feet, while the Premier rooms are larger, with over 600 square feet. The romantic deluxe suites, which range up to 5,000 square feet, offer Jacuzzi tubs, private fireplaces and common rooms, some in which one can entertain up to 200 people. Nestled in your cozy room, gaze out onto the majestic mountains, beautiful sprawling gardens or one of the lush golf courses.

SELECTION AND SATISFACTION

With a tasty variety of culinary styles, no one goes hungry or unsatisfied at The Wigwam. The Terrace dining room offers continental cuisine, while the Arizona Kitchen specializes in authentic southwestern entrees, and the Grille on the Greens serves up steaks and seafood in a country club setting. Executive Chef Jon Hill, who has served Kings, Queens and

Presidents, expertly guides the staff, assuring excellence and enjoyment. One treat which everyone must experience is the Chocolate Kahlua Taco... an ingenious, delectable delicacy.

RECREATIONAL RETREAT

The Wigwam is well known as one of the premier golf resorts in the Southwest with three championship courses. The club pro told us that they offer more golf than any other resort in Arizona. Two of the three courses were designed by legendary architect Robert Trent Jones, Sr., during his classical period in the mid 1960s. The gold course is the best known featuring classic Jones design with narrow fairways, small landing areas, elevated tees and strategically placed bunkers. This course currently ranks as Arizona's number one resort call course on *Golf Digest*'s list of Arizona's Best.The Wigwam is also rated by *Golf Magazine* as a Silver Medal Resort. Come and play and you will understand why they receive so much recognition.

On the resort the activity choices are wide and deep. While we head off to one of the nine tennis courts, our daughter makes a bee-line to the heated pool with the water slide. Horseback riding, trap and skeet shooting, or biking and walking the meandering trails provide abundant exercise.

Close at hand, you can river raft, bounce along on desert jeep tours, and hike in the nearby mountains. Both Phoenix and Scottsdale are convenient distances, providing a relaxed urban atmosphere to satisfy even the most dedicated shopper and explorer.

GETTING THERE

From Phoenix's Sky Harbor International Airport. Go west on I-10 to exit # 128. Turn right heading north to Wigwam Blvd. (the fourth stop light). Turn right, drive approximately 1/2 mile. The Wigwam Resort is on the left.

RANCHO DE LOS CABALLEROS
~ARIZONA ~

LOCATION: 54 MILES FROM PHOENIX'S SKY HARBOR INTERNATIONAL AIRPORT

ADDRESS: 1551 S. VULTURE MINE RD., WICKENBURG, AZ 85390

HOST: RUSTY GANT

TELEPHONE: 520.684.5484

TOLL FREE: 800.954.8585, EXT. 6012

FAX: 520-684-2267

ROOMS: 79 ROOMS AND SUITES

RATES: $266-$499 DOUBLE OCCUPANCY

REMARKS: OPEN OCTOBER 1 THROUGH MID-MAY. ALL MEALS INCLUDED. CHILDREN ESPECIALLY WELCOME TO THE CABALLEROS KIDS PROGRAM. 18- HOLE CHAMPIONSHIP GOLF COURSE RANKED AS ONE OF THE TOP FIVE COURSES IN THE STATE BY *GOLF DIGEST*. TENNIS COURTS WITH RESIDENT PRO. SWIMMING POOL. TRAP AND SKEET SHOOTING. WHEELCHAIR ACCESSIBLE. PERSONAL CHECKS ONLY.

Rancho de los Caballeros was designed and built as Arizona's premier ranch resort for the entire family. The ranch is located on 20,000 acres in the flowering Sonoran Desert of Wickenburg, 54 miles west of Phoenix. Surrounded by the beautiful Bradshaw Mountains, the setting is stunning.

Built in 1947, Rancho de los Caballeros has a long tradition of Southwest hospitality. The resort is owned and operated by the Gant family. The son of the founders, Dallas and his wife Edie manage the daily operations. Dallas "Rusty" Gant takes personal pride in seeing to it that your stay is as relaxing or as active as you want it to be.

Rancho de los Caballeros is a destination resort composed of a main lodge, 79 spacious guest rooms and suites, swimming pool, four tennis courts, conference facilities, hiking and riding trails and a corral for 90 horses. With adobe block construction and Mexican tile roofs, the effect is that of early Santa Fe style. Rooms and suites are clustered in small groups around the ranch, creating a sense of old homestead life. The living room, card room, dining room, and saloon display an Old West feel while providing a relaxing, inviting common area.

COMFORT FOR THE ENTIRE FAMILY

Southwestern decor with Mexican accents give the rooms a Southwest regional flavor. You can choose from single or double rooms, suites and multiple adjoining rooms. Rooms offer modern conveniences such as private bath, phone, TV, king-or queen- size beds, and a private sun terrace while the gorgeous new Maricopa luxury suites provide a fireplace, refrigerator, game table, wet bar and spa tub. As the ranch is surrounded by beautiful, rugged territory, views from all the rooms of both the mountains and desert are astounding.

DELICIOUS AND HEARTY

At Ranchos de los Caballeros the fabulous meals are fully inclusive and served in the beautiful, Santa Fe-style dining room. Choose from the breakfast and lunch buffets, while dinner is a more traditional occasion, featuring a choice of five entrees. Chef Dan Martin has worked for over 20 years on the ranch and uses fresh local produce to create the delightful meals. The Pastry Chef will make certain you don't leave without sampling at least one of her delectable freshly-baked desserts.

One evening each week, guests may climb on a hay wagon for a short ride out into the desert to participate in a cook-out. Steaks, ribs and chicken grilled over mesquite wood fire, baked beans and corn bread are served and savored under the open night sky.

ADVENTURES

Horseback rides are organized twice daily. Ranch wranglers accompany all rides. Our daughter's first choice, "Shorty" is a favorite pony for kids. The wranglers can handle all levels of riding abilities and make the rides fun for everyone. The Vulture Peak cook-out ride takes you out into the Sonoran foothills around Vulture Peak, with stops along the way to view spectacular plant and animal life. There is a welcome lunch waiting at the end of the trail.

The ranch's 18-hole golf course has been rated one of the top five in Arizona. The par 72 championship course plays 7,025 yards and features strategic bunkering and rolling Bermuda fairways. The hilly back nine put all of our clubs to work. There is also a putting green and driving range.

A few sets of tennis, a hike through the Bradshaw mountains, or skeet shooting are some of the other outdoor opportunities. To spend an exciting day steeped in history, explore the nearby gold mines, and ghost towns which surround Wickenburg, the oldest town in Arizona north of Tucson.

GETTING THERE

From Phoenix's Sky Harbor International Airport. Exit westbound via 24th Street to I-17. Go north 29 miles to State Route 74 (Carefree Highway). Follow Route 74 west 30 miles to U.S. Route 60. Turn right on Route 60, drive through Wickenburg to second stop light and turn left on Vulture Mine Road and go south 1.5 miles to ranch entrance.

CANYON VILLA
~ ARIZONA ~

LOCATION: ADJACENT TO THE COCONINO NATIONAL FOREST, HOME OF SEDONA'S RED ROCK FORMATIONS.

ADDRESS: 125 CANYON CIRCLE DRIVE, SEDONA, AZ 86351

HOSTS: CHUCK & MARION YADON

TELEPHONE: 520.284.1226

TOLL FREE: 800.954.8585, EXT. 1025

FAX: 520.284.2114

ROOMS: 11

RATES: $135-$2145

REMARKS: NO SMOKING. TWO-NIGHT MINIMUM STAY ON WEEKENDS.

Sedona is the gateway to Oak Creek Canyon, where 16 miles of creekside splendor attract both serious hikers and people who come to enjoy the changing of the seasons. It is here in Sedona that Chuck and Marion Yadon chose to build their inn after years of research. Opened in July of 1992, Canyon Villa is in the foothills of Coconino National Forest, directly adjacent to the giant red rocks for which the area is famous. The Yadons have created an outdoor statuary, as the dining room, lounge and guest rooms offer unobstructed views of Bell Rock and Courthouse Butte.

The sandy white walls of this mission-styled inn stand in stark contrast with both the rusted sandstone bluffs and brilliant blue skies. The view side of Canyon Villa offers a spacious deck with a swimming pool and thick green lawn, plus an outdoor fireplace for cool fall evenings. You don't need to go outside to enjoy the surrounding terrain since vaulted ceilings and tall windows in the dining room and lounge admit the full impact of the peaks and spires. On our most recent visit, we had the room shown in this photo.

VARIETY AND LUXURY

Of Canyon Villa's 11 guest rooms, 10 face north to the forest and rocks. Some of these view rooms have a fireplace, and a private patio or balcony through clear-paned French doors. In the event that you wish to access the outside world, all rooms are equipped with telephones and televisions. Room decor ranges from intricate Victorian to country French, native Southwestern to elegant Oriental, incorporating family heirlooms, art and rich antiques. Stained glass windows color the streaming sunlight in several of the rooms, all of which offer private baths with ceramic tile and large whirlpool tubs. We find these tubs to be especially inviting after a full day of clambering over rocks and wandering through Sedona's many enticing galleries and shops.

A PLACE TO UNWIND

In the morning, take your seat in one of the plush upholstered chairs in the dining room and prepare to experience one of the very special gourmet breakfasts that are Marion's trademark. Sour cream waffles and mushroom-artichoke bakes served with fresh fruit and home made breads are our breakfast favorites. Fresh coffee, fresh air and the spectacular view will make your meal taste all the better.

In the afternoons, relax around the large fireplace that separates the comfortable lounge from the dining room, take a leisurely swim or carry a book from the inn's extensive library into the reading garden outside. We like to schedule our return for around 5 p.m., to enjoy afternoon refreshments with our hosts and fellow guests.

As evening breaks over the red rock horizon, Chuck and Marion will be glad to make reservations for you at one of several excellent restaurants they recommend. Sedona has no shortage of dining attractions from causual fare to fine dining.

RED ROCKS AND MORE

Chuck and Marion can help you arrange Jeep tours of Sedona, the National Forest & Red Rocks, hot air balloon rides, golf or hiking. Two championship golf courses are located just a short drive from the inn. These courses offer spectacular scenery and a challenge for golfers at any skill level. There are many art galleries and shops in Sedona which feature the best of the local artists and artisans. For a historic look at the Oak Creek Canyon area, visit the nearby Tuzigoot, Montezuma's Castle and other ancient Indian ruins.

Red Rock State Park, also just west of town, provides insight into Sedona's natural history and the phenomena behind the imposing red rock formations.

GETTING THERE

From Phoenix, take Interstate 17 north for 120 miles to exit #298; take a left onto Highway 179. Drive north for 8.2 miles and turn left onto Bell Rock Boulevard. Straight to Canyon Circle Drive, then turn right. From Flagstaff, drive south on Highway 89A for approximately 27 miles to the signal for Highway 179 in Sedona. Turn left onto Highway 179, then drive south 6 miles and turn right onto Bell Rock Blvd. Straight to Canyon Circle Drive; turn right to the inn.

CASA SEDONA
~ ARIZONA ~

LOCATION: WEST OF CENTRAL SEDONA
ADDRESS: 55 HOZONI DRIVE, SEDONA AZ 86336
HOSTS: JOHN AND NANCY TRUE
TELEPHONE: 520.282.2938
TOLL FREE: 800.954.8585, EXT. 1026
FAX: 520.282.2259
ROOMS: 16
RATES: $120 TO $195 DOUBLE
REMARKS: NON-SMOKING BOTH INSIDE AND OUTSIDE.

Nestled amidst an ancient forest of juniper and pine, Sedona is surrounded by the monuments and pinnacles of Arizona's Red Rock country. It is here, in an area many call "the Eden of America," that Casa Sedona was built in 1992. Conceived by Frank Lloyd Wright protege, Mani Subra, the inn was designed to become one with its environment and to maximize the surrounding view from every possible perspective.

John and Nancy True came to Casa Sedona after managing inns across North America. Nancy had come to Sedona for childhood vacations, and her fond memories of the spectacular area were still fresh. She introduced John to the area when they were newlyweds, and over the years they often brought their three sons here for hiking and fishing in nearby Oak Creek Canyon. Sedona is a perfect setting, with a peaceful beauty that John and Nancy now joyfully share with their guests.

A WONDER AMONG WONDERS

The grandeur of the area is an integral part of the inn, which is comprised of two Spanish-style haciendas built of Sedona Red Rock stucco. A sculpted Native American maiden presides over the cascading fountain in the inn's main courtyard, while the thick hand-hewn door at the inn's entrance bears Native American carvings. Wrought iron accents in a subdued shade of teal mirror the area's extraordinarily blue sky. Colorful flowers and native plants bloom throughout the grounds and weathered wicker furniture beckons under large shady trees.

All around, you will enjoy the unparalleled landscape architecture of Mother Nature. Thunder Mountain seems to be in Casa Sedona's backyard, surrounded by neighboring Cathedral Rock, Coffee Pot and Mogollan Rim.

A VIEW FROM EVERY ROOM

Once inside, the inn's common area boasts a large fireplace crowned with talismans characteristic of the culture of the Southwest. Under high, pine-beamed ceilings, this room also has a hidden television and a music center, and a selection of books for you to enjoy during your stay.

All 16 rooms offer queen or king beds, including four-poster beds ingeniously crafted from wrought iron and, in one room, a richly polished Oak sleigh bed. Each room has a fireplace, a private patio or ter-

race and a luxurious private bath. Many of the rooms offer a whirlpool tub for two. Guests enjoy spectacular Red Rock views from room balconies. Plush robes, hair dryers, refrigerators and ceiling fans are also among the amenities provided.

SOUTHWESTERN BREAKFAST

Casa Sedona is known for wonderful Southwest-style breakfasts served in the Sunrise Alcove, which catches the first rays of the sun as they break over the horizon. During the summer months, dine on the patio overlooking the colorful garden. Begin your day of adventure with coffee, juice and fresh fruit, followed by entrees such as Stuffed French Toast, Huevos Rancheros, or Nancy's delicious granola. On any morning, the choices will spark your appetite for a day of exploring or just plain relaxing. Afternoon appetizers are served by the fireplace in front of a crackling fire.

John will create a customized map of top sites to visit in the area, or help organize a day trip to the Grand Canyon.

FAIR SKIES FOR EVERY PURSUIT

Sedona enjoys one of the most consistently temperate climates in North America, making it especially conducive for exploring the surrounding countryside. The town has become increasingly recognized as a creative center, and has attracted artists and writers from around the world. Outside the city limits, back country off-road jeep trips are a kick. Our favorite escape is to take a picnic to Slide Rock State Park in Oak Creek Canyon. When going to the Grand Canyon, be sure to drive the canyon route to Flagstaff. It's beautiful.

GETTING THERE

From Phoenix, take I-17 north 120 miles to Sedona exit. From Flagstaff, take 89-A south for 30 miles.

TERRITORIAL INN
~ NEW MEXICO ~

LOCATION: ONE BLOCK FROM SANTA FE'S HISTORIC
  PLAZA
ADDRESS: 215 WASHINGTON AVENUE, SANTA FE, NM
  87501
HOSTS: MARY HOKOM, GENERAL MANAGER
TELEPHONE: 505.989.7737
TOLL FREE: 800.954.8585, EXT. 1024
FAX: 505.986.9212
ROOMS: 10
RATES: $80 TO $160 DOUBLE
REMARKS: BREAKFAST, AFTERNOON SNACKS, AND
  EVENING BRANDY AND SWEETS INCLUDED. NON-SMOK-
  ING ROOMS AVAILABLE. FREE PARKING.

Once the tumultuous seat of power for the northern Spanish Empire, Santa Fe is characterized today by its smooth blend of diverse lifestyles and cultures. The city's narrow streets, some still unpaved, sequester enclaves of southwestern tradition; the Historic Plaza is at the city's heart. As you approach this low-rising city surrounded by rolling hills, pueblos and the Pecos river to the east, the sense of imminent discovery builds-and discover you will. Just one block from the Plaza in downtown Santa Fe, you'll find the Territorial Inn, a restored Victorian home that dates from 1896.

After traveling for 10 months, educating themselves about the world of inns and innkeeping, Lela and Mark McFerrin purchased and restored the inn in 1989, creating an elegant home atmosphere with a touch of southwestern style.

PERFECT LOCATION

"The first thing that draws people to the Territorial is its location," Lela notes. "But once they've experienced our personal service and the comfort of the inn, they always come back." The house itself is a blend of New Mexico's stone and adobe "Territorial-style" construction. Park your car in the lot behind the inn, then come through the private rose garden to the main house. Inside you'll find the building's southwestern design softened by a thoughtfully wrought Victorian decor. The large, comfortable living room provides a warm spot to enjoy afternoon snacks, or brandy and sweets before a roaring fire in the evening. On sunny days, guests gather on the patio for breakfast or in the six-person outdoor Jacuzzi cloistered behind the latticework fence and roses.

PLUSH AND COMFORTABLE

Of the Territorial's 10 guest rooms, all but one echo the Victorian decor of the inn. All guest rooms are plush and comfortable, with work from local artists on the walls. Traditional furnishings include a lovely mahogany sleigh bed, a marble-topped wash stand reminiscent of the one in many grandmothers' homes and an impressive canopied four-poster bed of rich cherrywood. Two guest rooms have woodburning fireplaces, and the private bath in Room One has a Greek soaking tub.

IN AND OUT OF TOWN

Santa Fe's Plaza is the center of the city's social and cultural life. The scene of gunfights and political upheavals four centuries ago, the Plaza has evolved into a civilized site for a variety of holiday and cultural celebrations, summer markets, dining and shopping. For a look into local history, visit the Palace of the Governors and the Indian Arts Museum. St. Francis Cathedral, though never finished, marks the upper limit of building height in Santa Fe. The Fine Arts Museum harbors a wealth of work by Georgia O'Keefe and other local artists.

ART-LOVERS PARADISE

You'll find countless handcrafted treasures to enhance your home at the semi-annual Spanish Market in July and December, a judged show of traditional Spanish colonial style art. Another favorite is the Indian Market in August, which is the country's largest juried show and sale of authentic jewelry, textiles, kachina dolls and other Indian artwork. Year-round offerings include more than 200 art galleries, most of which are on Canyon Road, ranging from contemporary work to traditional Hispanic and Indian paintings and sculpture.

When you've had your fill of the area's urban offerings, head out to one of the McFerrin's high mountain cabins, near the Pecos Wilderness. The hand-hewn log cabins are in close proximity to the Pecos River; one is so close that you can fish from the veranda that wraps around the cabin's exterior. Under 2,000-foot cathedral ceilings and endless New Mexico skies, you can get away from it all. Cabins may be rented for three-day to month-long periods during the months of March through October.

GETTING THERE

From I-25, exit at Old Pecos Trail (Exit 284) toward Santa Fe. Turn right at third light to stay on Old Pecos Trail. It becomes Old Santa Fe Trail, go to second stop light and turn right onto Paseo de Peralta. Go one mile and turn left on Washington. The Inn is on the left.

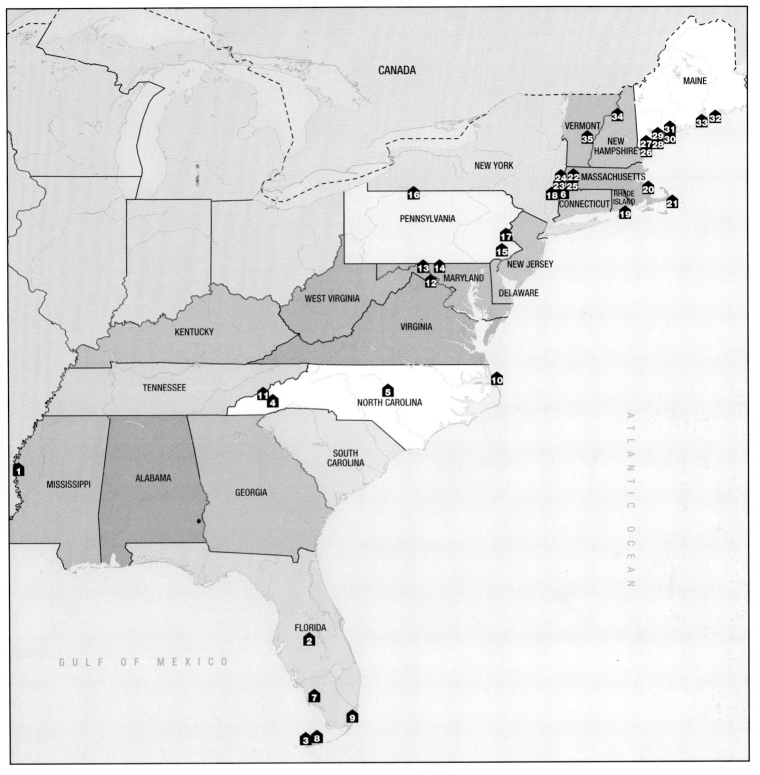

EASTERN UNITED STATES

1. MONMOUTH PLANTATION - Natches, MS
2. CHALET SUZANNE - Lake Wales, FL
3. MARQUESA HOTEL - Key West, FL
4. GREYSTONE - Lake Toxaway, NC
5. FEARRINGTON HOUSE - Pittsboro, NC
6. BOULDERS - New Preston, CT
7. INN AT PELICAN BAY - Naples, FL
8. PARADISE INN - Key West, FL
9. HOTEL PLACE ST. MICHEL - Coral Gables, FL
10. FIRST COLONY INN - Nags Head, NC
11. THE SWAG - Waynesville, NC
12. L'AUBERGE PROVENÇALE - White Post, VA

13. THOMAS SHEPHERD - Shepherdstown, WV
14. INN AT ANTIETAM - Sharpsburg, MD
15. THE RITTENHOUSE - Philadelphia, PA
16. GLENDORN - Bradford, PA
17. EVER MAY ON THE DELAWARE - Erwinna, PA
18. TROUTBECK - Amenia, NY
19. CLIFFSIDE INN - Newport, RI
20. CAPTAIN EZRA NYE HOUSE - Sandwich, MA
21. OLD HARBOR INN - Chatham, MA
22. OLD INN ON THE GREEN - New Marlborough, MA
23. EGREMONT INN - South Egremont, MA
24. CHAMBERY INN - Lee, MA

25. HISTORIC MERRELL INN - Stockbridge, MA
26. STAGE NECK INN - Kittery, ME
27. CAPTAIN LORD MANSION - Kennebunkport, ME
28. OLD FORT INN - Kennebunkport, ME
29. BLACK POINT INN - Scarborough, ME
30. INN BY THE SEA - Cape Elizabeth, ME
31. HARRASEEKET INN - Freeport, ME
32. INN AT CANOE POINT - Bar Harbor, ME
33. LINDENWOOD INN - Southwest Harbor, ME
34. ADAIR COUNTRY INN - Bethlehem, NH
35. KEDRON VALLEY INN - South Woodstock, VT

MONMOUTH PLANTATION

~ MISSISSIPPI ~

LOCATION: IN THE HISTORIC DISTRICT OF NATCHEZ.

ADDRESS: 36 MELROSE AVENUE, NATCHEZ, MS, 39120

HOSTS: JIM ANDERSON, MANAGER; RON AND LANI RICHES, PROPRIETORS

TELEPHONE: 601.442.5852

TOLL FREE: 800.954.8585, EXT. 2011

FAX: 601.446.7762

ROOMS: 28

RATES: $120 TO $350. BREAKFAST INCLUDED.

REMARKS: NO SMOKING. NO PETS. NO CHILDREN UNDER 14. FREE PARKING. WHEELCHAIR ACCESSIBLE. RESERVATIONS RECOMMENDED. NAMED "ONE OF THE MOST ROMANTIC SPOTS ANYWHERE" BY *VICTORIAN BRIDE MAGAZINE*. AAA FOUR DIAMOND AWARD.

For those of us with a fascination for the Civil War era, there is no better place to begin exploring than in the river-front town of Natchez. It seems that most residents of the town not only revere the era, they live it. Twice a year they have "Pilgrimages." During this time the historic homes are open for tours and many of the proud locals dress in period-correct finery.

For those who can't attend one of these semi-annual events, there is Monmouth Plantation. This lovely country inn's sumptuous grounds—some 26 acres of meticulously cared-for gardens, nature trails, pond and gazebo–are rich with history. Built in 1818 in Greek revival style, this was once the home of the first Mississippi governor. Eighteen years ago, it was restored to include its lovely Victorian decor through the perseverance of Ron and Lani Riches. After years of hard work and with a sense for the dramatic, they completed the restoration, much to everyone's delight. Located just five minutes from the Mississippi river, this property shows its guests what true southern hospitality is all about. Guests may spend their days leisurely playing croquet or fishing on the grounds. And the diligent staff, including manager Jim Anderson, all do their part to make guests feel welcome. Marguerite Guercio, who has been the hostess at Monmouth for the past 18 years, greets all guests and tours, and likes to provide an atmosphere where her guests feel cared for and loved. Arriving honeymooners are treated with champagne.

ACCENT ON AUTHENTICITY

The decorations in the main house and the restored outbuildings are perfect in detail. They give the visitor a glimpse of what the house was like in its Pre-civil War heyday. The common rooms have a formal atmosphere and the imported French wallpaper is the same pattern that hangs in the Diplomatic Room of the White House.

BEAUTIFUL DECOR

Impeccable decor and comfort beckons guests. The 13 suites, 12 rooms, two Victorian parlors and study that make up Monmouth Plantation are a treat for the senses. Antiques and reproductions adorn the inn. Some guest rooms have spectacular views of the gardens; many offer fireplaces; some have private patios; all have phones and televisions; all offer private baths; and 8 of the suites have jacuzzi tubs.

The Riches have provided five guest rooms and one suite, with a kitchen in the main house. Three rooms and a suite are nestled into the former servants quarters and four rooms are in the Garden Cottages. Lastly, they have recently added four suites in the old coach house and six suites in the old barn.

CANDLELIT DINNERS

The formal dining room uses a center table dating from 1826, which is set with Ron and Lani's collection of Sevres china. Large and elaborate floral arrangements are brought in daily.

Each night you may make a reservation to participate in a wonderful ritual. The staff prepares and serves a romantic five-course dinner by candlelight.

The next morning these same lucky guests receive a full southern breakfast in the informal dining room. During our recent visit, breakfast consisted of sausages, eggs, grits, freshly baked breads, biscuits, fruit, coffee and juice.

After a breakfast like that it is no wonder the grounds are walkways leading to tranquil ponds and along past beautiful flower beds. Also on the grounds are a full-service bar, a fully equipped conference room, great spaces for retreats and weddings, and a gift shop offering many Victorian items.

OFF THE PLANTATION

Though it's tempting not to leave Monmouth Plantation's ground, there are Gambling Boats, tours of ante-bellum homes, and walking tours through the historic district to consider.

GETTING THERE

From the south on Hwy. 61, continue through Natchez to the fifth light. Take a left on Melrose Montebello Parkway. Go through flashing yellow light and the drive to the Plantation will be on the left.

CHALET SUZANNE COUNTRY INN

~ FLORIDA ~

LOCATION: 45 MILES SOUTHWEST OF ORLANDO, 60 MILES EAST OF TAMPA.

ADDRESS: 3800 CHALET SUZANNE DRIVE, LAKE WALES, FL 33853-7060

HOSTS: CARL AND VITA HINSHAW

TELEPHONE: 941.676.6011

TOLL FREE: 800.954.8585, EXT. 2014

FAX: 941.676.1814

ROOMS: 30

RATES: $139 TO $195 DOUBLE, INCLUDES FULL BREAKFAST. MODIFIED AMERICAN PLAN AVAILABLE IN SUMMER.

REMARKS: CHILDREN AND PETS WELCOME. WHEELCHAIR ACCESSIBLE. PRIVATE 2,450-FOOT AIRSTRIP, POOL, LAKE, ANTIQUE AND GIFT SHOPS. AWARD-WINNING RESTAURANT SERVING BREAKFAST, LUNCH AND DINNER. GOLF AND TENNIS NEARBY. *WINE SPECTATOR* "AWARD OF EXCELLENCE"

Ideally situated on a lush 70-acre estate, and surrounded by fragrant orange groves, Chalet Suzanne is a stunning privately owned country inn that is guided by deep family values. The roots of this inn go back to 1924, when Carl and Bertha Hinshaw built their home here. When her husband died suddenly in 1931, Bertha opened her home as a bed and breakfast to help support her two young children. She steadfastly clung to the conviction that if she created something special, if she served exceptional food, people would come. Bertha's son Carl and his wife Vita have carried on that dream, managing the inn and the restaurant and the family tradition with the help of their children Eric and Tina. And the people are still coming.

A SMALL KINGDOM

Over the years, the Hinshaws have continued to create a small kingdom of towers, turrets, spires and steeples surrounding a world class restaurant. The architecture is reminiscent of Bavarian style, with a dash of whimsy thrown in for good measure. Chalet Suzanne has been listed as its own National Historic District, and is on the National Register of Historic Places.

ECLECTIC AND ELEGANT

Each of the rooms and suites are individually decorated in authentic antiques and fine reproductions. All have air conditioners, telephones and private baths, and most have patios or balconies. Several of the rooms have a view of the sparkling lake. One room has its own private dining balcony with a private dumbwaiter overlooking the Swiss Dining Room.

OUT OF THIS WORLD SOUP

Chalet Suzanne has been voted among the "Top Ten Restaurants" in Florida for over 20 years and the inn has been nationally honored numerous times. The restaurant, which has received the Golden Spoon for 28 years from *Florida Trend* magazine, is on several levels and faces the shimmering waters of the lake. Here, you will find no two tables set alike. The atmosphere is elegant and cozy with candlelight, fresh flowers and family china. The food is uniformly wonderful, in fact it is out of this world. Astronauts aboard the Apollo space flight took Chalet Suzanne's soups with them to the moon in 1973. Carl makes the Moon Soup and many other varieties of soup and sauces in the inn's own cannery, where they are available for visitors' memorable meals back home.

Breakfast is a full country affair, with items such as Swedish Pancakes with Wild Lingonberries, Scrambled Eggs with Chives and Fresh Grapefruit, or Eggs Benedict on Puff Pastry. The dinner menu is a six-course fixed price menu. The house specialties include slow-cooked Chicken Suzanne, Romaine Soup and broiled grapefruit. The signature dessert of Chalet Suzanne is Gateau Christina, a chocaholics delight. There are flourishing grapefruit trees on the property, and many of the herbs used in the restaurant are grown in the inn's gardens. Evening wine tastings are conducted in the inn cellar, the Wine Dungeon, which features over 300 fine wines. Chalet Suzanne's wine list received the 1997 "Award of Excellence" from *Wine Spectator* magazine.

ARTISTRY AND AMBIANCE

Chalet Suzanne also has a ceramic studio where the hand-crafted dishes used in the restaurant and tiles for the Autograph Garden are made. The Autograph Garden has a wall filled with tiles autographed by some of the many celebrities and guests who have stayed here over the years.

One of the most unique features of Chalet Suzanne is the relaxed and romantic atmosphere. The grounds are spacious and beautiful, and with a careful eye, there is an abundance of wildlife to watch: turtles, alligators, Blue Herons, Ibis, foxes, rabbits, mockingbirds and squirrels. The most popular day trip from Chalet Suzanne is Cypress Gardens. An easy drive, the gardens and the incredible water ski shows have made this central Florida attraction world-famous. Other close attractions include Box Tower Gardens, Fantasy of Flight and Disney World.

GETTING THERE

From Orlando take Interstate 4 west to Hwy. 27, exit 23. Head south on Hwy. 27 for 23 miles and turn left (east) on Chalet Suzanne Drive (County road 17A). Chalet Suzanne is one mile down the lane on the right.

MARQUESA HOTEL
~ FLORIDA ~

LOCATION: KEY WEST IS THE LAST ISLAND IN THE FLORIDA KEYS, 160 MILES SOUTHWEST OF MIAMI.

ADDRESS: 600 FLEMING STREET, KEY WEST, FL 33040

HOST: CAROL WIGHTMAN

TELEPHONE: 305.292.1919

TOLL FREE: 800.954.8585 EXT. 4002

FAX: 305.294.2121

ROOMS: 27

RATES: $140 TO $235 LOW SEASON, $190 TO $275 MID SEASON, $205 TO $315 HIGH SEASON.

REMARKS: FREE PARKING FOR HOTEL GUESTS, RESERVATIONS SUGGESTED FOR CAFE MARQUESA. CAFE IS COMPLETELY NON-SMOKING, BUT SMOKING IS PERMITTED IN THE GUEST ROOMS. NO PETS, TWO ROOMS WHEELCHAIR ACCESSIBLE. NAMED ONE OF FLORIDA'S TEN BEST INNS BY THE *MIAMI HERALD*.

Built on a prominent corner in the downtown historic district, the Marquesa Hotel was originally built as a private home, but was later turned into a boarding house. The cafe served as a grocery store, bicycle shop and clothing store. Both the hotel and cafe were in disrepair in 1987 when Marquesa was bought and converted by Erik deBoer and Richard Manley, who specialize in historic preservation. They had already renovated over 75 homes in Key West's historic district and welcomed the challenge of restoring this site.

The extensive renovation took eight months to

complete. After removing 10 decades of accumulated debris and any improvements that were not original or authentic, they found the heart of the building still beautifully intact. This original portion of the hotel was restored, reducing 21 cramped rooms to nine spacious ones. An additional expansion in 1994 transformed two neighboring historic buildings into an additional 12 suites, bring the number of accommodations to 27. The Marquesa Hotel has received numerous design awards, including the Master Craftsmanship Award from the Historic Keys Preservation Board.

The hotel is located in the heart of the Key West's historic district, close to all area attractions, and only one block from Duval Street, where shops, galleries and restaurants are located. The Gulf of Mexico is five blocks to the east, while the Atlantic Ocean is 11 blocks west.

WEST INDIES AUTHENTICITY AND ELEGANCE

The main building is Greek Revival, built in 1884. Two adjoining buildings, also from the late 1800s, are West Indies-island wood-frame construction, typical of the Bahamas. All buildings have some of the classic wood "conch house" elements–tin roofs, wide wraparound porches and gingerbread railings.

The lobby has floor-to-ceiling windows with large bouquets of flowers and historic prints of old Key West, interspersed with prints from local artists. The main meeting places are the garden and two pools, where pitchers of iced tea are set out each day for sunbathing guests. Decor is an eclectic mixture of antiques and reproductions, with modern and tropical cotton fabrics throughout.

LUXURIOUS COMFORT AND IMPECCABLE SERVICE

All rooms have Italian green-marble baths with crisp white porcelain fixtures and Caswell-Massey

bath amenities, telephones, cable television, hairdryers, small personal safes, embroidered cotton bathrobes, and individually controlled air conditioning and heat. Most rooms have spectacular views.

Rooms range in size and style from a queen-size bed to those with queen-size bed and living area. Junior Suites have king-size bed, comfortable living area and private outdoor porches that overlook the two pools and lush gardens. Larger suites offer separate bedroom with king-size bed and an elegant living room. The pool fountain and a waterfall ensures that the sound of water is ever-present.

IMAGINATIVE, UNIQUELY AMERICAN CUISINE

Cuisine at Cafe Marquesa is called Food of the Americas. Here, local seafood specialties such as grouper, snapper, stone crabs and lobster are brought in fresh from the sea. Indigenous fruits, such as mango and papaya, are frequently used for distinctively warm-weather American flavors. Full bar is available, including a complete wine selection. Breakfast is served via room service or in the pool/courtyard area for a nominal charge.

SUN OR HISTORY

Just a few minutes away are bicycles for rent or catamarans and sailboats to take you to the coral reef six miles off shore for snorkeling or scuba diving to view tropical fish and brilliantly-colored corals. Visit the Mel Fisher Atocha Treasure Museum with booty from a Spanish ship, wrecked off of Key West in 1622.

GETTING THERE

Enter the Island and go right onto North Roosevelt Blvd. Take the first right at Palm Ave. Go over bridge. Palm Ave merges into Eaton St. From Eaton, take a left at Simonton Street and left at the next corner (Fleming Street.) Hotel is on the right hand side of Fleming.

GREYSTONE INN
~ NORTH CAROLINA ~

LOCATION: 50 MILES SOUTH OF ASHEVILLE ON U.S. 64.

ADDRESS: GREYSTONE LANE, LAKE TOXAWAY, NC 28747

HOSTS: TIM AND BOO BOO LOVELACE

TELEPHONE: 704.966.4700

TOLL FREE: 800.954.8585, EXT. 2018

FAX: 704.862.5689

ROOMS: 33

RATES: $255 - $420 FOR TWO PEOPLE. RATES INCLUDE GOURMET DINNER AND FULL BREAKFAST. RESERVATIONS RECOMMENDED.

REMARKS: GOLF, TENNIS AND SWIMMING RIGHT OUTSIDE YOUR DOOR. NO PETS. RECEIVED THE FOUR DIAMOND AWARD FROM AAA FOR THE LAST 11 YEARS.

Listed on the National Register of Historic Places, the Greystone Inn sits gracefully on a peninsula jutting into beautiful Lake Toxaway. Built in 1915 as a summer lake home, the Greystone Inn has six levels and is reminiscent of a Swiss Chalet, reflected in the cool waters of a mountain lake. The beautiful lake has an allure which has long attracted a host of interesting people, among them Thomas Edison, J.P. Morgan and the Rockefellers, all of whom came by train to spend their relaxing time along the shore of the lake. Modern visitors now arrive by car, after a scenic drive in the surrounding Blue Ridge mountains. Many return each year to relax and unwind at the Greystone Inn. After our first visit we can understand why this inn is so special and the number of returing guests is so high.

Host Tim Lovelace had retired early from a career in investment banking when he and his wife Boo Boo fell in love with the old historic mansion. They bought and restored it, converting it into an intimate charming inn with all the of amenities of a large resort.

Tim and Boo Boo work diligently to make certain that their guests "feel the relaxation of being in their own home, while being pampered like royalty. We want to anticipate every need, make every outdoor activity available and provide memorable, romantic dining experiences." And they do.

Guests do relax in wicker chairs on the sun porch, they lounge on the terrace and gather in the library for cocktails. We timed our arrival so we could join the nightly sunset champagne cruise on the pristine lake, one of the truly romantic features of this elegant inn.

HISTORIC CHARM AND ROMANCE

The oak-paneled parlor, lounge and guest rooms are furnished with antiques and fine period reproductions. All the rooms at the Greystone Inn are individually decorated and feature king- or queen-size beds, Jacuzzi baths and hardwood floors with area rugs. Most rooms have views of the lake and nearby mountains, and many rooms have fireplaces and private balconies. The Presidential Suite has even won the *Harper's Hideaway Report* "Guest Room of the Year."

INTIMATE AND INNOVATIVE DINING

Each afternoon, tea and cakes are served on the sun porch, and in the evening, the library is our favorite place to gather for cocktails. Every table in the dining room of the Greystone Inn has a view of Lake Toxaway. While the emphasis is on classic southern cuisine, the menu is innovative and seasonal. Both breakfast and dinner are included in your room rates, so be prepared for a delightful and delicious dining experience. Plan to be treated like a house guest instead of a hotel guest.

HEALTHFUL, FRESH, FUN

There is no shortage of activities for you while staying at the Greystone Inn. Your choices include a romantic picnic on a mountain top overlooking Lake Toxaway, or by a private waterfall. There is an 18-hole championship course for the avid golfer, while tennis buffs can play on five clay courts. The water-oriented guests can paddle a canoe, water-ski, swim in the lake or the pool, or fish from the bass boat. Land-lubbers can enjoy mountain biking, or hiking to secluded waterfalls nearby. Other activities available include whitewater rafting, rock climbing, and for those seeking to be totally pampered, the sauna and spa services, which include massages, facials and full body treatment.

The most popular day trip from Greystone Inn is to the Smoky Mountains Historical Park or to the Biltmore Mansion in nearby Asheville. However, many guests check in for a week, relax into the charm and luxury of the inn, and never leave the grounds until their stay is over.

GETTING THERE

From Asheville take I-26 east to Highway 280. Travel west on 280 to Brevard, where 280 becomes US 64 west. Travel approximately 17 miles to the entrance and security gate to the Lake Toxaway Country Club. The Greystone Inn will be on your right. Follow the drive approximately 3.5 miles to the inn.

FEARRINGTON HOUSE COUNTRY INN

~ NORTH CAROLINA ~

LOCATION: EIGHT MILES SOUTH OF CHAPEL HILL

ADDRESS: 2000 FEARRINGTON VILLAGE CENTER, PITTSBORO, NC 27312

HOST: RICHARD DELANY, GENERAL MANAGER

TELEPHONE: 919.542.2121

TOLL FREE: 800.954.8585, EXT. 2015

FAX: 919.542.4202

ROOMS: 30

RATES: $165 TO $275. ALL RATES ARE DOUBLE OCCUPANCY AND INCLUDE A FULL BREAKFAST.

REMARKS: THE RESTAURANT SERVES FIXED-PRICE DINNER TUESDAY THROUGH SATURDAY, 6:00PM UNTIL 9:00PM, AND SUNDAY 6:00PM UNTIL 8:00PM. RESERVATIONS ARE REQUIRED. THE MARKET CAFE SERVES DINNER MONDAY THROUGH FRIDAY FROM 6:00PM TO 8:00PM. GOLF, TENNIS AND KENNEL NEARBY. FIVE DIAMOND RATING BY AAA NO SMOKING IN GUEST ROOMS.

For two centuries the large Fearrington farm has been an important part of the North Carolina landscape between Chapel Hill and Pittsboro. In 1786, Jesse Fearrington's great-great grandfather purchased the 640-acre farm that has been passed from generation to generation. In 1974, the transformation of the old dairy farm into a country village began. Today, the barn and the silo still dominate the landscape and black and white Belted Galloway cows still graze the green pastures. The village has grown to include the award-winning Fearrington House Inn and Restaurant, as well as unique shops, homes, a market, a medical center and a cafe.

At the center of this village is the Fearrington House Restaurant and Country Inn. The Inn is the only AAA five Diamond award winner in North Carolina and one of only a few country inns to earn this highest of accolades.

The 30-room inn has been tastefully decorated with English pine antiques and original art, inspired by many visits to fine inns and small villages in England and France. Our restful and elegant room had a pair of ecclesiastical doors tastefully used as a headboard. Pine flooring from a workhouse along the Thames was used in our bath room. The inn rooms are either clustered around a private courtyard, look into the beautiful 17-acre Camden Park or overlook the village center. Marble vanities, heated towel racks and individual sound systems cater to personal comfort.

Two public rooms are available to you. In the Garden House, you and other guests will have a chance to enjoy the formal afternoon tea service and relax before a warm fireplace. The Sun Room opens onto a terrace that in turn leads to "Jenny's Garden." A water sculpture is the centerpiece of the garden, which is also outlined by trellises. This secret garden is alive with roses, climbing vines, a variety of flowers and has a view of Bynum Ridge.

ELEGANT SOUTHERN CUISINE

While staying in the inn, you will have two excellent choices for dining. The original 1927 Fearrington home now contains the nationally acclaimed Fearrington House Restaurant where fresh garden herbs enhance the flavor of the ever-changing menu. During the remodel, they were able to save much of the building and in turn this act of preservation created a warm and wonderful collection of small and inti-

mate dining rooms. We gathered in the lounge which was the family living room, with other guests to drink a glass of wine before being seated for dinner. We discovered exceptional Southern cuisine served in a gracious manner without being intrusive. It was a treat to experience the roast loin of lamb with bourbon molasses sauce with fresh garden herbs. The extensive wine list has won the *Wine Spectator*'s Award of Excellence for several years.

Across the square in the old granary is the informal Market Cafe. The seating is upstairs with great views of the pastures. The dishes are fresh and home-made. Downstairs is a country store and deli featuring speciality foods, baked goods and a selection of wines.

In the village, you have lots of interesting places to browse. Mardi loved the Dovecote and the Potting Shed. She was missing for hours shopping among the garden supplies, dried flowers, and garden ornaments. She filled a basket with seeds and a selection of herbs propagated in the lands around the village.

VERDANT VIEWS

Enjoy the acres of lush gardens, displays of wildflowers, the thousands of planted azaleas, and the cattle which graze in the surrounding pasture land. In addition to enjoying the scenic attractions, you can bicycle down the lane to the Swim and Croquet Club or play a game of tennis.

Day trips from Fearrington include the University of North Carolina at Chapel Hill, Duke University, antique shopping, and boating on nearby Jordan Lake.

GETTING THERE

Take the Chapel Hill exit from I-40, continue south on 15-501 for approximately eight miles. The village is on the left. Airport transportation can be arranged.

THE BOULDERS INN

~ CONNECTICUT ~

LOCATION: IN THE BERKSHIRE HILLS OF NORTHWESTERN
  CONNECTICUT

ADDRESS: EAST SHORE ROAD, NEW PRESTON, CT 06777

HOSTS: KEES AND ULLA ADEMA

TELEPHONE: 860.868.0541

TOLL FREE: 800.954.8585, EXT. 2013

FAX: 860.868.1925

ROOMS: 17

RATES: MAP ON HOLIDAY WEEKENDS YEAR-ROUND AND
  WEEK DAYS FROM MAY 1 TO NOVEMBER 1

$200 TO $250 B&B, DOUBLE; ADD $50 ON PREMIUM
  WEEKENDS FROM MEMORIAL DAY THROUGH OCTOBER.
  DEDUCT $50 MID WEEK FROM NOVEMBER 1 TO MAY 1.

REMARKS: CHILDREN OVER 12 WELCOME. NO SMOKING
  IN THE DINING ROOM. GOLF NEARBY.

Nestled in the Berkshire Hills of northwestern Connecticut, the Boulders Inn began as a private residence in 1895. The striking Victorian home was constructed to provide breathtaking views of Lake Waramaug as well as the natural splendors of Pinnacle Mountain, which rises behind the inn.

The award-winning inn is the creation of an international team. Dutch-born Kees Adema and his German- born wife Ulla, who run the inn with a relaxed European flair. Under their professional scrutiny, the inn and the restaurant have garnered exceptional reviews from numerous domestic and international publications.

A Choice of Styles

All of the 17 individually appointed guest rooms are decorated to ensure a warm and pleasant atmosphere. All have private baths and are air conditioned. The six rooms in the main house are furnished with a combination of country classics and antiques. Several of these rooms overlook the lake and garden and feature comfortable sitting areas with windowseats or a small balcony. There are three large suites with sitting areas.

Located directly behind the inn are four secluded guest houses. These are our favorite places to spend our visits, especially the ones with the double whirlpool baths. The guest houses are decorated with a country decor and have great views down the hill on to the lake. We love watching the sun set while relaxed on the private deck. The houses are equipped with wood-burning fireplaces with a ready supply of dry wood.

The Carriage House has three traditionally furnished and spacious guest rooms, each with its own stone fireplace.. All are just a short stroll along well-maintained paths to the main house.

Massive Boulders

One of the first things we noticed about the inn was the massive stone work. We learned from Kees that early in the 20th century, Pinnacle Mountain behind the inn was bare of trees and grazed by sheep. This made for an ideal vantage point to see and collect the stunning boulders you will now see in and around the inn. The huge rocks that were selected for use in the inn were transported down Pinnacle during the winter on sledges pulled by oxen. Then under the

guidance of a master stonemason, the "boulders" part of the building was added to parts of the original structure. Those boulders used in the porch pillars seem to radiate a sense of peace, harmony and relaxation. They certainly set the tone for each visit to this wonderful inn.

The Outdoors in Harmony

The Boulders has become renown for its fine dining. Fresh and creative cuisine is prepared by Chef David Anderson. From the glass-enclosed Lake Room diners can view the spectacular sunsets over Lake Waramaug while they savor the best of North American cuisine. The restaurant seats 60 and there is a private dining room which will seat 15 to 20 people.

During the warm seasons of the year, you can also dine on the outdoor terrace. The cuisine is matched by a very impressive wine list. With over 400 selections, the list is quite comprehensive. Apparently the *Wine Spectator* agrees, because they gave their Award of Excellence in both 1995 and 1996.

Most of the quests stay on the Modified American Plan and have unlimited choice of the complete dinner menu, as well as breakfast.

Guests make good use of the tennis courts and the inn's private beach, boats, hiking trails and bicycles. The surrounding Litchfield Hills hold many inducements to stay in the area longer. There are 18th-century villages to explore, antiques to find, craft shops to browse and in the fall there is the world-renowned autumn colors courtesy of the local trees.

Getting There

From New Preston, drive north on Hwy. 45 along the east side of the lake. The inn is on the right side of the road.

Inn At Pelican Bay
- Florida -

LOCATION: 10 MINUTES FROM THE NAPLES AIRPORT AND NEAR THE BEACH.

ADDRESS: 800 VANDERBILT BEACH ROAD, NAPLES, FL 33963

HOST: PHILIP McCABE

TELEPHONE: 941.597.8777

TOLL FREE: 800.954.8585, EXT. 4010

ROOMS: 100

RATES: $75 TO $250

REMARKS: INCLUDES CONTINENTAL BREAKFAST. NO PETS. NO SMOKING. SPANISH AND GERMAN SPOKEN. ON-SITE GOLF, TENNIS AND SWIMMING. PRIVATE BOARDROOM FOR MEETINGS AND EVENTS.

Hotel Place St. Michel
- Florida -

LOCATION: THREE MILES SOUTH OF MIAMI INTERNATIONAL AIRPORT

ADDRESS: 162 ALCAZAR AVENUE, CORAL GABLES, FL 33134

HOST: STUART BORNSTEIN

TELEPHONE: 305.444.1666

TOLL FREE: 800.954.8585, EXT. 4006

FAX: 305.529.0074

ROOMS: 27

RATES: $165 TO $200

REMARKS: INCLUDES CONTINENTAL BREAKFAST. NO PETS. NO SMOKING. RESERVATIONS MUST BE GUARANTEED.

The Paradise Inn
- Florida -

LOCATION: 150 MILES SOUTH OF MIAMI

ADDRESS: 819 SIMONTON STREET, KEY WEST, FL 33040

HOST: SHEL SEGEL

TELEPHONE: 305.293.8007

TOLL FREE: 800.954.8585, EXT. 1044

FAX: 305.293.0807

ROOMS: 18 SUITES AND COTTAGES

RATES: $160 TO $475

REMARKS: INCLUDES CONTINENTAL BREAKFAST. NO PETS. WHEELCHAIR ACCESSIBLE. FREE PARKING. SPANISH, GERMAN, ITALIAN, PORTUGUESE AND POLISH SPOKEN.

FIRST COLONY INN
- North Carolina -

LOCATION: ON THE OUTER BANKS OFF THE NORTH CAROLINA COAST

ADDRESS: 6720 SOUTH VIRGINIA DARE TRAIL, NAGS HEAD, NC 27959

HOSTS: THE LAWRENCE FAMILY

TELEPHONE: 919.441.2343

TOLL FREE: 800.954.8585, EXT. 1037

FAX: 919.441.9234

ROOMS: 26

RATES: $110 TO $190 FROM MARCH 30 TO MAY 21 AND SEPTEMBER 1 TO NOVEMBER 1; $130 TO $240 MAY 22 TO AUGUST 31; $60 TO $125 NOVEMBER 2 TO MARCH 30TH.

REMARKS: INCLUDES CONTINENTAL PLUS BREAKFAST. NO PETS. NO SMOKING. OCEAN BEACH AND POOL ON-SITE. GOLF, TENNIS, WATER SPORTS AND KENNELS NEARBY.

THE SWAG COUNTRY INN
- North Carolina -

LOCATION: ON A MOUNTAIN RIDGE ON THE EDGE OF THE GREAT SMOKY MOUNTAINS NATIONAL PARK.

ADDRESS: 2300 SWAY ROAD, WAYNESVILLE, NC 28786-9624

HOST: DEENER MATTHEWS

TELEPHONE: 704.926.0430

TOLL FREE: 800.954.8585, EXT.2039

FAX: 704.926.2036

ROOMS: 16

RATES: $235 TO $490

REMARKS: INCLUDES THREE MEALS A DAY FOR TWO PEOPLE. NO PETS. NO SMOKING. FOUR STAR RATING BY MOBIL.

L'AUBERGE PROVENÇALE
- VIRGINIA -

LOCATION: 60 MILES SOUTHWEST OF WASHINGTON D.C.

ADDRESS: RT. 340, WHITE POST, VA 22663

HOSTS: ALAIN AND CELESTE BOREL

TELEPHONE: 540.837.1375

TOLL FREE: 800.954.8585, EXT. 2020

FAX: 540.837.2004

ROOMS: 11

RATES: $145 TO $250

REMARKS: INCLUDES FULL GOURMET BREAKFAST. NO
PETS. NO SMOKING. CHILDREN OVER 10 WELCOME.
FOUR DIAMOND RATING BY AAA. RESERVATIONS REC-
OMMENDED FOR DINING.

THOMAS SHEPHERD INN
- WEST VIRGINIA -

LOCATION: 75 MINUTES FROM WASHINGTON D.C.

ADDRESS: 300 WEST GERMAN STREET, SHEPHERDSTOWN,
WV 25443

HOST: MARGARET PERRY

TELEPHONE: 304.876.3715

TOLL FREE: 800.954.8585, EXT. 1052

FAX: 304.876.3313

ROOMS: 7

RATES: $75 TO $130

REMARKS: INCLUDES FULL GOURMET BREAKFAST. NO
PETS. NO SMOKING. CHILDREN OVER 8 WELCOME.

INN AT ANTIETAM
- MARYLAND -

LOCATION: 17 MILES WEST OF FREDERICK AND 13 MILES
SOUTH OF HAGERSTOWN, MD

ADDRESS: 220 EAST MAIN STREET, SHARPESBURG, MD
21782

HOST: BETTY N. FAIRBOURN

TELEPHONE: 301.432.6601

TOLL FREE: 800.954.8585, EXT. 1054

FAX: 301.432.5981

ROOMS: 4 SUITES

RATES: $95 WEEKDAYS AND $105 WEEKENDS.

REMARKS: COMPLIMENTARY BREAKFAST. NO PETS. NO
SMOKING .CHILDREN OVER 6 WELCOME.

THE RITTENHOUSE
- PENNSYLVANIA -

LOCATION: DOWNTOWN PHILADELPHIA

ADDRESS: 210 W. RITTENHOUSE SQUARE, PHILADELPHIA, PA 19103

HOST: DAVID BENTON, VICE PRESIDENT & GENERAL MANAGER

TELEPHONE: 215.546.9000

TOLL FREE: 800.954.8585, EXT. 4003

FAX: 215.732.3364

ROOMS: 98

RATES: $170 TO $285

REMARKS: CHILDREN WELCOME. SPANISH, ITALIAN, FRENCH, RUSSIAN, GERMAN, JAPANESE, PORTUGUESE, DUTCH AND CHINESE SPOKEN. WHEELCHAIR ACCESSIBLE. ROOM SERVICE, BEAUTY SALON, FLORIST, SWIMMING POOL, FITNESS CENTER AND SPA AVAILABLE. VALET PARKING. 8,000 FT OF MEETING SPACE. DOGS ARE ALLOWED. FIVE DIAMOND RATING BY AAA AND FOUR STAR BY MOBIL. INCLUDED IN CONDE NAST, THE *GOLD LIST/ BEST PLACES TO STAY IN THE WORLD.*

GLENDORN
A LODGE IN THE COUNTRY
- PENNSYLVANIA -

LOCATION: NORTHWESTERN PENNSYLVANIA, 1 1/2 HOURS SOUTH OF BUFFALO, NY.

ADDRESS: 1032 W. CORYDON STREET, BRADFORD, PA 16701

HOSTS: GENE AND LINDA SPINNER

TELEPHONE: 814.362.6511

TOLL FREE: 800.954.8585, EXT. 2025

FAX: 814.368.9923

ROOMS: 11 ROOMS, SUITES AND LUXURY CABINS

RATES: $345 TO $545 PER COUPLE.

REMARKS: INCLUDES ALL MEALS AND ON-SITE ACTIVITIES. NO PETS. ON-SITE SWIMMING POOL, TENNIS, TRAP AND SKEET SHOOTING. BICYCLING AND HIKING NEARBY.

EVER MAY ON THE
DELAWARE
- PENNSYLVANIA -

LOCATION: 13.5 MILES NORTH OF NEW HOPE ON DELAWARE RIVER.

ADDRESS: RIVER ROAD, PO BOX 60, ERWINNA, PA 18920

HOSTS: WILLIAM AND DANIELLE MOFFLY

TELEPHONE: 610.294.9100

TOLL FREE: 800.954.8585, EXT. 2026

FAX: 610.294.8249

ROOMS: 16 WITH PRIVATE BATHS

RATES: $90 TO $180

REMARKS: INCLUDES CONTINENTAL BREAKFAST AND AFTERNOON TEA. NO PETS. NO SMOKING. CHILDREN OVER 12 WELCOME. WHEELCHAIR ACCESSIBLE. RESERVATIONS FOR DINNER ARE RECOMMENDED. MEETING AND EVENTS FACILITIES AVAILABLE.

TROUTBECK
- NEW YORK -

LOCATION: 92 MILES NORTH OF NEW YORK CITY.

ADDRESS: LEEDSVILLE ROAD, AMENIA, NY 12501

HOST: JIM FLAHERTY, INNKEEPER

TELEPHONE: 914.373.9681

TOLL FREE: 800.954.8585, EXT. 6011

FAX: 914.373.7080

ROOMS: 42

RATES: $650 TO $1050, PER COUPLE, TWO NIGHTS

REMARKS: INCLUDES ALL MEALS AND OPEN BAR. THIS IS A CORPORATE RETREAT FACILITY, OPEN TO RESORT TRAVELERS ON WEEKENDS. CHILDREN OVER 12 WELCOME. SPANISH, PORTUGUESE, ITALIAN AND FRENCH SPOKEN. WHEELCHAIR ACCESSIBLE.

CLIFFSIDE INN
- RHODE ISLAND -

LOCATION: 50 MILES SOUTH OF BOSTON

ADDRESS: 2 SEAVIEW AVENUE, NEWPORT, RI 02840

HOST: STEPHAN NICOLAS, INNKEEPER

TELEPHONE: 401.847.1811

TOLL FREE: 800.954.8585, EXT. 2027

FAX: 401.848.5850

ROOMS: 15

RATES: $175 TO $325

REMARKS: COMPLIMENTARY FULL GOURMET BREAKFAST AND AFTERNOON VICTORIAN TEA. ROOMS FEATURE WHIRLPOOLS AND WORKING FIREPLACES. NO PETS. NO SMOKING. CHILDREN OVER 13 WELCOME. ADJACENT TO NEWPORT'S FAMOUS CLIFFWALK AND TWO BLOCKS FROM THE BEACH.

CAPTAIN EZRA NYE HOUSE
- MASSACHUSETTS -

LOCATION: 60 MILES SOUTH OF BOSTON, THE FIRST TOWN ON CAPE COD.

ADDRESS: 152 MAIN STREET, SANDWICH, MA 02563

HOSTS: ELAINE AND HARRY DICKSON

TELEPHONE: 508.888.6142

TOLL FREE: 800.954.8585, EXT. 1059

FAX: 508.833.2897

ROOMS: SIX ROOMS AND ONE SUITE

RATES: $85 TO $110

REMARKS: COMPLIMENTARY HYANNIS AIRPORT PICK UP. INCLUDES BREAKFAST. NO PETS. NO SMOKING. CHILDREN OVER SIX WELCOME. TWO NIGHT WEEKEND MINIMUM JUNE THROUGH OCTOBER. SPANISH SPOKEN.

Old Harbor Inn
- Massachusetts -

LOCATION: ON CAPE COD, 100 MILES SOUTHEAST OF
    BOSTON

ADDRESS: 22 OLD HARBOR ROAD, CHATHAM, MA 02633

HOSTS: JUDY AND RAY BRAZ

TELEPHONE: 508.945.4434

TOLL FREE: 800.954.8585, EXT. 1056

FAX: 508.945.7665

ROOMS: 8

RATES: $145 TO $195 HIGH SEASON; $135 TO $185
    FALL; $105 TO $170 WINTER AND SPRING

REMARKS: INCLUDES CONTINENTAL BREAKFAST. NO PETS.
    NO SMOKING.

Old Inn On The Green
- Massachusetts -

LOCATION: SIX MILES EAST OF ROUTE 23

ADDRESS: ROUTE 57, VILLAGE GREEN, NEW
    MARLBOROUGH, MA 01230

HOSTS: BRAFORD WAGSTAFF AND LESLIE MILLER

TELEPHONE: 413.229.3131

TOLL FREE: 800.954.8585, EXT. 2028

FAX: 413.229.2053

ROOMS: 21

RATES: $120 TO $285

REMARKS: INCLUDES GENEROUS CONTINENTAL BREAK-
    FAST. NO SMOKING. CHILDREN WELCOME. GOLF, SWIM-
    MING AND TENNIS NEARBY. FRENCH AND GERMAN SPO-
    KEN. RESERVATIONS RECOMMENDED FOR DINING.

The Egremont Inn
- Massachusetts -

LOCATION: IN THE HEART OF THE SOUTHERN
    BERKSHIRES.

ADDRESS: 10 OLD SHEFFIELD ROAD, SOUTH EGREMONT,
    MA 01258

HOSTS: STEVE AND KAREN WALLER

TELEPHONE: 413.528.2111

TOLL FREE: 800.954.8585, EXT. 2030

FAX: 413.528.3284

ROOMS: 21

RATES: $80 TO $165

REMARKS: INCLUDES FULL BREAKFAST. SWIMMING POOL
    AND TENNIS COURTS. CHILDREN WELCOME. NO PETS.
    NO SMOKING. RESERVATIONS RECOMMENDED FOR DIN-
    ING.

THE CHAMBERY INN
- MASSACHUSETTS -

LOCATION: IN HEART OF THE BERKSHIRES, TWO HOURS FROM BOSTON, ONE HOUR FROM ALBANY AND HARTFORD.

ADDRESS: 199 MAIN STREET, LEE, MA 01238

HOSTS: JOE AND LYNN TOOLE, PROPRIETORS

TELEPHONE: 413.243.2221

TOLL FREE: 800.954.8585, EXT. 2038

FAX: 413.243.3600

ROOMS: 9

RATES: $99 TO $265 IN SEASON, $75 TO $220 OFF SEASON.

REMARKS: COMPLIMENTARY BREAKFAST DELIVERED TO YOUR ROOM. NO PETS. NO SMOKING. CHILDREN OVER 15 WELCOME. HANDICAPPED EQUIPPED ROOM. THREE NIGHT MINIMUM ON WEEKENDS IN SEASON, TWO NIGHT MINIMUM ON WEEKENDS DURING OFF SEASON. FEATURING 500 SQ. FT. FIREPLACE SUITES. MEETING FACILITIES. THREE DIAMOND RATING BY AAA AND THREE STAR RATING BY MOBIL.

HISTORIC MERRELL INN
- MASSACHUSETTS -

LOCATION: ALONG THE BANKS OF THE HOUSATONIC RIVER NEAR VILLAGE OF STOCKBRIDGE

ADDRESS: 1565 PLEASANT STREET, SOUTH LEE, MA 01260

HOST: PAM HURST

TELEPHONE: 413.243.1794

TOLL FREE: 800.954.8585, EXT. 1057

FAX: 413.242.2669

ROOMS: 9

RATES: $75 TO $165

REMARKS: INCLUDES FULL COUNTRY BREAKFAST. CHILDREN WELCOME. NO PETS. NO SMOKING. LISTED ON NATIONAL REGISTER OF HISTORIC PLACES

THE STAGE NECK INN
- MAINE -

LOCATION: ONE HOUR NORTH OF BOSTON AND 45 MINUTES SOUTH OF PORTLAND.

ADDRESS: STAGE NECK ROAD, YORK HARBOR, ME 03911

HOST: MARK FOSTER

TELEPHONE: 207.363.3850

TOLL FREE: 800.954.8585, EXT. 2031

FAX: 207.363.2221

ROOMS: 58

RATES: $130 TO $220

REMARKS: RESERVATIONS RECOMMENDED. SPECIAL PACKAGES AVAILABLE OCTOBER THROUGH MID-JUNE. INDOOR POOL AND SPA. MEMBERSHIP PRIVILEGES AT STAGE NECK POOL AND TENNIS CLUB. GOLF AVAILABLE AT YORK COUNTRY CLUB.

CAPTAIN LORD MANSION
- MAINE -

LOCATION: 80 MILES NORTH OF BOSTON. 35 MILES SOUTH OF PORTLAND.

ADDRESS: P. O. BOX 800, KENNEBUNKPORT, ME 04046-0800

HOSTS: BEV DAVIS AND RICK LITCHFIELD

TELEPHONE: 207. 967.3142

TOLL FREE: 800.954.8585, EXT. 1048

FAX: 207.967.3172

ROOMS: 16

RATES: $175 TO $349 FALL; $125 TO $299 WINTER

REMARKS: INCLUDES FULL BREAKFAST. NO PETS. NO SMOKING. FOUR DIAMOND RATING BY AAA AND FOUR STAR RATING BY MOBIL

THE OLD FORT INN
- MAINE -

LOCATION: 80 MILES NORTH OF BOSTON, 35 MILES SOUTH OF PORTLAND.

ADDRESS: 8 OLD FORT AVE. KENNEBUNKPORT, ME 04046

HOSTS: SHEILA AND DAVID ALDRICH

TELEPHONE: 207.967.5353

TOLL FREE: 800.954.8585, EXT. 2035

FAX: 207.967.4547

ROOMS: 16

RATES: $135 TO $2875

REMARKS: INCLUDES BREAKFAST. RESERVATIONS RECOMMENDED. NO SMOKING. FREE PARKING. SWIMMING POOL AND TENNIS COURT. ON-SITE MEETING FACILITIES. FOUR DIAMOND RATING BY AAA AND MOBIL THREE STAR.

BLACK POINT INN
- MAINE -

LOCATION: EIGHT MILES SOUTH OF PORTLAND

ADDRESS: 510 BLACK POINT RD., SCARBOROUGH, ME 04074

HOSTS: NORMAND AND AGNES DUGAS

TELEPHONE: 207.883.4126

TOLL FREE: 800.954.8585, EXT. 3009

FAX: 207.883.9976

ROOMS: 80

RATES: $250 TO $400

REMARKS: INCLUDES BREAKFAST AND DINNER. NO PETS. NO SMOKING. POOL, TENNIS AND GOLF ON SITE. TWO PRIVATE BEACHES. FITNESS CENTER AND MEETING FACILITIES.

INN BY THE SEA
- MAINE -

LOCATION: SEVEN MILE SOUTH OF PORTLAND

ADDRESS: 40 BOWERY BEACH ROAD, CAPE ELIZABETH, ME 04107

HOST: MAUREEN McQUADE

TELEPHONE: 207.799.3134

TOLL FREE: 800.954.8585, EXT. 1064

FAX: 207.799.4779

ROOMS: 43 SUITES

RATES: $100 TO $410

REMARKS: RESERVATIONS RECOMMENDED. NO SMOKING. PETS WELCOME. CHILDREN FREE. FREE PARKING. FOUR DIAMOND RATING FROM AAA AND MOBIL FOUR STAR.

HARRASEEKET INN
- MAINE -

LOCATION: 15 MILES NORTH OF PORTLAND

ADDRESS: 162 MAIN ST., FREEPORT, ME 04032

HOST: NANCY GRAY

TELEPHONE: 207.865.9377

TOLL FREE: 800.954.8585, EXT. 4009

FAX: 207.865.1684

ROOMS: 84

RATES: $100 TO $230

REMARKS: INCLUDES FULL BUFFET BREAKFAST AND AFTER NOON TEA. IN-DOOR POOL. NO PETS. LIMITED SMOKING. TWO RESTAURANTS. FREE PARKING. FOUR DIAMOND RATING BY AAA. LISTED AMONG THE "400 BEST PLACES TO STAY IN THE WORLD" BY *CONDE NAST TRAVELER*.

THE INN AT CANOE POINT
- MAINE -

LOCATION: ON THE WATER'S EDGE, 43 MILES FROM BANGOR AIRPORT

ADDRESS: ROUTE 3, EDEN STREET, BAR HARBOR, ME 04609

HOSTS: TOM & NANCY CERVELLI

TELEPHONE: 207.288.9511

TOLL FREE: 800.954.8585, EXT. 1065

FAX: 207.288.2870

ROOMS: 5

RATES: LOW SEASON $80 TO $150, HIGH SEASON $135 TO $245 .

REMARKS: BREAKFAST INCLUDED. NOT APPROPRIATE FOR CHILDREN. NO PETS. NO SMOKING. TRANSPORTATION AVAILABLE.

THE LINDENWOOD INN
- MAINE -

LOCATION: 50 MILES EAST OF BANGOR

ADDRESS: 118 CLARK POINT RD.(PO BOX 1328), SOUTHWEST HARBOR, ME 04679

HOST: JAMES KING

TELEPHONE: 207.244.5335

TOLL FREE: 800.954.8585, EXT. 2032

FAX: 207.244.3643

ROOMS: 23

RATES: $75 TO $225

REMARKS: INCLUDES FULL BREAKFAST. RESERVATIONS RECOMMENDED FOR GOURMET RESTAURANT. NO SMOKING. POOL, HOT TUB ON-SITE.

ADAIR COUNTRY INN
- NEW HAMPSHIRE -

LOCATION: 155 MILES NORTH OF BOSTON, BETWEEN THE VILLAGE OF BETHLEHEM AND TOWN OF LITTLETON.

ADDRESS: 80 GUIDER LANE, BETHLEHEM, NH 03574

HOSTS: PATRICIA, HARDY & NANCY BANFIELD

TELEPHONE: 603.444.2600

TOLL FREE: 800.954.8585, EXT. 2033

FAX: 603.444.4823

ROOMS: 9

RATES: $135 TO $220

REMARKS: COMPLIMENTARY FULL BREAKFAST. NO PETS. NO SMOKING. NOT RECOMMENDED FOR CHILDREN. FOUR DIAMOND RATING BY AAA.

KEDRON VALLEY INN
- VERMONT -

LOCATION: FIVE MILES SOUTH OF WOODSTOCK, VT

ADDRESS: ROUTE 106, SOUTH WOODSTOCK, VT 05071

HOSTS: MAX AND MERRILY COMINS

TELEPHONE: 802.457.1473

TOLL FREE: 800.954.8585, EXT. 2029

FAX: 802.457.4469

ROOMS: 27

RATES: $120 TO $195

REMARKS: BREAKFAST INCLUDED. IN-ROOM FIREPLACES, JACUZZIS, QUEEN CANOPY BEDS. MUSEUM-CALIBER HEIRLOOM QUILT COLLECTION. GERMAN SPOKEN. WHEELCHAIR ACCESSIBLE. WELL-BEHAVED CHILDREN WELCOME. PETS ACCEPTED BY SPECIAL ARRANGEMENT. VOTED TOP TEN INN NATIONALLY BY TRAVEL WRITERS; AWARD OF EXCELLENCE FOR WINE LIST.

To Reorder

If you would like additional copies of Special Places, please use the attached mailing card. If the card has already been used, send your name, address and a personal check for $19.95 plus $1.80 for postage to:

Special Places
PO. Box 378
Issaquah, WA 98027

Tel: 425.392.0451
Fax: 425.392.7597

Please Help

Your reactions to the Special Places in this book are very important to us. Please complete one of the attached review cards after you have experienced one of the places in this edition. Give us your impression of their overall quality, service and attention to your needs. We will use your information to help in our ongoing process of ensuring the continuing quality of the places we select to include in our books.

Your Personal Discoveries

Try as we might, we just cannot keep up with all of the new places. If, during your travels, you discover a place you feel is quite special, we would appreciate your letting us know. Any suggestions in North America will be personally inspected by us for consideration for future editions and for our web site.

Keep Up With Fred & Mardi

We continue to travel and select new places throughout the year. These new selections end up on our web site at www.specialplaces.com well before they make it into a printed book. For the latest information always check our web site before making your travel plans.

Thanks,

Fred & Mardi Nystrom
Issaquah, WA

Send me a copy!

THE DISCERNING TRAVELER'S GUIDE TO
Special Places
7TH WESTERN EDITION

Name _____

Address _____

City _____

State _____ Zip _____

Please send me _____ copies of Special Places at $19.95 each plus $1.80 for postage.

$19.95
x _____ (QTY)
= _____ subtotal
+ $ 1.80 postage
_____ TOTAL

Send me a copy!

THE DISCERNING TRAVELER'S GUIDE TO
Special Places
7TH WESTERN EDITION

Name _____

Address _____

City _____

State _____ Zip _____

Please send me _____ copies of Special Places at $19.95 each plus $1.80 for postage.

$19.95
x _____ (QTY)
= _____ subtotal
+ $ 1.80 postage
_____ TOTAL

THE DISCERNING TRAVELER'S GUIDE TO
Special Places
7TH WESTERN EDITION

Dear Fred & Mardi,

We experienced the following Special Place, and would like to share our impression with you.

Special Place: _____

reservation date: _____

our comments: _____
_____
_____
_____
_____
_____

We experienced a place we feel is Special and think you should see:
_____
_____
_____
_____

THE DISCERNING TRAVELER'S GUIDE TO
Special Places
7TH WESTERN EDITION

Dear Fred & Mardi,

We experienced the following Special Place, and would like to share our impression with you.

Special Place: _____

reservation date: _____

our comments: _____
_____
_____
_____
_____
_____

We experienced a place we feel is Special and think you should see:
_____
_____
_____
_____

Special Places

P.O. Box 378

Issaquah, WA 98027

Special Places

P.O. Box 378

Issaquah, WA 98027

Special Places

P.O. Box 378

Issaquah, WA 98027

Special Places

P.O. Box 378

Issaquah, WA 98027